Single on Purpose

Jordi Bostock

*To Asha,
God Bless you!
Just know, be heard
you! Be Ready!
Jordi. B.*

Legals

Contents

INTRODUCTION 1

SECTION 1 – WHY AM I SINGLE? 9

CHAPTER 1 WHY AM I SINGLE? 11

CHAPTER 2 YOU CAN'T HAVE WHAT YOU *WANT!* 25

CHAPTER 3 NO MORE DATING 37

CHAPTER 4 SOMETHING ABOUT MARY 53

CHAPTER 5 HIDE AND SEEK: WHAT HAPPENS WHEN GOD HIDES YOU … 67

CHAPTER 6 NAMES: YOU *CAN* CHANGE A WHORE INTO A HOUSEWIFE! 81

CHAPTER 7: YOUR PURPOSE PART 1 99

CHAPTER 8: YOUR PURPOSE PART 2 107

SECTION 2 – GIVE ME BODY 129

CHAPTER 9 "*I*" GIVE UP! 131

CHAPTER 10 CHICKEN HEAD: GET YOUR MIND RIGHT 151

CHAPTER 11 YOUR BODY *IS* THE TEMPLE 171

SECTION 3 – WANT HIM TO PUT A RING ON IT? READ THIS … 197

CHAPTER 12: GOD'S SYSTEM: MATCHMADEINHEAVEN.COM 199

CHAPTER 13 GOD'S PRENUPTIAL AGREEMENTS 207

SECTION 4 - GIRL, YOU BETTER WORK! 243

CHAPTER 14 YOUR ASSIGNMENT 245

CHAPTER 15 FRUIT 255

CHAPTER 16 MULTIPLY: IF "*I*" DIE, YOU WILL MULTIPLY 263

CHAPTER 17 SUBDUE 271

SECTION 5 - WHERE DID I GO WRONG? 279

CHAPTER 18 DISCERNMENT: MR RIGHT FROM MR WRONG 281

CHAPTER 19 HE THAT FINDS A WIFE … 291

CHAPTER 20 KEEPING YOUR WORD 313

CHAPTER 21 THE IDOL OF RELATIONSHIP	325
CHAPTER 22 THE THIEF	337
CHAPTER 23 HIGH PLACES, STRONGHOLDS & SOUL TIES	351
CHAPTER 24 ADULTERY	361
SECTION 6 – WAITING … OMG WHERE IS HE?!	375
CHAPTER 25 THE PROCESS	377
CHAPTER 26 TIRED OF WAITING	389
A WORD TO MY DAUGHTERS:	399
PURPOSE PRINCIPLES	421
ACKNOWLEDGMENTS	433
ABOUT THE AUTHOR	437
REFERENCES	441
WORKS CITED	442

INTRODUCTION

Who are you?

There has been a widespread epidemic amongst women commonly known as *singlewomanitus*. Apparently, you catch this disease when you *think* nobody wants you or your fat and ugly, broke, got kids or if you're too old. This so called disease has affected millions of unsuspecting women and no one knows where it came from. Some speculate that it's the men; they're dogs, mean, cheap, insecure, selfish and worthless (that's what most of the female experts say). But my studies show a very different and interesting factor…*you. You* are the common denominator in all of your relationships.

Single on purpose puts *you* on the examination table and gets to work. Perhaps what has caused you to be single did not afflict you from the outside but resulted from an ingredient lacking on the inside. In other words, it wasn't that the man was a cheater or treated you bad or was intimidated by you. Although he may have done those things, you are still to blame. Why? The reason is if you were more in tune with the Holy Spirit and his guidance, you wouldn't have chosen that man in the first place. Single on purpose helps uncover what's going on *inside of you*, so that you can change the world *around you*! You've been missing the mark, relationship after relationship, looking outside of yourself for answers, when the answer already resides within (you just wasn't listening).

Which leads to the qualifying question… who are you? To whom do you belong? Who is your master? The absence of proper identity explains why so many women give themselves away mind, body and soul so cheaply. How in the world can you become one with someone if you're not complete within yourself first? And who can make you whole...you? No, you must go to your *creator* to find your true self, discover your name and *purpose*. Single women have wasted valuable time solely focused on finding a mate, while neglecting to find themselves.

Now before you say "she's getting all churchy on me", its important you understand where I'm coming from. There's no way you can obtain a genuine love relationship without God because God *is* love. Today's society wants to have a relationship outside of the confines of the word of God, then fall to their knees crying out to him when things don't work out. When you ignored the word of God and did things your way, you pushed God out of the picture. Coincidentally, you simultaneously pushed out all opportunity for love (because God *is* Love). Whether you acknowledge God's way of doing things or not, you'll realize (if you haven't already) there are consequences to disobedience. Wisdom, blessings, miracles and divine strategies are awarded to the obedient.

If you're single and depressed it only means that you have misunderstood your worth. This time alone should not be a dismal one with you drawing lines on a wall in the dungeon of your house counting down to the day you find mister right. You're special and have been selected for a divine assignment. Did it ever occur to you that your singleness has nothing to do with you? Perhaps divine intervention prevented you from being involved with someone because of a greater purpose.

Single on purpose, establishes the fact that the latter statement is true. God does have a greater purpose in mind for you. If you're single at this time it's certainly not an accident. It seems strange that it would take women so long to figure this out, especially Christian women because we are no longer our own. But that's exactly where we went wrong. Christian women have forgotten that they are no longer their own and are violating the word of God in pursuit of their own lust. The fact is, most people don't pursue *love*...they seek romance, the *illusion* of love. Romance in the grand scheme of things is superficial, short lived and cheap. Love is free but it's not cheap.

Women of God, your father blessed you with beauty, gifts and talents, for *his will and purpose* not to seduce and manipulate men to get what you want. There is so much work to be done in the kingdom that only you can do. Did you know that a man becomes a king through marriage to you? You are a daughter of the King of Kings and when God is ready to expand his kingdom he searches for a man that's willing to please him by laying down his life. When he finds that man, he gives *you* to him as a reward. If he never marries you, he only remains a son. Therefore, you are very valuable to the kingdom. God uses you to enlarge his territory. Single on Purpose will help you realize and tap into what God intends for you to have and do. It's through the process of handling God's business that he takes care of yours, positioning you for your future.

Now if you're not saved, you're living in sin. Everyone was born into sin, no matter how good you think you are. The father of sin and lies is Satan. His kingdom is the world system. Satan's job is to lie, steal, kill and destroy. His operation is designed to ultimately take as many people to hell as he can with him. And while you're here on earth he wants to have you live in hell as well. Of course, he's not obvious with it. He uses things you *want* to seduce you. You may say you don't worship or serve Satan. But you must understand, if you're not born again through Jesus, you're a loyal subject of Satan's kingdom automatically by default.

What does this have to do with being *Single on Purpose*? The unforeseen battle going on in the spirit, preventing you from having the love you desire is over your purpose. The real reason we are all on this earth is to do the will of God (that's our purpose). The enemy doesn't want you to come into the fullness of that reality. Because if you ever stop seeking man and pursue God's interest, the devil knows that he won't be able to abort your mission because you'll be off his radar. You will be hidden at the right place at the right time with the right people. You'll be more attractive than ever without effort. People all around you will be blessed because you'll be more loving and supportive. There's so much connected to your purpose and position in Christ that transcends far beyond what you see. We're talking about generations, governments, nations and communities. But most women are oblivious to this fact. Their world has been so small. The all consuming thought is "why am I single"? It's through the daughters of God that kings are birthed and nations are born.

Unfortunately, Christian singles have walking around lost and heartbroken as a result of direct violation of the word of God and they don't even realize it. Disobedience has opened the door to the failures they've experienced in relationships. The word of God is the manual he left for us to find our way to him (LOVE), not to a man (that's key). When you chase a man, you're operating in the world system of pursuing what *you want*. God doesn't make you work that hard. He simply instructs us please *him* and he'll *give* you the *desires* of your heart.

If you're a Christian, you've chosen God to be your Lord and Master. Believe it or not, the game of life is set and you have almost nothing to do with it. You're just a piece on the board. The only option you can exercise is *whose* going to play you. Will it be God or the devil? God's system is designed for you to have life and have it more abundantly. If you follow the rules of the Kingdom of God it will yield success, love, happiness, joy, peace, health and wealth.

Don't get me wrong, it's natural for a woman to desire a man. We've been groomed that way since little girls. For many that's been the primary focus. And when it doesn't happen in the time frame we expected, we panic. This untamed emotion has thrust literally thousands, maybe millions of single Christian women into panic mode, sending them on a misguided mission to take matters into their own hands. This massive manhunt has single handedly destroyed the self esteem of countless women.

Single on Purpose interrupts that false mission with questions I rarely, if ever hear women ask. Ironically, these questions contain the answers. What does *God* want from *me*? What is his purpose for me being single at this time in my life? Am I supposed to help someone? Is there a ministry that I should be doing? Do I have talents that need to be given or developed? Since we understand God is omniscient, omnipotent and perfect, obviously, we're not single accidentally, it's on purpose. So it is incumbent on you to realize what God has in mind for you while single. Purpose holds the answers to your position in life.

Have you ever given that any consideration? Don't feel bad most people haven't. *Single on Purpose* is different, instead of me telling you what I think about relationships, you'll see what God has in mind for you through scriptures. This map will reveal to you where you are, where you've been, what you need for the journey, what you need to let go of to fulfill your destiny and find your way to true LOVE & purpose.

Ignorance of the word and its application has been, for many of you, a major factor as to why you're still single. God's kingdom principles are simply God's way of doing things. Since God is perfect, your way will be perfect if you follow his plan. Even though you may struggle with faith from time to time, the principles never change and it will work every time you apply them.

God's Kingdom

I've been raised in the church all of my life. I am a born again believer. Unfortunately, for years I have heard preachers talk about the kingdom of God but it didn't register in my mind until recently what that really meant. Understanding your relationship within the kingdom of God will be the foundation that will change everything! It certainly did for me.

Before you gave your life to Jesus, you were in the world system. In the world system anything goes. You work for your wages, nothings free. You can fornicate, live with someone without being married, it's ok to be homosexual, commit adultery if you feel like it (you're in love, so you have the right to succumb to your desires). You can sleep your way to the top. This kingdom is self serving and self destructive. At the end of doing all the things that the flesh can conceive there's a heavy price to be paid. The bible says that the wages of sin is death. I mean death in the literal sense (disease, murder, etc) or spiritual death, separation from God. Yes, satan has devised a counterfeit world based on lies, seduction, murder and deception.

Satan is the taskmaster of this kingdom. He'll do whatever he has to do to keep you in his kingdom because he wants to take you to hell with him. Do you know that he has demonic power to make you rich? He also has demonic seduction powers to encourage you to give into lust and perversion. He lies to you to keep you in bondage. With the limited powers he has to give you, he will *never* satisfy you. He gives you just enough to keep you imprisoned.

When you give your life to Christ, you instantly change systems/kingdoms. It's as if you were first born and raised in America for 30 years, then moved to China and are not allowed to go back, ever! Now, you must learn the language, culture, food, people, currency, laws and their way of life in order to survive. Not learning these things (and quickly) will lead to starvation, homelessness, depression, punishment, loneliness and possibly death. Since you're now a citizen of China you no longer have the protection of America, as far as they're concerned, you're considered a traitor and the enemy. That's how satan views you when you get saved. That's why you cannot turn back to worldly living. You are officially on satan's hit list.

Considering that analogy, now that you're part of the body of Christ and a citizen of Gods kingdom you need to know your rights. When you became a Christian you became part of the royal priesthood. You are now royalty! You're now daughters of The Most High God. It is imperative that you learn the ways of your kingdom. No longer do you behave like a peasant, servant, sinner girl. You're a royal princess. Knowledge of your prestigious position should change the perception of yourself and the world around you. Armed with purpose, you deepen your relationship with the Lord.

So what does this have to do with being single? Everything! The sinful, fleshly mentality and living has deprived you of the love you deserve and desire. There are spiritual laws that you have intrinsically been breaking. There are reasons why you are single beyond what you may think or feel. Some of which may surprise you. The enemy has launched an all out attempt to abort your destiny. Upon completion of Single on Purpose, you'll see how God most certainly has a purpose and plan for you! It's not an accident that you are single. You're *Single on Purpose*!

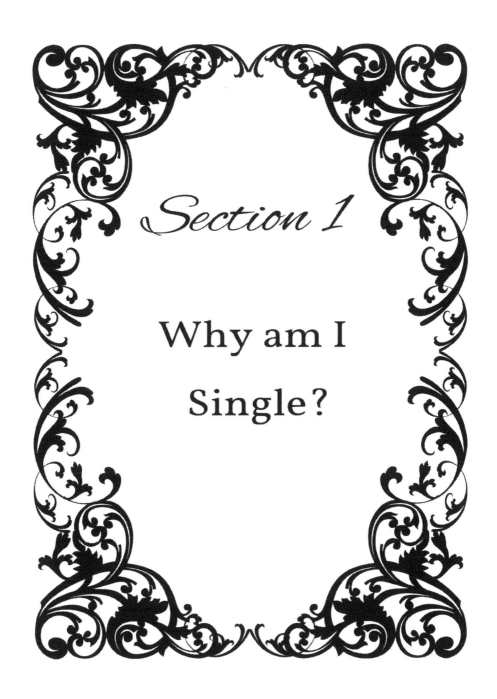

Section 1

Why am I Single?

WHY AM I SINGLE?

Dear God, I know I'm not supposed to question your judgment or anything but errr uhmmm, I couldn't help but notice *I am still* single. Now, *I* know you have perfect timing and all but *I* kinda had a time frame *I* was working with. You know *I'm* almost forty and *I* thought *I* would be married with kids by now. Soooo… *my* biological clock is ticking and *I* don't even have a date, much less a bun in the oven! God, I'm aware you're eternal and a thousand years is but a day but here on earth, *I* don't have a thousand years to spare. (Respectfully). *I* know *I* have some flaws…but *I'm* not as a bad as….you know who, and she got a man. Not just any man, but a good man! And everybody knows she's a ho! *I* might not be a beauty queen but *I'm* prettier than… you know who. And not to go off into a tangent but *I* kinda liked the last guy I was with but he ended up sleeping with me and left me for that girl who was straight up fat and ugly (God forgive me) but she was and *I* JUST DON'T GET IT!!! What do all these other women have that *I* don't? God…why is it taking so long? Why aren't *my* relationships working?!! What is wrong with me?!! WHERE IS HE?!!!!

You might not have prayed that prayer but I bet you thought something like it! I know I have. Upon reading that hypothetical prayer, you'll notice there's one word that's mentioned more than any other and that is "*I*". Everything has been about you; your thoughts, feelings, perceptions and point of view. Yet, you did not create "you" so how can you be sure your thoughts, feelings, perceptions and point of view are accurate? Did it ever occur to you that maybe God *allowed* you to be single on purpose? Sure you're hot and got it going on, but really, could it be that God had different intentions for your beauty and intelligence beyond attracting a man?

When we think about how we feel about being alone, most of us focus on loneliness. Other times, the thought goes through our minds that we're not good enough, nobody wants us and there must be something wrong. We're not really asking "*why* am *I* single?" Deep within our heart the real question is "when will I find the one?" In this book I'm going to share the answer God gave me to the question that every single person *should be asking* in the context that it ought to be asked. "*Why* are you single"?

Where does this instinctive sense of entitlement come from anyway? Single people whine all the time about not having a partner, talking about how lonely and miserable they are. They converse about how much better/easier their life would be if they were married. Ironically, if you examine the lives of most married couples, I don't see how you can get that picture! Half of them wish they were single again themselves! Basically, who ever promised you that you would get married anyway? (Just a thought)

Now, I don't want to get off on the wrong foot here, because I'm single too. What I'm attempting to do is to create a paradigm shift in your thinking when it comes to *being* single. Or, let me be more specific, a Christian single. As a Christian, you're no longer your own. It's not about you anymore. And if you really want to know *why* you're single, the reason in one word is "purpose".

There is a saying, "if you run toward your shadow it will run from you". The opposite happens when you change directions. If you run away from your shadow, not only does it follows you, the shadow gets bigger and bigger!

C'mon, we've all been there. The man that you wanted so badly was the one that gave you the hardest time, did the least with you and for you. But when you decided to stop chasing them, changed your interest, the tables turned. Now the hunter became the hunted. You see, when you run *toward* the things *you want*, you miss the opportunity to receive the experience of love and relationship from the

> ### Interesting note about "shadow chasing":
>
> The flesh will never chase love because the carnal mind is sensual. Characteristics of love, transcends the flesh to where the body cannot comprehend. A great example of this is the love a mother has for a child. The things a mother would do to provide, protect and nurture is not limited to how she's *feeling* about her child. Even if the child behaved badly, she may discipline them but her love will not move. Why? Real love is not about *feelings*, *love is a spirit*, love is a person... God *is* love.
>
> Flesh pursues anything that gratifies the lust of the senses, anything that *feels* good. That's what Satan appeals to, your senses. Lust, like the shadow it is, never satisfies. Therefore, if you ever find yourself chasing someone, recognize the fact that it's not love you're running after. Upon deeper, introspection you'll discover the pursuit was really about:
> 1. Lust of the eyes
> 2. Lust of the flesh
> 3. The Pride of Life
>
> True Love on the other hand, is immutable! For God is Love, he never runs from you. Love stands in front of you, waiting on you, making the shadow you are chasing.

giver. When you genuinely run to the giver, (God), you find true love. Therefore, the reason why love has escaped you is because you weren't looking *for him*. How do you find love WITHOUT GOD?!!!!

If you're reading this book, it is not by accident. Nothing just happens and God doesn't make mistakes. God is a God of purpose and it's imperative you understand that. With that being said, I'll give you the second answer to the question "why am I single"? You are single because of your assignment.

❧ Purpose Principle #1 ❧

You're not single by accident, you're single on purpose!

> Jeremiah 1:5
>
> Before I formed you in the womb I *knew you*, before you were born *I set you apart*; I *appointed you* as a *prophet* to the nations.

> Jeremiah 29:11 (NIV)
>
> For I know the *plans* I have for *you*, declares the Lord, plans to prosper you and not to harm you, plans to give you hope and a future

> **Romans 8:29**
>
> For those God *foreknew* he also *predestined* to be conformed to the likeness of his Son, that he might be the firstborn among many brothers.

This entire time people have been looking at singlehood one-dimensionally. Meaning, we're looking from a self centered point of view. "I want a husband", "I'm lonely", "I need help" and "companionship", "I need sex"...etc.

Regardless your reasons, it always results in what YOU want. Other times the question, "why am I single" comes from a place of lack, insecurity and a feeling of being left out. When in actuality it should be a *position* of empowerment. Yes, you should be *enjoying* this time and place in your life!

❧ PURPOSE PRINCIPLE #2 ❧

IF YOU'RE SINGLE, YOU ARE IN A HIGHLY FAVORED POWER POSITION

I use the word "empowerment" because singlehood leaves room for the freedom of choice to do whatever you want without distraction and obligation. God is a purposeful, strategic, omnipotent, omniscient God. Every relationship he ordains has a purpose.

Honestly, the relationships you had in the past weren't about how your union would serve God. More than likely those relationships were your own personal gratification.

There's nothing wrong with desiring a relationship. The caveat is your *motives, the true intentions of the heart. Since those affairs were all about you, there was *no divine purpose* for you to be in a relationship.

> **James 4:3**
>
> When you ask, you do not receive,
> because you ask with **wrong motives*,
> that you may spend what you get on *your pleasures.*

> **1 Corinthians 16:14**
>
> Let all that you do be done from **motives* of love.

> **Proverbs 16:2**
>
> All a man's ways seem innocent to him,
> but **motives* are weighed by the LORD.

> ***Motives**
>
> Have you ever considered your motives for wanting to be in a relationship? What is it about a relationship that you want so bad? Within your reasoning for having a man, you can temperature check yourself and really see where you are. Do you want a man just for money, easy lifestyle, sex, or sense of security? Or are you the type that cannot stand the idea of not being in a relationship (what's that *really* about)? Why is it so hard for you to be alone? Seriously, think about these things. Do you want a family? Why? What are your plans for this family? Regardless if your reasoning is noble, selfish or borderline crazy, ask yourself does any of my motives include God or his plans for my future? If God isn't in your plans then maybe God isn't in your plans.

Because God is sovereign and Lord over our lives, we must to allow him to be just that. Not only with the things that we feel comfortable with but with everything. When we do so, it allows us to be transparent. We don't have to keep up appearances lying to ourselves and people, sending a false representation of who we are. Impure motives build an idol that men can see, that's why they're not comfortable enough to marry you. God's ways are past finding out. That's why commitment, obedience and complete surrender to God tears that idol down and reveals his glory in you (which is terribly attractive).

God has a master plan that spans vertically and horizontally like the cross. His plan covers the past, present and future. He created everything therefore he knows everything. It's to our advantage to operate properly in our purpose because we become recipients of the benefits of his plan. Our purpose on this planet is simple; *to do the will of God.*

∾ PURPOSE PRINCIPLE #3 ∾

GOD'S PLAN FOR YOUR LIFE IS TO DO HIS WILL.

Realize one of the biggest mistakes we've made was chasing and worshiping the dead idol of relationship instead of pursuing the true and living God's purpose for Christian women. It should be a special time and place of unobstructed, uninterrupted direct relationship with you and God! You can serve God freely. That is why I used the word "position". The status of marriage and singlehood is like a job position. For instance, if you're married, the bible says that your job description is to care for the things of the *world*. If you're single, your job is to care for the things of *the Lord*. We are married to God in the spirit through the covenant of being born again; it is our job to produce spiritual Godly offspring with ministry, which is the manifestation of God's purpose in our lives.

Until now, women of God have been asking the world how to find a man, keep a relationship etc. You will always find the "shadow chasing" system in the world. Let me segue for a minute and talk about the old system that you were living in and why it hasn't worked for you. The world system is formerly known as the Babylonian system. The Babylonian system is told in the bible to have been started by Nimrod. Nimrod was a mighty hunter whose name literally means "Rebel". He was also the great grandson of Noah and his grandfather was Ham. Ham was *cursed* for looking upon his father Noah's nakedness when he was drunk. This cursed bloodline continued through Ham to Nimrod and still continues today.

Basically, Nimrod rebelled against *God's system* by attempting to emancipate man from God. Prior to Nimrod's reign, people were under a patriarchal system where the father, the head of the family, consulted God for answers. This was the original system God ordained for this world. When Nimrod came into power he made *himself* a king, thus the beginning of an organized system where people allowed man to rule *instead* of God. This system is the also the beginning of idolatry and rebellion.

~ PURPOSE PRINCIPLE #4 ~

DESTRUCTION BEGINS WHEN YOU DECIDE TO DEPEND ON YOURSELF.

The Babylonian system is the world system we see today. People have decided to take their life into their own hands, doing what they want to do without Gods leadership. The worship of one's own self; ideals, thoughts and effort is prevalent in the world today, "what about me", "what can you do for me", "I want", "I'm not happy" etc.. Once you're born again, you are no longer part of this cursed wicked kingdom. You no longer depend on yourself, money is not your source and you don't worship at the altar of relationships. These things were idolatry and rebellion.

Is this you?

Have you decided to rebel against God? I'm sure on a conscious level you will say "NO"! But when you get tired of being single and decide to form your "find a man campaign" by hitting up the bars or online dating sites etc...you have begun to rebel. Why? Because God never told you to "Go find a man". Never!

When you meet a man you like and start sleeping with him, that's rebellion against God and his way because the word says it's a sin to fornicate. Our bodies are the temple of the Holy Spirit. Therefore when we make these kinds of decisions with our life and bodies, we commit rebellion and idolatry! Rebellion and idolatry because you're worshiping and satisfying the desires of the flesh instead of the will of the Lord. Again, this is why many are single. Just like the children of Israel some people have been wandering for 40yrs on a journey that should have been 3 days due to disobedience and rebellion. Could it be that you could have had a husband a long time ago but your "husband" has been held up due to your rebellion & disobedience? Hmmmm.

As you enter into the presence of God you change directions from chasing shadows, (which like the things of the world is nothing), to pursuing Jesus, the actual person your heart was really reaching for; the light in front of you making the shadow. This is exactly what God tells single people to do. Ultimately, in order to find Love, *you* must decrease so that *he* may increase.

> **1 Corinthians 7:34**
>
> The *unmarried woman* careth for the things of the Lord, that she may be holy both in body and in spirit.

There is a method to this madness. God's intricate system is so complete that it's designed to nourish every area of the body: physical body, spiritual body and the body of Christ. The mysteries of God's way is locked inside the word; opened up with the key of worship, faith and obedience. When you cancel your "find a man campaign" and decide to pursue him, you step into another principle that gives you your heart's desire.

> **Matthew 6:33**
>
> But seek ye first *the kingdom of God*, and his righteousness; and all these things shall be added unto *you*.

You're probably thinking, look, I love the Lord and all that but I want some physical, tangible companionship in my life. Now! LOL! I get it, trust me I get it. But we can both admit that your way hasn't worked and it won't. Yes, you can go get a man but can you keep him? Matter of fact, do you even want the work of having to "keep him"? You probably could get a man to marry you but if he's not God's choice, you'll be paying for the duration of the relationship. The point I'm making is we must, especially as Christians, realize God's word and way really is true! And if his way is true, it is incumbent on us to discover his kingdom system. The world's way (Satan's way) is a lie! He defies everything of God. That is why he wants you to *think* that you have to take matters into your own hands to get what you want. He wants you to think that you are in control. *You* can make things happen. The funny thing is, the Holy Spirit told me every time we do things our way, we're working too hard!

> **Matthew 11:30**
>
> For my yoke is *easy*, and my burden is light.

ꙮ PURPOSE PRINCIPLE #6 ꙮ

**IF YOU'RE DO THINGS YOUR WAY,
YOU ARE WORKING TOO HARD.**

> **Proverbs 16:25**
>
> There is a way that seems right to a man, but in the end it leads to death.

In order to successfully do his will and receive the desires of your heart you must operate by faith. So in this book you'll be asked to do just that. Therefore, if you want a man, don't go for a man; go for God and the man will follow. That's how the system works.

◈ PURPOSE PRINCIPLE #7 ◈

YOU'RE REWARD COMES AFTER YOU COMPLETE YOUR ASSIGNMENT

Our approach to a loving union has essentially been screwed. We want answers to relationships as if we can really control the results. To control another person's will or manipulate them to do what you want them to do is witchcraft. This book is not about how to get and keep a man. Single on purpose is about being single according to biblical principles which will lead you to your *own husband*.

The desire you have in your heart for a husband is hinged on the foundation of the word. If you want God to give you the desires of your heart you have to delight yourself in *him*. It's not about how you wear your hair, clothes or how nice your body is. God joins his sons/kings only to daughters of kings. We're like Esther. She wasn't born a queen; she had to go through developmental exercises to learn *how* to be one *before* she met the king. Likewise, *our process begins before we get married not after*.

It's in this single-on-purpose process that our mind is renewed and transformed. Upon completion of your assignment you will be in position to give and receive. For this reason God sifts you while single, purifies your thoughts and motives to create in you a Holy vessel. It is Love (God) himself who becomes your father and gives you away to his son (your king).

We're here on this earth as ambassadors for God. When your assignment has been completed, you will be rewarded. Not with what you want but with the desires of your heart. You see, in this system, the good things that we desire, follows those that follows God.

> **1 Peter 2:11**
>
> Dear friends, I urge you, as aliens and *strangers in the world*, to abstain from sinful desires, which war against your soul.

> **2 Corinthians 5:20**
>
> Now then we are ambassadors for Christ, as though God did beseech you by us: we pray you on Christ's behalf, be reconciled to God.

2

You Can't Have What You Want!

For many years, I wanted to get married. One way or the other, it seemed to have escaped me. After each failed relationship I thought to myself, "God, you know how badly I have wanted this, what's going on?"

Time after time I would give new relationships a chance only to run into a dead end. I kept asking God, "what was I doing wrong"? He may have been answering me all along, either I didn't hear or I wasn't listening, not sure. Nevertheless, I like many of you, was extremely frustrated!

The last relationship I was in, got off to a great start. I was excited and felt like he was the one. Ironically, each man that I felt I had a connection with, I thought could be "the one". Crazy as it sounds, I sincerely felt that. Partially because we would have so many things in common, we got along easily or for a period we would be inseparable.

The other reason they felt like kindred spirits was they would tell me what I wanted to hear because I consciously and unconsciously, *told them* what I wanted to hear.

> Stop looking for "the one", "your soul mate", just stop *looking*! The enemy already knows what you're "looking" for so he sends a demon in that package. When you stop looking it confuses the enemy because he doesn't know what you *want*. God wants you to realize that it's impossible to seduce a satisfied person. He desires to satisfy your soul, so you no longer have to be out there "thirsty". We all know what that looks like! LOL

Inevitably, the relationship failed and I was done! I went to church that Sunday, with an attitude like God had forsaken me. Frustrated, at my breaking point, I sowed a seed. I told God, I don't want money back I want an answer! I want to know why haven't my relationships worked?!

Now I know I'm not perfect, but I see plenty of less than perfect women get wonderful husbands that ignore their imperfections and stay with them. Half of these women are carnal Christians shacking up, nasty attitude, don't go to church, tithe or anything but they get what they want! All I wanted was my own husband, my own children, a family of my own.

As I was on my complaining tantrum, God said, "Say it again". So I repeated, "All I wanted was my own husband, my own children, a family of my own."

God answered me, "That's the problem". I didn't get it at first because I believed what I wanted was normal, honorable and noble. There was nothing wrong with the idea of having a family of my own. The problem was that *I wanted it*!

❧ PURPOSE PRINCIPLE #8 ❧

THE MAIN REASON MANY PEOPLE HAVE NOT GOTTEN THE RELATIONSHIP THEY WANTED IS *BECAUSE THEY WANTED IT*!

> **Psalm 23**
>
> The Lord is my shepherd *I shall not want.*

Want, for many people is the driving force in their life. It becomes a high place and a stronghold. The enemy uses the things we want to seduce and imprison us into a holding pattern. *Want* is one of the sneakiest tactics the enemy uses to lure people into compromising positions. The key is not to *want* but to *desire*. There is as distinct difference between the two.

The posture for want is defined as "destitute, needy, lacking", or worst "hunt or seek in order to apprehend". The definition that really got my attention was "to fail to possess especially in

Definition of WANT (Merriam Webster dictionary)

1 to be needy or destitute
2 to have or feel need
3 to be necessary or needed
4. to fail to possess especially in customary or required amount : lack
5. to have need of : require
6. to hunt or seek in order to apprehend

Definition of DESIRE (Merriam Webster dictionary)

1. to long or hope for : exhibit or feel desire for
2 to express a wish for : request <they *desire* an immediate answer> b archaic

customary or required amount: lack". *Now I understand* why God instructs us not to "want". He is our heavenly father, King of Kings, Lord of Lords. The earth is the Lord's and the fullness thereof! He is my shepherd, he takes care of me, I shall not want! Wanting is so beneath him and his children!

What has happened with many single people is they've been bound by their *want* for a partner. We have been seeking the lord, asking for a partner. God has not granted the request because the *wanting* is *faithless*. Deep inside your want and request is riddled with unbelief.

If you knew and believed that God would actually give you what you wanted there would be no need to want it. God put the desire in your heart for companionship. But because you tried to fulfill the desire within the flesh (on your own), you kept the desire in the natural realm which always results in death.

In order for any God given desire to materialize it requires "now faith". That "now faith" is the *substance* needed to make the desire appear. The fact that you have been wanting proves you don't believe.

How do I know? Answer; *now faith* is *the evidence* of things not seen. If your husband hasn't manifested yet but you believe in your spirit God has granted your petition, your heart, attitude and conviction would be the *evidence* that you have faith it will come to pass.

> Sometimes, when you've been single for a long time, it's hard to believe that you will ever get the love your heart so desperately crave. Don't let that fear kill your faith. Remember, God hasn't forgotten you. He chose you for this assignment. When your assignment is over, if you have it in your heart to be married, you will be! Never forget who God is. NOTHING is impossible for him! Never, ever, stop believing! For if you believe it won't happen for you, YOU ARE THE REASON THAT IS HASN'T! Instead, take a deep breath, smile, get happy because now you know it's about to happen FOR YOU. Don't limit God, he's the creator of the universe, surely if he created you and all of mankind, he can provide a husband just for you!

Mark 4:19

And the cares of this life, and the deceits of wealth, and the *desire* for *other things* coming in, put a *stop to the growth of the word*, and it gives *no fruit*.

James 4:3

Ye ask, and receive not, because ye ask amiss, that ye may consume *it* upon your lusts.

What God desires from us is to love him with understanding, trust with childlike faith and follow *Him*. When we do that, then He knows that He can trust us. In turn we acknowledge within ourselves that He can trust us as well. Why? In order to totally focus on God and follow Him, we must crucify our own flesh. That's when we learn to be satisfied and content in Him. Then something powerful happens…He gives us the desires of our heart!

> **Matthew 5:6**
>
> Happy are those whose heart's *desire* is for righteousness: for they will have their desire.

This is a process that takes time. In the beginning of our walk with the Lord we feel strong and faithful. We're willing to walk alone, for a while. We're willing to abstain, for a while. But when it looks like the dating pool is drying up and it seems like everybody else is getting married, while you're getting older, that's when we entertain giving up. Then *"want"* creeps back in. What needs to be done in order to remain in purpose, we must go through the process entirely. Never, give up!

> **James 1:4**
>
> But *let patience* have her perfect work, that ye may be perfect and entire, *wanting nothing*.

Your patience is going to work for you! After patience has done her job you will *want* nothing! It's not about "want" it's about "desire". To desire is to request, hope or long for, to invite. God longs for you to desire the things of God; he doesn't expect his children to want. There is no need!

Desire is part of his system. God is the author and finisher of our faith. When we delight ourselves in Him, he gives us the desire of our hearts. Once that desire deposit hits our spirit, it is our duty to respond with faith. That is the transaction that must take place in order to receive from heaven to earth. Once God gets the faith (substance) from you, He uses it to cloth your desire and deliver it to you. Think like this, faith is to your desire like clothes on the body.

God's word will not return to him void, it will accomplish all that it is set out to do. Since God is that *autho*r of your faith, that means he started it. He gets your faith started with a desire.

We are in two separate kingdoms. On earth, in order for a spirit to reside here it needs a body. In heaven, only spirits can reside, no bodies. Each kingdom has laws. On earth a body makes a spirit visible and tangible. Anything that comes from heaven to earth has to have the substance of faith. That's what makes heavenly things tangible to us. So God gives you a desire which is spiritual (his word), you clothe that desire with your faith in order to manifest it. Belief in His word is what he was waiting for so that *He* can be *the finisher* of your faith.

Isaiah 57:10

You grew weary in your search, but you never gave up. *Desire* gave you renewed strength, and you did not grow weary.

> **Psalm 37:4**
>
> Delight yourself in the LORD and he will give you the desires of your heart.

Remember, our purpose is to do the will of the Lord. It's not our purpose to find a mate. That search is empty and futile. When you are in the will of God, you are one with God. You are operating the way that you were designed to function in the earth realm. That is to manifest the sons of God.

When we are caring for the things of the Lord, there will be obstacles and hurdles to get over. God will give us the desires of our heart. This desire is for his purpose. It is in his will and purpose that we align ourselves with the power of God and do exploits.

When Jesus was on earth, he was always doing the will of God. He was healing the sick, raising the dead, making the blind see, feeding multitudes, etc... That's what we should be doing with our single time and position.

When Jesus was working, doing God's will, you never hear him pray to God for selfish gain. His request was for things that pertained to the growth, edification of the kingdom of God.

> **Job 23:13**
>
> But he is in one mind, and who can turn him? and what his soul *desireth*, even that he doeth.

> **John 5:30**
>
> *Of myself I am unable to do anything*: as the voice comes to me so I give a decision: and my decision is right because I have no *desire* to do what is pleasing to myself, but only what is pleasing to him who sent me.

> **John 15:16**
>
> You did not choose me, but I chose you and appointed you to go and bear fruit--fruit that will last. Then the Father will give you whatever you ask in my name.

> Reevaluate the use of your time and resources. You have a lot to give to the Lord for his use that you have given to men that are not interested. Begin to open your eyes to a world beyond self. Start genuinely, loving others selflessly by giving yourself, time and resources.

For example, let's say you were working with an outreach at your church. You also have a full time job. Even though you're tired you press your way to help the ministry. For months you've had an idea for the ministry that you believe will help them grow. But, you need money, time and favor.

This idea you have, is a desire of your heart. It is a selfless act that God put in your heart that will edify the body of Christ. When you ask

God for what you need to accomplish this desire he will give it to you because *you're in his will* by caring for the things of the Lord!

❧ PURPOSE PRINCIPLE #9 ❧

WORK ON PLEASING THE LORD SO THAT HE WILL GIVE YOU THE DESIRES OF YOUR HEART. WITH THE DESIRE COMES PURPOSE AND PROVISION.

That is how the system works. We misunderstood the scriptures thinking we can just ask for whatever we want and we'll just get it. It's not about our wants; it's about the will and the word of God, *His desires*. God gives us what we really desire when we sincerely give our request in accordance to His word.

This revelation of not wanting was so simple that I could not believe that I missed it. I often say, "It's simple but it's not easy". The idea of not wanting and focusing on self is so hard, because we have been brainwashed by the world system. For some, what I'm saying here is just religious rhetoric because they cannot fathom releasing control in order to receive. The world deceives many into thinking that you have the power to get what you want. And guess what, you do have that power. But what you want is not always what you need (I'm sure your track record in relationships will prove it). God in his infinite wisdom knows exactly what you need, what will satisfy you and make you happy. Your hands cannot receive anything if there's something already in it. You must release control and trust God.

We have to trust that God's way *really is true*. If you believe the word is true, *stop operating by sight*. You *see* time passing, you *see* other people getting married, having children etc.. Don't look at that. Focus on God and your purpose. They're people out there in the world that are waiting for you. They're waiting for you to give them a timely word or to be a friend that's available for them in their time of need. They're looking for someone who is the real deal, willing to walk with a standard, to be an example. They're looking for someone they can trust who is available to minister to them. Someone who has gone through fiery trials that's willing to be transparent enough to show them the way out of their situation.

Caring for the things of the Lord is rewarding and satisfying. But how can you get the strength you need for your life ministry if you keep wearing yourself out trying to get what you want? God is not depriving you. You must believe that because Satan will use that thought against you if you don't.

> **1 Peter 2:2**
>
> As newborn babes, *desire* the sincere milk of the word that ye *may grow* thereby:

> **John 15:7**
>
> If you remain in me, and my words remain in you, you will ask whatever you *desire*, and it will be done for you.

❧ PURPOSE PRINCIPLE #10 ❧

THE MORE YOU READ THE WORD, THE MORE YOU WILL DESIRE GOD AND THE THINGS OF THE LORD.

Your defense in keeping the faith, while letting patience have her perfect work is to stay in the word. The more you get in the word, the more you desire what God desires. The more you will understand his mission and love toward people. It's not just about you and your want. God loves his people and so should you. No one wants to *suffer. I know it's not fun being single when your heart craves to be married. But when you lay down your want for God's desire, he gives you the desire of your heart.

---

*Matthew 26:39

He went forward a little, fell on his face, and prayed, saying, "My Father, if it is possible, let this cup pass away from me; nevertheless, not what I *desire*, but what *you desire*.

John 5:30

Of myself I am unable to do anything: as the voice comes to me so I give a decision: and my decision is right because I have no desire to do what is pleasing to *myself*, but only what is pleasing to him who sent me.

No More Dating

∽

1 John 4:16 states that God is Love. Then, why is it when we're looking for love we look for a man/woman? Why is it when we have questions about love we ask our friends and family? Or, why do we turn to self help books on love instead of asking Love himself?

The reason is, unfortunately, many do not know *who* Love is. How can you find someone or something if you don't know what it is you're looking for? In order to find love you must know where he is and *who* he is.

∽ Purpose Principle #11 ∽

God is Love. There is no love relationship without God.

As I began researching the scriptures regarding this subject, God started giving me revelation. He showed to me that there was no dating in the bible. I was like WHAT?

He showed me that there was no dating. He reminded me that in the bible the marriages were arranged.

Also, women who were about to be married were predominantly found in one of three places:

- The temple (church)
- The field (work)
- Home

God arranges *marriages and he accomplishes this in an unorthodox way. Through our obedience, his system leads us to be in the right place at the right time doing the right thing. It also simultaneously develops our character.

> ***Mark 10:9**
>
> What therefore God hath joined together,
> let not man put asunder.

❧ Purpose Principle #12 ❧

While you're caring for the things of the Lord, God is processing and preparing your husband on how to care for you.

> **1 Corinthians 7:34**
>
> I would like you to be free from concern. An unmarried man is concerned about the Lords affairs-how he can please the Lord.

Most men would say that they just don't understand women, they're too complex. Or they're too irrational and emotional.

God knew men would feel that way and he's showing men through their relationship with him, how to be with their wife. Men have to be concerned with ways to please his wife. You don't believe me? Let's go to the word:

> **1 Corinthians 7:33**
>
> But a *married man* is concerned about the affairs of this world - *how he can please his wife.*

> **1 Peter 3:7**
>
> *Husbands*, in the same way *be considerate as you live with your wives*, and treat them with respect as the weaker vessel.

Here you see a snap shot of the skills men learn in their relationship with the Lord reflected in marriage.

1 Peter 3:7, talks about how they have to consider their wives and 1 Corinthians 7:33 reveals how to please her.

> Both men and women have different paths they have to take to in order to get to their appointed destinations. Therefore, it's not wise to focus on the development of the opposite sex. Let God complete the work he started with the man without you. While you're single, focus on what God is building in you. You can't tell a man to "be a man" or " real men don't do..." etc. You barely know what women are supposed to do! Let's encourage our brothers and use this developmental time to let God make you a wife!

Women on the other hand, have a different mandate:

> **1 Corinthians 7:34**
>
> An unmarried woman or virgin is concerned about the Lords affairs: *Her aim* is to be devoted to the Lord in both body and spirit.

Not only are single women suppose to be concerned about the Lords affairs, he says that her AIM is to be *devoted to the Lord in both body and spirit.*

For men and women, concerning yourself with the Lords affairs is part of the process. Within this system he has a multiplicity of things going on. For one, he's strengthening your relationship with him while simultaneously preparing you for marriage. Second, he uses unmarried women to care for the things of the Lord. In other words, he uses you to take care of his business.

Therefore, single women in particular, the Lord expects devotion in both body and spirit. Devotion in both body and spirit is a form of worship, faith and commitment. These are qualities that every *man* desires in his wife! God commands a clean pure vessel and so does your future husband.

ᚼ PURPOSE PRINCIPLE #13 ᚼ

IN GOD'S SYSTEM, CARING FOR THE THINGS OF THE LORD PREPARES YOU TO BE A WIFE.

Romans 12:1

Offer your bodies as living sacrifices, holy and *pleasing to God*-this is your reasonable *spiritual act of worship*.

---

1 Peter 3:7

Husbands, in the same way be considerate as you live with your wives, and treat them with respect as the weaker *vessel*.

In your relationship with the Lord you'll develop a humble, quiet spirit. Your very nature will be based on faith and commitment. Since you've turned your heart to God, he become your source. You have faith in *him*. Therefore, later on, you can have faith in your husband *because* you have faith in God. Submission to your husband will be easy for you because you've been taught submission through your relationship with the heavenly father. And honestly, what man alive can resist praise? We see here that God does have a system of process before you get married.

The world system today tells you otherwise. They say to date whomever you want, do what you want, as often as you want to. Information about sex is so prevalent, you can find it anywhere whether you're looking for it or not. You could be in line at the grocery store, looking at the magazines and right on the cover you'll see "10 ways to the best sex", "how to have an orgasm". You don't have to look far. We're constantly being bombarded on television. It's sexual overload! Even in children/teen programs they talk about kissing boys, who wants to have sex with them, and teenage pregnancy.

So being up to par sexually has become part of the dating game. You may have even gossiped with your friends about sexual escapades, talking about whom you thought was good sexually or not. We as a society have accepted this culture. To consider another way outside of this system feels unnatural, weird and too far out. But in actuality, look around...the worlds way *is* unnatural, weird and too far out!

Think about a date in itself. You meet someone you like, he calls you or you call him, chat for a while, set a date to go out. It may be to dinner, movie, dancing etc... You're doing this to get to know the person, understandable. But what ends up happening is the physical attraction grows every time you see each other. 9 times out of 10, this dating leads to physical contact and I would go as far as to say it eventually leads to sex 6 times out of 10 (I'm being generous here). Then you break up, later meet someone new and the dating cycle continue.

According to the word, sex before marriage is fornication. Fornication is a sin. A woman who fornicates is a whore, according to the word. If you go out with a man and have sex with the intent for him to give you money, guess what, that's prostitution. This sounds harsh but we need to expose the devil and get to the truth. The truth shall set you free. Dating is a trap! I know, I know, this sounds insane. You're probably thinking, "how can I get to know someone if I don't spend time with them?" The answer is just that. You spend time with them, that's it.

> Now I'm not trying to condemn anyone. My goal is for people to gain understanding. If you have one man and you are sleeping with him out of wedlock, that's still considered fornication. Therefore, you are no different from the next woman who has several men. Sin is sin. And sin means separation from God. If you are separated from God, then you are separated from love. If the man you are with really loved you, he would honor you by waiting and make you his wife.

It simply goes back to the bible way. First of all, you are one person. You only need one partner. That's it. You're the rib from the man's side. There's a specific man that you belong to. God said when you're single, you are to care for the things of the Lord. That's where your focus should be.

When your focus lines up with his will, that's when the process begins. Now, you're learning *Gods way* of doing things, by building faith, Godly character and discernment. He makes you whole and satisfied. Nowhere did he tell you to look for a man. Nor does he mention in his word anything about "dating".

God, while you're doing his will, is arranging your marriage. He's preparing you for your husband and your husband for you. This way you both are whole spiritually, have the same Godly character and speak the same language. Your husband will find you and call you by your name. And when you hear him, you'll know his voice. The voice I'm referring to is the Holy Spirit in him and in you. The Lord said my sheep shall know my voice. God is perfect; there's no confusion in his program; it works every time.

❧ PURPOSE PRINCIPLE #14 ☙

IF YOU LET HIM, GOD THE FATHER WILL ARRANGE YOUR MARRIAGE.

Think about it. When you meet someone of interest, you have no idea if they have unfinished business with other women. As far as you are concerned, it shouldn't even matter to you because they're not your focus, nor are they your man. You are free to talk and spend time with them without pressure. God's system allows you to focus on him, as he helps you get your life in order while allowing the other person to do the same. If, while caring for the things of the Lord, the man really wants you he will have to pursue and wait for you. Generally, most men today, if they're not serious about a future with you, will not wait for you, period. God's "no dating" system is a filter for imposters and captures "your husband". It's about spending time getting to know someone and seeing if they're part of your purpose. And when it is right, I don't believe it takes long.

Ok, I know what you're thinking. How can I marry someone that I don't know and haven't dated? Generally when dating someone, you say "that's my girlfriend" or "that's my boyfriend", etc... What I'm saying is when it is right, things will flow naturally. There is no preliminary title of boyfriend/girlfriend. You both are simply in agreement in spirit. In other words you both "will just know". I'm not saying that it will be easy but you'll agree to wait because both of you are believers and God is not the author of confusion. Confusion is a signal that the enemy is present and someone doesn't agree.

> **Hebrews 11:3**
>
> Through faith we understand that the worlds were framed by the word of God, so that things which are seen were not made of things which do appear. In God's system, relationships are formed in the spirit first. That's why when it's right, the Holy Spirit will confirm it within you and you'll just know.

✿ PURPOSE PRINCIPLE #15 ✿

CONFUSION IS A SIGNAL THAT SOMEONE DOESN'T AGREE. HOW CAN TWO WALK TOGETHER UNLESS THEY AGREE?

> **Amos 3:3**
>
> Can two walk together except they agreed?

Don't be deceived as you have been in the past by the dating game. The devil *is* a liar. God is not mocked! Even if you're engaged, the word says it's not good for a man to touch a woman. Whoaa! I know you are ready to throw this book in the trash now! But it's true, you're not married yet so premarital sex is still illegal! Hugging, kissing, touching, as wonderful as it is, are gateways to the lust of the eyes, of the flesh and the pride of life. So keep physical contact at a minimum. All these things lead to premarital sex (sin). How? When you're dating, those simple gestures of affection get boring. Your flesh after while craves for more. Eventually, you will do more.

Make no mistake, sin is sin! Let's really pull the covers off this thing. How many people (I don't mean you of course, lol) do you know who were engaged but never got married? Now you have sinned against the Lord with your body and the man is no longer there. That's just like the devil; he will always leave you holding the bag. Don't you see it's all a set up? In the grand scheme of things, all that matters is the bottom line. The bottom line is that you want to be pleasing to God and have your own husband. You want to love and be loved the right way. You want to enjoy sex and intimacy the way God intended. God is not trying to deprive you. He understands covenants, agreements, and rights. If you legally own something, you have the right to do what you please with it and no one can take that right from you. That's the type of relationship God has for you. Not like the world, who gives and takes away. You don't want to be used up by various men nor do you want to disgrace your father. For the bible says, did you not know that your body is the temple for the Holy Spirit? The devil wants to separate you from your blessings and God given right then leave you with a counterfeit. If you don't believe what I'm telling you, think about your own life. If what I was saying wasn't true you probably wouldn't have this book. You would already be married to your H.S. sweetheart!

The Lord's rules of engagement, requires faith. You must believe that God can and will do his part. Once you do that God's peace settles into your spirit and you're no longer thirsting after the flesh. No more dating. Wait on the Lord to show you who your husband is. Spend this time getting to know God and his voice. Start doing his will.

Love is the Principle Thing

In *Single on Purpose*, all of the answers come from the word and revelation, not from me. I personally, don't have the answers and I'm flawed like you therefore, I feel I would be doing a great disservice just giving my point of view. So, what's the answer?" "How does one have a good relationship?"

This is the million dollar question most of us want to know. First, I have to address the dating concept. The more popular school of thought says that women should date multiple men. I disagree because there's no dating in the bible. The danger in the dating relationship model is people commit to being what they call "in love" without a covenant. Because both parties have verbally agreed to be joined in a relationship, the world leaves a "break up clause" if they *feel* differently for any reason.

The fact is *feelings do change*! Satan the god of this world system operates through the senses; the lust of the eyes, and lust of the flesh and the pride of life. Wherefore, you will experience feelings and circumstances that causes changes. Our heavenly father is not a God of "like". He *is* Love. Love *is* the principle thing. God designed marriage for love and intimacy not "like". He has specific instructions for married couples. The instructions are designed for love, procreation, purpose, protection, multiplication, endurance and worship. For the wife, he commands her to respect and submit to *her own husband*.

God instructs the husband to *love his wife* like Christ loves the church. Then he tells them to love one another. But what is love?

> **Love is patient**
>
> **Love is kind**
>
> **Love, it does not envy**
>
> **It does not boast**
>
> **It is not proud**
>
> **It is not rude**
>
> **It is not self seeking**
>
> **It is not easily angered**
>
> **It keeps no record of wrong**
>
> **Love does not delight in evil but rejoices in truth**
>
> **It always protect**
>
> **Believeth all things**
>
> **Always hopes always perseveres**
>
> **Love never fails**

God is love, he *never changes*! The Lord is bound to his word, covenant and principles. Dating is a man made concept God has not approved, therefore he's not obligated to support it. If you choose this route you're responsible for all that comes with it.

In God's system, he requires both of you to love each other. He's not talking about feelings. He is talking about being responsible with your walk *with him* by manifesting *his character* in your relationship. Having his character and his Holy Spirit reign in your life, your relationship will have the ability to survive anything.

It's a major commitment to love someone in this intimate kind of way. When most people date/live with someone, they're really in "like a lot" not love. If they were genuinely *in love*, like the above scripture, feelings would not take preeminence in their relationship. They would get married.

I also hear a lot of women say they have a problem trusting men. God never told us to trust our partners. Actually, he said that we should *not* trust man but put your trust in God.

You see, people are going into dating relationships with marriage concepts. This is out of order and you have no protection. There's no one protecting your feelings!

God knows that we all fall short and have the capacity to sin, hurt feelings and disappoint. For this reason, in all successful relationships agape love is required.

A WORD ABOUT TRUST:

If you have trust issues, you have a faith issue. Therefore, your best line of defense is to drench yourself in the word and put your trust in God. Complete trust in man is unstable and unreliable. It's virtually impossible for any person to be completely trustworthy because we're not perfect. Sometimes, we violate trust when we're not trying too. Other times, people commit to terms they believed they could keep...then life happens. Oh yes, you could say "that's unfair" until it's you who've done the violating! Putting your trust in God allows people the space to make mistakes and bad decisions, which we all will do from time to time. It frees you up as well as others. If you're believing God for someone who is trustworthy, ask God for more faith. That's the substance of what you are hoping for. Then you must be what you want to attract.

> **Psalm 118:8**
>
> *It is* better to trust in the LORD than to put confidence in man.

Now you have people in a dating relationship experiencing "like a lot" mistaking it for "love". Love is the principle thing. There's unbalance in the dating model because one party is treating the other like a spouse without "covenant". Why would you engage in any agreement where you feel obligated to give your all without the assurance of a mutual agreement? Could it be that your relationships have failed because you were "acting married" to someone who is "dating" you? Are you submitting to someone who is not your own husband and expecting "love" in return? If so, you've been cheating yourself. Ask yourself, are you even "in love"? To be "in love" would mean that you are "in God" and "in God" means "in the word". Is your relationship in writing?

❦ Purpose Principle #16 ❧

Love is Free But it Ain't Cheap!

Real love relationships are easy to identify. Just check the biblical definition of Love. As a Christian, since you're not dating, spend time with whomever the Holy Spirit directs you to. Don't give the relationship a title until it has one… "Husband or wife".

Before anything is materialized in the natural it starts in the spiritual. If you truly love a person, you'll love them in your spirit first. The tell tale sign is the manifestation of the character attributes listed in 1 Corinthians 13. The one who is right for you will also exemplify the same spirit and both of you will agree.

God's love will always agree with his word. He will lead you to the righteous relationship of marriage. Love is free but it's not cheap! It is extremely valuable; that's why God houses your union in a secured, meaningful environment called marriage. How else do you think your relationship can survive?

Feelings *do change*…for all of us! We grow, we're happy today, sad tomorrow. I like you today and I don't tomorrow. This is inevitable. But when you truly love someone, it allows room for all of those changes. If you really love someone, you'll be long suffering, forgive, and hold no record of wrong. God knows, a boyfriend doesn't deserve the throne because he hasn't paid the price to be king.

Only a husband, the man that paid the price with his name and life, deserves that level of love, respect and submission from you. This is why women of God feel cheated within the dating, boyfriend/girlfriend model.

SOMETHING ABOUT MARY

Why is it so important that you understand your position in the body of Christ while single? God has purposefully designed you to be a vessel. You're carrying the most precious cargo in the universe. We carry the seed of the Holy Spirit. The spirit is in the seed and life is in the blood.

Ha ha ha, you thought it was about you, huh?! No, the purpose for marriage between Christ and the church is to join together blood and spirit, in order to produce Godly offspring.

> **Malachi 2:15**
>
> Has not the Lord made them one? In *flesh and spirit* they are his. And why one? Because he was seeking *Godly offspring*.

Now, we're starting to get to the real nuts and bolts of this thing. This is so significant! We're here to establish God's kingdom on earth in his likeness and image. What does that look like? You and I as Jesus walking the earth! *We* are Jesus in the flesh! Let's look at the birth of Jesus:

> **Matthew 1:18**
>
> *This is how* the birth of Jesus came about: His mother Mary was pledged to be married to Joseph but *before they came together, she was found to be with child through the Holy Spirit.*

You're not just here on this planet to be pretty and fulfill the desires of the flesh. There's a clear purpose which is very serious. It's sad because people are so used to the world system that they are totally disconnected from the will of God for their lives. You're so much more significant than superficial things. God has honored women with the capacity to give birth in the earth realm as well as in the spirit with the word (the seed) of the Holy Spirit.

✿ PURPOSE PRINCIPLE #17 ✿

YOU ARE WORTH SO MUCH MORE THAN YOU CAN IMAGINE. YOU ARE PREGNANT WITH DESTINY AND PURPOSE

> **Matthew 1:20**
>
> But after he had considered this and angel of the Lord appeared to him in a dream and said, "Joseph son of David (This is the bloodline) do not be afraid to take Mary home as your wife, because what is *conceived in her is from the Holy Spirit.* 21she will give birth to a son, and you are to give him the name Jesus, because he will save *his people* from their sins.

The Holy Spirit is the seed and Jesus is the baby! Jesus is also the word. So when you minister to people with your life, words and actions, you're speaking into their spirit.

When a person accepts Jesus (the word), they receive the divine deposit (the Holy Spirit). This is Holy matrimony, the joining of spirit and flesh. This is part of your purpose! Reproduce Jesus in the flesh and establish the kingdom of God! Be fruitful and multiply! Mary's life provides this example.

> **Matthew 1:18-23**
>
> *This is how the birth of Jesus Christ came about*: His mother Mary was pledged to be married to Joseph, but *before they came together, she was found to be with child through the Holy Spirit.* [19]Because Joseph her husband was a *righteous* man and did not want to expose her to public disgrace, he had in mind to divorce her quietly.
> [20]But after he had considered this, an angel of the Lord appeared to him in a dream and said, "Joseph son of David, do not be afraid to take *Mary* home as your *wife*, because *what is conceived in her is from the Holy Spirit.* [21]She will give birth to a *son*, and you are to give him the name *Jesus*, because he will save his people from their sins." [22]All this took place to fulfill what the Lord had said through the prophet: [23]"*The virgin will be with child and will give birth to a son*, and they will call him Immanuel - which means, 'God with us'."

What does Mary has to do with our purpose? Everything. Consider, what has the Holy Spirit imparted in you? What assignment has he given and asked you to carry to term? God used Mary to assist in the birth of his son Jesus in the earth. Loving people, imparting the word of God into their lives is the process of reproducing Jesus on earth through us. He knew Mary was perfect for the task that's why he chose her. God knows that you're single and he's equipped you to be perfect for the purpose he has in mind for you. It's all in your willingness to serve.

Mary's experience also reveals through Christ we become:

1. Virgins: Born again, pure in spirit
2. Wives: God is our husband
3. Mothers: We carry, birth, manifest the word of God
4. Daughters: God is our Father
5. Sisters: In the body of Christ

We're wives because of our covenant relationship with God. He's our *husband, father and God while single. Mary the mother of Jesus was betrothed to Joseph, which meant that the marriage was pre-arranged. Mary wasn't concerned about *getting married* because she already knew that she was going to get married.

So what was her concern? Her concern was her assignment given to her by the angel of the Lord. Carry to term, birth and take care of this Holy baby. Baby?! What baby? How could she be pregnant and still a virgin? How can she be a wife and not married? The answer is found in the scriptures:

> ***Isaiah 54:5**
>
> For your Maker *is your husband--the LORD Almighty is his name*--the Holy One of Israel is your Redeemer; he is called the God of all the earth.

CHAPTER 4 – SOMETHING ABOUT MARY

> **Matthew 1:18**
>
> 18This is how the birth of Jesus Christ came about: His mother Mary was pledged to be married to Joseph, but *before they came together*, she was found to be *with child through the Holy Spirit*.

Mary became pregnant by *hearing and receiving* the word of the Lord and her faith (the substance of things hoped for) in the word conceived the seed in her womb. She accepted the terms of her assignment from the angel of the Lord and agreed to serve.

Her selfless, sacrificial act is a divine example of how single women of God ought to be. With one word from the Lord, she was prepared to sacrifice everything for what she believed in. She was willing to lose Joseph, risk persecution by the people, etc. to fulfill her God given purpose.

That's the attitude Christian singles need to adopt.

PURPOSE PRINCIPLE #17

WHEN YOU DECIDE TO HEAR AND OBEY THE WORD OF THE LORD MIRACLES BEGIN TO HAPPEN.

Whether you realize it or not, we're like Mary. As a single woman of God, Mary was part of the covenant. When we get born again, we become virgins in the spirit. Therefore, we're virgins, wives and mothers at the same time.

What is the purpose?

1. Wife: To produce Godly offspring
2. Mother: To birth Jesus in the flesh
3. Virgin: To be used as a hallowed vessel
4. Daughter: To serve the father by caring for the things of the Lord
5. Sisters: To anoint the body of Christ

Initially, this information may seem over the top spiritual and it is. The revelation of our relationship with the will of God has been the crucial element we've ignored.

Honestly, most women operate off of what they see. That directly violates the system of the Kingdom of God. If you're a woman of God, the only way that will work for you is Gods way. You are no longer part of the world system. Please allow yourself to understand the spiritual process so that you can manifest the desire God placed in your heart like he did with Mary.

God the Father is our husband and we are intimate with him through the word/the Holy Spirit. Our lives should birth Christ. The reproduction of the spirit of Christ in your life is confirmation of who you are. That's the evidence your future husband needs to solidify the fact that you're a wife in the spirit.

As a man spends time with you, if you profess to be a Christian, he's looking for the manifestation of Jesus in your *life. Mary had to birth Jesus first!*

Yes, your future husband should find you married and pregnant (Pregnant with the word and a wife through covenant).

> **Matthew 1:21**
>
> ²¹She will give birth to *a son* and you are to give him the name *Jesus*, because he will save his people from their sins.

The reason you must complete your assignment of birthing Jesus in your life is because people will be led to him through you. That's what single on purpose is all about!

You're running around trying to find a man when God has appointed you to manifest the son of God on this earth to keep people from going to hell! It doesn't matter how old you are, divorced, widowed, single mom or what your situation may be.

If you're a believer and you're single, we must be like Mary! Birth Jesus in your life!

✧ PURPOSE PRINCIPLE #18 ✧

WHEN YOU MEET YOUR HUSBAND, HE SHOULD FIND YOU ALREADY MARRIED AND PREGNANT (IN THE SPIRIT).

When Mary became pregnant, Joseph was prepared to divorce her. This is the initial reaction most carnal men have when you decide to realign you life in proper order with the Lord. They'll notice something different about you.

Your belly is protruding in the spirit with the word, revelation, the Holy Ghost and it's become obvious! Life came inside of you from God; not from man. In other words, things that bothered you before won't and things that used to be acceptable are not because the Holy Spirit removed that taste from you. A worldly man cannot understand nor accept these drastic changes without resistance.

In Mary's case, the bible was clear that Joseph was a *righteous* man, which made the difference. The word of the Lord came to Joseph in a dream and when he woke up, he knew exactly what to do with Mary.

He took her home and had *no union with her* until she gave birth! He had to wake up to the word in order to truly see her *and know how to treat her*.

In order for Mary to transition as a wife in the physical world, she had to birth Christ in the spirit!

❧ PURPOSE PRINCIPLE #19 ❧

IF YOU'RE ALREADY IN A RELATIONSHIP WITH A GOOD MAN AND YOU DECIDE TO START OBEYING GOD, DON'T WORRY. IF HE IS FOR YOU GOD WILL WAKE HIM UP. THEN, HE WILL KNOW WHAT TO DO WITH YOU. IF NOT, LET HIM GO. GOD WILL LEAD YOU TO THE RIGHT ONE.

Luke 1:27-38

to *a virgin pledged to be married* to a man named Joseph, *a descendant of David*. The virgin's name was Mary. [28]The angel went to her and said, "Greetings, *you who are highly favored! The Lord is with you.*" [29]Mary was greatly troubled at his words and wondered what kind of greeting this might be. [30]But the angel said to her, "*Do not be afraid*, Mary; *you have found favor with God.*

> ³¹*You will conceive and give birth to a son,* and you are to call him *Jesus.* ³²He will be great and will be called the Son of the Most High. *The Lord God will give him the throne* of his father David, ³³and he will reign over Jacob's descendants forever; *his kingdom* will never end." ³⁴"How will this be," Mary asked the angel, "since I am a virgin?" ³⁵The angel answered, *"The Holy Spirit will come on you,* and *the power of the Most High will overshadow you. So the holy one to be born will be called the Son of God.* ³⁶*Even Elizabeth your relative is going to have a child in her old age,* and she who was said to be unable to conceive is in her sixth month. ³⁷*For no word from God will ever fail."* ³⁸*"I am the Lord's servant,"* Mary answered. *"May your word to me be fulfilled."* Then the angel left her.

In the above text the angel of the Lord is giving Mary her assignment. Although he's talking to Mary, he's also speaking to you. He's saying, *"this is how the birth of the Lord came about"*. This is how the system of betrothal and Godly offspring is produced. Below, I list the chain of events in the order according to the conversation between Mary and the angel of the Lord. It's through this order we begin to witness the blueprint for single women of God develop:

- The angel identified her as a virgin.
- She was betrothed.
- Joseph was descendant of David. (this means he was part of the royal lineage/bloodline and descendent of the children of Israel).
- "You're highly favored" (The angel is telling Mary that her being single is good news and that she has been chosen, preferred to do a special assignment at this moment in her life.).
- The Lord is with you. (He's letting her know that she is not alone.).

- Don't be afraid. (This can appear to be a word of consolation but it's actually a command. DON'T BE AFRAID).
- You have found favor with God.
- You will conceive and give birth to a son (here's her assignment).
- You are to call him Jesus (when you birth Christ in your life, call him Jesus (God). It's not about you).
- God will give him a throne (purpose).
- He will reign forever, his kingdom will never end (purpose).
- The Holy Spirit will come upon you (this is how you're going to conceive).
- The power of the Most high will over shadow you (process and protection).
- The Holy one born will be called the son of God (manifestation of the sons of God on earth).
- Elizabeth, your relative will give birth in her old age (He's letting us know there's no age limit. No matter what age you are you can still give birth in the spirit).
- The angel of the Lord says his word never fails (your assurance that God will do what he said he will do in your life).
- Mary says, "I am the Lords servant" (Here Mary accepts the mantle of her calling and begins to serve).
- Mary responds, "may your word to me be fulfilled" (Mary agrees and has faith in the word of God).

✌ PURPOSE PRINCIPLE #20 ✌

THE MANIFESTATION OF CHRIST IN YOUR LIFE IS PROOF TO MEN THAT YOU ACTUALLY ARE WHO YOU SAY YOU ARE.

Perception of what's going on in your life is so crucial. Mary could have easily misinterpreted what was happening. If Mary focused on herself more than the will of God, she would have never conceived. She would not have received the word of God because the answers to all of her questions were spiritual and required faith (this is happening to women of God in society today).

Also, it appears as if the Lord's request came at an inopportune time because she was already scheduled to get married. How would she explain her pregnancy to Joseph?

Fortunately, her perception was accurate because of her character. What she did before marriage is what made her blessed. Her heart and character got the attention of the Lord. He favored her so much that he used her for an amazing assignment.

God has highly favored us just like Mary and will use us to manifest his son on this earth as well. While you're waiting on your Joseph, remember what the angel of the Lord said in Luke 1:37, "For no word from God will ever fail".

> **Genesis 35:11**
>
> God said to him, "I am God Almighty. Be fruitful and *multiply*. A nation and a *company of nations will be from you*, and *kings will come out of your body.*

Mary understood very well that it was not about her. She understood her purpose. Inside her was the most precious cargo; The King of Kings! Today we have the same royal mandate. God spoke this to us back in Genesis when he told us to be fruitful and multiply. He says a *company of nations* will be from you and kings will come out of *your body*! Single women, this is our purpose, to carry, birth, nurture and marry the King!

Mary the mother of Jesus is not the only Mary in the bible we can learn from. Look at Mary Magdalene, who was very close to Jesus. She anointed his feet with expensive perfumed oil and wiped it with her hair and tears. When the disciples saw what she was doing they tried to stop her. Yes, they tried to stop her because they didn't understand what she was doing and why.

The bible says that Jesus delivered her from 7 devils. Think about all the things God miraculously delivered you from that people aren't aware of or don't understand? They cannot comprehend how after all you been through, you still devote yourself to the Lord. Nor do they understand the level, depth or magnitude of your praise. Mary Magdalene knew who Jesus was *to her* therefore she humbled herself at his feet and worshiped him by anointing the body of Christ.

Mary Magdalene's demonstration of love shows single women how and why they should worship God through devotion. The "How" is on her knees in humble submission before the Lord in gratitude and love. The "why" is because of all the miraculous wonders Jesus has done in her life.

My sisters, when we realize how much God loves us and how he's been there all along…tears of love will flow out of you in gratitude. This is not a cute praise. Mary Magdalene tells us why.

The reason why you can't be cute here is because in order to stay in his presence like Mary, you must worship him in spirit and in *truth*. This is the place where you get naked and allow your hair to be disheveled because the truth is if it had not been for the Lord you wouldn't have made it. For that you're truly grateful!

Your testimony, praise, worship, your life…all of it was broken like that alabaster box to pour out the precious anointing that God has given you. In return, while you're single, your life testimony anoints the body of Christ.

> *** Mark 14:6**
>
> Let her alone; why trouble you her? *she has wrought a good work for me.* ⁷For you have the poor with you always, and whenever you will you may do them good: but me you have not always. ⁸She has done what she could: she has come beforehand to *anoint my body* for burying.

*Note about Mary Magdelene:

As she worshiped Jesus at his feet, Judas commented about the alabaster box. He felt there would have been better use for the ointment if she would have sold it and gave it to the poor.

You see, Jesus knows the heart of men. He knew that Judas was a thief and he could care less about the poor.

That's how worldly men will approach you. Your alabaster box stores the precious anointing oil derived from all the trials and tribulations God has brought you though.

That ointment is precious and priceless. Don't give your alabaster box to Judas! He's a traitor! He doesn't care AT ALL about what you been through, all he wants to do is steal from you.

The bible says that any man that doesn't enter through the door is a thief and a robber. A man that wants your body, that which is precious from you without marrying you is trying to enter another way other than the door.

He is a thief and a robber. Ignore Judas. Stay at the feet of Jesus and anoint the body of Christ (the church).

Hide and Seek: What happens when God hides you ...

OK, here's where things get really interesting! In God's divine system, everything must be done in spirit and in truth. In other words, you will not see his blueprint with your physical eyes. This has been the problem all along. Flesh has natural inclination to pursue what it wants. Not a spiritual attraction but by what you see or what you *want* to see.

Many women have a long detailed wish list of what they're looking for in a man. Men also have an ideal picture in their mind on what they think they want. So what happens? You go out looking for what you find appealing. This is a trap! What you see with your eyes is the bait and like gullible little fish you go for it. But did God tell you to do that? If he didn't then you weren't operating in spirit and truth, you were operating in the flesh.

> **Genesis 3:6**
>
> When the woman *saw* that the fruit of the tree was *good* for food and *pleasing to the eye*, and also desirable *for gaining wisdom, she took some* and ate it. She also gave some to her husband who was with her and he ate it.

The lust of the eyes, my dear friends is a set up. The enemy has familiar spirits that he assigned to follow you since birth. Spiritual assassins that study your weaknesses then inform the appropriate demons to come and attack you in that area.

Satan understands that we have the proclivity to be vulnerable to our physical senses. Once he knows your preference he dispatches that handsome kryptonite your way.

Haven't you ever notice how people seem to attract the same type of person over and over again? This is not an coincidence, different body, same spirit!

⚘ Purpose Principle #21 ⚘

Remember, you are a spirit being with a body because God is a spirit. We walk by faith not by *sight*.

Oftentimes, we refer to ourselves as "human". We make excuses for our weak decisions by saying "I'm only human". God never called us that. When we were born again, we became spiritual beings with bodies of flesh. Understanding your spiritual nature will help you grasp spiritual concepts.

God is a spirit, which means you are a spirit. The spirit realm is more real and vast than the physical realm we see. It's hard to fathom that but how I do it is to close my eyes and think. When you do that, in that moment, there are no limits or boundaries to your thoughts or what you can see. In your mind you can see, be, do, and have anything you desire. That is the nature of the spirit realm (at least one aspect of it). Our strength is through the Holy Spirit who lives inside of us.

> **John 4:24**
>
> God is a Spirit: and they that worship him must worship him in spirit and in truth.

> **2:Corinthians 10:4**
>
> For the weapons of our warfare are not carnal, but mighty through God to the pulling down of strongholds

> **Ephesians 6:12**
>
> For we wrestle not against flesh and blood, but against principalities, against powers, against the rulers of the darkness of this world, against spiritual wickedness in heavenly places.

I'm establishing the fact that we're spiritual beings because that's the realm in which we must operate. We're to walk by faith (substance of things hoped for, the evidence of things not seen) not by sight (the physical realm). God uses foolish things to confound the wise. People who are worldly will only respond to what they see with their physical eyes and what they understand with worldly thinking. This is why women often choose a man that's physically attractive, who treats them horrible over a man who is not as appealing that treats them like a queen. Carnal people will always crave things of the flesh instead of the substance of the spirit.

> Listen, my sisters, I couldn't get more serious than this! It is not play time anymore. God is requiring us to live a Holy and righteous lifestyle. Going to church on Sunday as usual is not going to cut it. You want to know why you're single but you're still thinking worldly thoughts. If I told you to date, you would be comfortable with that. Now that I'm challenging you to live like the word commanded I could feel right now in the spirit, the resistance. You must understand as long as you are a Christian you are the enemy of the world. Whenever, you go the world's way, IT WILL NOT WORK. You can resist what I'm showing you the word is saying but I guarantee, you'll find it's true because it is. Please, please, please take God's way to heart and do it. IT DOESN'T MATTER WHAT AGE OR STAGE YOU ARE IN EITHER! Understanding this chapter will help you see what God is trying to do for you while you're single on purpose.

In God's system, and I'm talking about his principles found in the word, he hides "the wife" in him. You lose your "self" in him. This is the time when God processes you, inducing growth personally and spiritually. During this period it often seems like no man is interested or paying attention to you. God is not allowing men to find you because you're "under construction". Remember when God created Eve? He put Adam to sleep. He woke Adam up after the work in her was done. You see, all the while when you're feeling isolated and rejected, God is making you a wife. As he sets you aside for his purpose, your development should be in tandem with service in the kingdom.

One of the reasons God employs this method is to make the woman prudent. The bible says that a prudent wife is from the Lord. God is going to "present you" to your husband. The man God chooses for you has to earn God's favor. Once the man completes his assignment, he has earned the rest of his body. Remember, you're the rib from *his side*. In other words, "you" are the rest of his body. In order for the man to win God's favor, he had to die himself and put on the perfect body of Christ. Single women must do the same so that God can join you *together. The two shall become one. The new you must be righteous and prudent. Devoting yourself body and spirit makes you righteous and after the process is over, you'll be prudent.

PRU·DENT

1. Wise in handling practical matters; exercising good judgment or common sense.
2. Careful in regard to one's own interests; provident.
3. Careful about one's conduct; circumspect.

*Mark 10:9

Therefore what God has joined together, let man not separate

> ***Ephesians 5:31**
>
> "For this reason a man will leave his father and mother and be united to his wife, and the two will become one flesh."

Why prudent? God's intention for creating the woman in the first place was for her to be a *suitable helper*. A woman who is prudent is defined as competent, wise in handling matters, can exercise good judgment and simply has good common sense! This manner of character is what a husband needs in a wife to operate at maximum capacity in home, business and government.

The process women must go through to become "prudent" is a spiritual process that's intimate and private between themselves and God. For that reason, the last time you probably got any attention was when you were the "old you".

What you attracted in the past was the person you were at that time. If you were full of lust, you attracted men with the spirit of lust. If you were selfish, then you attracted selfish men. You may not have realized these negative characteristics belonged to you because people rarely consider themselves in such an ugly light.

> Generally, God hides you, you won't get a lot of attention from men because they cannot see you (the real you). God has you hidden in plain sight. Don't get discouraged, this is only part of the process. You don't need a bunch of men, you only need one, *the right one*. The one God has chosen from the beginning of time at the appointed time that God has predetermined.

Nevertheless, kind attracts kind. The world says "opposite attracts" but that's not what the word says. In order for you to attract the man of God that he has for you, you must "be" who you are attracting.

So God has to change who you were and he does so through Christ. All of this is done right before our physical eyes but no one can see it until the butterfly (you) emerges from the cocoon (spirit realm).

When you're hidden, the enemy is out there desperately looking to destroy you. The enemy cannot see you because when he looks at you he's blinded by the light of Jesus! His job is to get you to move out of position. If you're in Christ, he *cannot* move you nor can he see the real you! That's why when you've committed to devoting yourself to God an imposter *will show up* at your door. This is the enemy's

- Be Righteousness
- Stay obedient to the word
- Test the spirits according to the word
- Look at the fruit
- Ask the Lord for clarity
- Remember that your body is the temple for the Holy Spirit
- Remember you are Jesus in the flesh

attempt to draw you out of position. So how do you know the real deal from the imposter?

You will know an authentic man of God through your spiritual eye. Your spiritual eye is the "Holy Spirit, the spirit of truth". Sometimes, you may not be sensitive to what the Holy Spirit is saying or showing you. So when you can't see, hear or understand the voice Holy Spirit, how do you avoid entrapment of the enemy? Simply obey the word!

If you remain obedient to the word, you'll win by default. Beware, just because a man is saved doesn't mean that he's the one. This is why sometimes women get so frustrated. They meet a nice man of God; hit it off then nothing.

Let me tell you what that is. That man did not fit the purpose you and your future husband will have together. You don't need a lot of men, you only need one. God has a man specially made for you, for his purpose.

Another reason some men do not make the cut is they are not worthy of you. God test the spirits, he knows who is who.

He said in proverbs:

> **Proverbs 18:22**
>
> 22He that finds a wife finds what is good and receives favor from the Lord.

If you're with a man whose heart is not right or demonic, he will not see "you". He will only perceive the flesh. That man will not have the ability, the "spiritual eye" of the Holy Spirit to see you. He doesn't recognize you as a wife.

If he cannot identify the real you, he disqualifies *himself* from receiving what is good from you and favor from the Lord!

❧ PURPOSE PRINCIPLE #22 ☙

A WORLDLY MAN IS BLINDED BY SIN. HE CANNOT DISCERN WHO YOU REALLY ARE AND LOVE YOU FOR IT.

The man God designated for you will have the spirit of discernment. First, he will have to "seek the kingdom of God and his righteousness". Second, in order for him to gain discernment, he has to, "care for the affairs of the Lord; and find how he can please the Lord".

If a man is caring for the things of the Lord, he's being obedient, faithful and loving. He's led by the Holy Spirit. As a result, his eyes are wide open. You cannot be in sin and see clearly.

A true man of God that is chosen for you will SEE YOU! In order to find you he has to be looking for Jesus in you. His spirit will agree with your spirit. The exchange that occurs is spiritual!

> **Proverbs 25:2**
>
> It is the glory of God to conceal a thing: but the honor of kings is to search out a matter.

One of the things that God conceals is *you*! God *reveals you* to *your betrothed* after he has earned you. Not by pursuing you but by pleasing God. Only a man with the heart of a king will search for God and find his good thing.

As a woman, your role is different from the man which is part of his match-making system. God requires devotion of our body and spirit. Men must find ways to please him. This system is a sophisticated game of hide and seek. After the man has worked and searched hard enough, God rewards him for his service. For your faithful devotion, God rewards your patience.

> **Hosea 12:12**
>
> Israel *served* to get a wife. And to pay for her he tended sheep.

> **Hebrews 11:6**
>
> But without faith it is impossible to please him: for he that comes to God *must believe that he is*, and that he is a rewarder of them that *diligently* seek him.

> **Matthew 7:7**
>
> Ask, and it shall be given you; *seek, and you shall find*; knock, and it shall be opened unto you:

The incongruity here is the man should not be seeking to find a wife. He should be seeking God. Nor should a daughter of Zion look for a husband but God. The Lord put desire in both hearts for love. When both men and women seek and find God they find each other in him, in love. *see illustration. Your obedience simultaneously protects you throughout your process and positions you. No time is wasted.

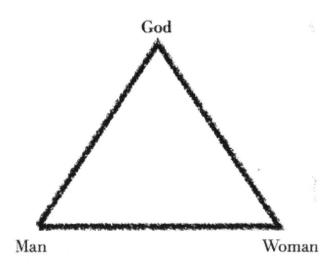

> **Psalms 84:11**
>
> For *the Lord God is a sun and shield*: the Lord will give grace and glory; *no good thing will he withhold from them that walk uprightly.*

> **2 Corinthians 4:4**
>
> in whom the god of this present age has *blinded their unbelieving minds* so as to *shut out the sunshine* of the Good News of the glory of the Christ, who is the image of God.

> **Acts 28:26**
>
> Go to this people and say, "you will be ever hearing but never understanding; you will be *ever seeing but never perceiving*." For this people's heart has become calloused; they hardly hear with their ears. And *they have closed their eyes*. Otherwise they might see with their eyes, hear with their ears, understand with their hearts and turn, and I would heal them."

God does not make mistakes, people do. If the Lord decided for you to be single at this time, then you should obey his instruction to care for the things of the Lord and devote yourself body and spirit. The moment you disobey this command you begin to move out of the hiding place. Then bam! The devil got you!

That enemy will try to make you feel like God made a mistake, he didn't know what he was doing. Didn't he know that you wanted to be married with children by now? Didn't he know that you were getting older and if you're going to have kids you need to start now?

Yes, he does know and it's all good! Just remember, thoughts like these are designed to distract and seduce you out of your power position in the Father.

There's no wisdom outside of God! You don't know what's best for your life more than him. He's hiding you on purpose for your good. There's nothing wrong with you. This is simply part of the process. Trust God, in time you'll begin to see this is a wonderful, beautiful situation!

How Do You Get Off Track?

Sin will separate from God

Fear will make you hide from God

Disobedience will make you turn your back on God

How To Get Back On Track:

Love will make you turn to God.

Obedience will bring you to God

Faith will hide in God

NAMES: YOU CAN CHANGE A WHORE INTO A HOUSEWIFE!

> **Proverbs 22:1**
>
> A good name is more desirable than great riches; to be esteemed is better than silver or gold.

When God began to reveal biblical truths about being single, he told me to write a chapter about names. At first I thought he was actually talking about our birth name. But he took me much deeper, illuminating shocking truths about names that we were called by, call ourselves and the names given as a result of things we've done.

I'm sure you may be thinking what in the world does my name have to do with being single on purpose?! Stay with me, I'm going somewhere with this.

God himself said that a good name is to be desired. Why, because he knows the name that you're known by will define who you are and affect your relationships. He also wants us to understand that our name is what we'll be judged by (physically & spiritually) in the book of life. Your name should stand for and mean something positive.

❧ Purpose Principle #23 ☙

You're identified by the name you're called.
Make it a good one.

While you're walking out your purpose, God tells you to *desire* a good name. There are things that you must do along the way to achieve that. For him to mention that suggests some of us don't have good names.

For example, you may say, "I'm a good person, I'm nice, I have a good name". But how is your credit? Yes, what is your credit like? If your credit is not up to par then your name is not altogether in good standing. If you do not pay back what you owe, then your name alone is no good.

This fact has been a hindrance for many single people today because bad credit affects lots of opportunities in life. With the use of the internet, people can easily find out your credit history. As a matter of fact, this is how some employers are making their final decisions when hiring employees. They are judging people's character by their creditworthiness.

Many men and women today are doing the same thing when finding a mate! People find someone they're interested in, then go online and research their credit history. Basically they're trying to find more information about your character.

Although this method is unethical, people are taking their future very seriously. Everyone wants to find a partner who is responsible, competent and trustworthy. As you continue to 'care for the things of the Lord', he'll build your character and give you a good name.

The word is light and the closer you get to it, darkness is exposed. In other words, before you decided to be single on purpose, doing things God's way, you had little to no conviction about doing the wrong thing. It didn't bother you to owe people without intentions of paying back (especially men).

Now that you're born again, you're no longer comfortable lying or living a lie. Although it may take some time to completely change your character or to get out of debt etc., the most important thing is to never stop walking in righteousness.

God is so awesome that when he see's your effort, he will bless you. He can do anything! He can make all debt go away in an instant if he wants to. Nevertheless, the point is to allow your Father to change your name from negative to positive by *honoring his.*

Deuteronomy 15:6

For the LORD your God blesses you, as he promised you: and *you shall lend to many nations*, but *you shall not borrow*; and you shall reign over many nations, but they shall not reign over you.

❧ PURPOSE PRINCIPLE #24 ☙

DON'T IGNORE BAD CREDIT. YOUR NAME REPRESENTS YOUR CHARACTER. IF YOU DON'T PAY BACK WHAT YOU OWE, YOUR NAME IS NOT COMPLETELY GOOD.

> **Proverbs 3:3,4**
>
> Let love and faithfulness never leave you; bind them around your neck, write them down on the tablet of your heart. 4. Then you will win favor and a *good name* in the sight of God and man.

One of the things God expresses here is that if you hold steadfast to the word and keep it in your heart, you'll be transformed into a wife with a loving, faithful spirit. The word in your heart is truth and light. You literally have God living inside of you which wins favor with God and man. The bible tells us to "owe no man", "you will be a lender not a borrower". The obeying of the word transforms you. Your new nature will not allow you to be content with a bad name. Because your character is now God like, honest, true and faithful, your name will be associated with these characteristics. The word makes your name good.

Your old name represents who you used to be when you were in the world. In the bible, a woman who had sex before marriage was called a whore. A woman who committed adultery was called an adulterer. Whatever sin that was committed, had a name. The minute you habitually committed the sin (the action), you became that thing. If you lied, you were a liar. If you stole something, were a thief, etc...

> **1 Corinthians 6:11**
>
> And that is what some of us were. But you were washed, sanctified and justified in the name of the Lord Jesus Christ and by the Spirit of our God.

Of course, these names are ugly as that's what sin is. No one wants to face this reality. If I called a whore a whore, they'd be ready to claw my eyes out. They would be offended because that's not how they see themselves. But that's what the bible calls a woman who fornicates, if you're having sex out of wedlock that's what you're called.

The sad thing about this is that too many people only look at things with their physical eyes. Something happens spiritually when a woman sleeps with a man. They become spiritually married to that person.

Here's where it gets really deep. When you give your life to God, he becomes your Lord, father, kinsman redeemer and husband. The Lord personally gives you his name.

If you fornicate, this is unlawful intercourse. You are committing spiritual adultery. This changes your name! You go from wife to whore, blessed to curse.

And believe it or not, men pick up these things! Sometimes your name will precede you. Your name is attached to your reputation. Good or bad, you are called by your name.

> **Name defined:**
>
> 1. A word or words by which an entity is designated and distinguished from others.
> 2. A word or group of words used to describe or evaluate, often disparagingly.
> 3. Representation or repute, as opposed to reality
> 4. A reputation: has a bad name
> 5. A distinguished reputation: *made a name for himself as a drummer*
> 6. An illustrious or outstanding person: joined *several famous names for a photograph.*
> 7. To mention, specify, or cite by name
> 8. To call by an epithet: named them all cowards

Name or number?

Your name signifies who you are and whose you are. The Lord revealed to me one of the differences between his system and Satan's system. Gods system is designed by words and names. Satan's system is a numerical/mathematical system. Numbers are cold, impersonal and calculating. Numbers are never satisfied. One plus one is two and so on and so on. The numerical system is a formula for manipulation. Each move, equation is predicated on an outside element that will add, take away, multiply, divide or subtract. Whenever a number is manipulated it changes the original number to something totally different.

Satan's ultimate desire is to ascend his kingdom above God to be God. This is impossible because God is God of gods, King of kings and Lord of Lords. He's the original God, the creator. Satan is a creation. Since Satan is not a creator, he doesn't possess the ability to be original all he can do is be a counterfeit. That's why the numerical/mathematical system may sound very close to the word/name system but it's very different.

Names are a form of identification. So are numbers. The difference is names are personal, identifies bloodlines, lineage, seal contracts, validates inheritance. Jesus, his place as Lord and savior, messiah is sealed with his name and blood. Satan is identified by the mark of the beast, 666, nothing personal, no bloodline, lineage and no rights. Ultimately, after we die, on judgment day the book of life will be opened and the angel of the Lord will be looking for your name!

All this directly relates to you as a Christian person, period. But as it relates to a single woman, you should know God is your husband. When you get married in the physical world, you take on your husband's name. His family becomes your family. You now have rights to the family inheritance, you and your children (lineage). As a single person, you have to assume the name of your spiritual husband, Jesus. This means more than *saying* Jesus is my husband.

> **Genesis 2:24**
>
> For this reason a man will leave his father and mother
> and be united with his wife
> and they will become *one flesh*.

When you get married you and your husband become one flesh. The marriage itself is a contract/covenant that is sealed by your name. It is not considered official until the marriage is consummated (intercourse/intimacy/blood relationship). Since your name defines you and your character, when you accept Jesus as your Lord and savior, you are to manifest *his* character. God is Love. Being married to God is not about trying to be something. I don't try to be Jordi. *I am* Jordi. When I am Jordi Jesus, my character should reveal him in me; the fruit of the spirit:

> **Fruit of the Spirit:**
>
> But the fruit of the Spirit is love, joy, peace, longsuffering, gentleness, goodness, faith Meekness, temperance: against such there is no law.
>
> Galatians 5:22,23
>
> **Characteristics of Love:**
>
> [4]Love is patient, love is kind. It does not envy, it does not boast, it is not proud. [5]It is not rude, it is not self seeking, it is not easily angered, it keeps no record of wrongs. [6]Love does no delight in evil but rejoices with the truth. [7]it always protects, always trust, always hopes, always perseveres. [8]Love never fails.
>
> 1 Corinthians 13:4-8

The *character* traits listed above should be the manifestation, the sign that you've become one with *God. If you're not walking in the character of Jesus Christ and you sin, you'll experience separation. And if you don't have a name, you're just a number.

> ***Song of Solomon 1:3**
>
> Pleasing is the fragrance of your perfumes; your name is like perfume poured out. No wonder the maidens love you!

⁂ PURPOSE PRINCIPLE #25 ⁂

MEN WILL DATE ANY NUMBER OF WOMEN AT ANY GIVEN TIME. IT'S ALL A NUMBERS GAME FOR THEM. BUT WHEN A MAN REALLY DESIRES YOU, HE'LL CALL YOU BY NAME AND GIVE YOU HIS. DON'T CONCERN YOURSELF WITH THE NUMBERS.

An example of the name/numbers principle is found in Esther. King Xerxes was looking for a queen to replace Queen Vashti. So they held a huge pageant, recruiting women from all over the world to find the next queen. Esther was not proficient in the royal customs, as she was not raised a princess. Therefore she didn't know what a king would desire in a woman. However, her upbringing did teach a valuable skill. Her uncle Mordecai taught her how to listen to, and respect authority. Estjer *listened* to the Eunuch who was in charge and did whatever he told her to do.

The rules were simple. Each woman would *wait their turn* to be called in to see the king. After the king saw you, if he *liked* you (personal), he would request you by *name* (personal). Many women from the harem (numbers) entertained the king. But the only woman you heard about that won the favor of the king was called upon by her *name (official title)*! The other women were just numbers.

In Esther, there are a couple of key points. First, Queen Vashti lost the throne, her position as queen, because of her attitude. She forgot who she was. Her position had power but it wasn't *absolute*. Her role as queen required complete loyalty and submission to the king.

Vashti's grave mistake is one we often see women make, and that's the inability to submit to authority. She had a sense of entitlement, another bad character trait amongst many women today. If she knew her name, she would have known to give the king what he wanted.

Technically, Vashti's response wasn't as random a one may think. Here's the scenario: the king was drinking and decided he wanted Queen Vashti to leave her banquet and come to his event. Basically, he wanted to show her off in front of his drunken friends. She thought being strutted before a group of drunks was beneath a queen so she refused.

Right here is the fork in the road between worldly thinking and the thoughts of a believer. Queen Vashti thought she had a choice in the matter. But a queen who understands her name, role and position knows better. She would show up in her finest and throw the best fashion show she knew how because SHE DOESN'T HAVE A CHOICE! Why? Because she understands that the moment she became queen, she was SUBJECT to the King! Vashti didn't have the *character of a queen*.

Another important note is that Esther's uncle Mordecai instructed her *not to reveal her nationality or background*. Why is that? He knew that she was in enemy territory. When God brings you into a new dimension, until you learn it and get to a power position, less is more. Esther was in a worldly place, she wasn't surrounded by friends and family, but by the enemy. And he can and will use old information against you.

Take a look at Miriam Webster's dictionary defines harem:

> 1. A house or a section of a house reserved for women members of a Muslim household.
> 2. The wives, concubines, female relatives, and servants occupying such a place.
> 3. A group of women sexual partners for one man.

Mordecai understood that Ester had to live in the harem for a season. In the harem, Ester would be processed through 12 months of rigorous treatments with oil of myrrh, perfumes and cosmetics.

The harem is a "type" of world system; remember harem defined states, "a house or a section of a house reserved for women members of a *Muslim* household. Muslims were not in covenant with God, nor did they acknowledge his ways.

Those mandatory treatments were designed for external beauty but for Esther, this procedure was *already completed within her*. In the beginning of the book of Esther, the scriptures mentioned that she didn't have any parents, which means she didn't have a name. She was no stranger to rejection; her family was in exile, the tribe of Benjamin was in exile, and to top it off, she had no parents.

Needless to say, she has already gone through pressure and pain treatments of life which anointed her for her purpose, (the oil of myrrh) as a result she was clothed with humility (you see this through her obedience to her uncle and authority).

Therefore, her royal obligation was fulfilled *before meeting the king*. It was the *anointing oil derived from all God has brought her through that made her beautiful and attractive not the natural beauty treatments the world gives.

> **John 12:22**
>
> And I, if I be lifted up from the earth, will *draw all *men* unto *me*.

I believe her uncle Mordecai also knew that her previous name, background and past weren't relevant for the assignment at hand. It was about the purpose in front of her. Esther's obedience is confirmation to the point God wants us to understand. She didn't have to make a *verbal* announcement of who she used to be. Her spirit, character spoke volumes for who she is in the present. She was Jewish, not Muslim.

Mordecai gave her his name, which placed her in the lineage of the children of Israel. Through that relationship, the covenant of her ancestors, she became a woman of God entitled to the blessing and inheritance of the seed of Abraham.

Esther was a covenant wife, *not just a woman that's part of the harem*. Her name, who she was, wouldn't allow her to conform to the ways of the harem. Her name/character made her different, causing her to stand out!

That's why when the women of the harem would consult one another regarding how to impress the king, she instead asked *the King's servant*, the eunuch for advice. You see she was *in the world* but not *of the world*. Her strategy was to *please the king*.

Knowledge of your name *is* your strategy. Your role in that single position is to please *the King of Kings* (not men). Don't ask the women of the harem (unsaved/carnal women) for their advice. Don't tell them who you are, be who you are by walking in the favor of God. When your moment comes to see the king, you'll find favor with him because the heart of the king is in *his hands* (the King of Kings).

> **Esther 2:10**
>
> [10]Esther *had not revealed* her nationality and family background, because Mordecai had forbidden her to do so. [11]Every day he walked back and forth near the courtyard of the harem to find out how Esther was and what was happening to her. [12]*Before* a young *woman's* turn came to go in to King Xerxes, she had to complete twelve months of beauty treatments prescribed for the women, six months with oil of myrrh and six with perfumes and cosmetics. [13]And *this is how she would go to the king*: Anything she wanted was given her to take with her from the harem to the king's palace. [14]In the evening she would go there and in the morning return to another part of the harem to the care of Shaashgaz, the king's eunuch who was in charge of the concubines. *She would not return to the king unless he was pleased with her and summoned her by name.*

Prior to giving our life to Christ, we were part of the harem, "a group of women sexual partners for one man". Instead of asking God how to please the king, we've solicited advice from non believers, who are clamoring for the same spot. As we allow God to change our names, we must discover ways to please him because he is King of Kings! Then what happens? When you come out of obscurity, you will find favor with everyone, including the king. Not only will he call you by name, he will give you his!

~ PURPOSE PRINCIPLE #26 ~

IF YOU DON'T HAVE A NAME, YOU'RE JUST A NUMBER

Another point about the number system; it's one of witchcraft and manipulation. Mathematics includes formulas, values, calculations, symbols and figures. In order to change one number to another number is to manipulate it. This requires thought, planning, calculations and figures.

If you want a desired result aside from what you already have you must manipulate the figures. This is what we do when we decide to leave God and do things ourselves. We begin to calculate and manipulate…knowledge of good and evil.

God didn't begin our existence with good and evil, he just gave us good. Satan came along and *added* knowledge of evil. Once Adam and Eve ate of the tree of the knowledge of good and evil, that was the element that changed the equation.

> Manipulation is a form of witchcraft. All these books on "How to make a man fall in love with you", "how to find, seduce a keep the man you want" etc.. is glorified witchcraft. The advice given in these type of books is in rebellion to God's way. The bible says that rebellion is a form of witchcraft. When you feel like you're tired of waiting and you decide to just go out there and find you a man, you're violating your name. It is your Father's job to choose your husband for you and give you away, in due time. The husband God ordained for you has the SAME NAME! Therefore the lineage continues along with the blessings. But when you formulate your own system for getting a man, you violate the system and it won't work for you.

◢ Purpose Principle #27 ◣

YOU CANNOT OBTAIN TRUE LOVE THROUGH MANIPULATION. THE COST OF A RELATIONSHIP FORMULATED BY YOU OWN DEVICES WILL BE PAID BY YOU FOR THE DURATION OF THE RELATIONSHIP AND POSSIBLY GENERATIONS TO COME.

When we're struggling with sin, I believe God's mercy and grace abounds. But when you eat (receive, digest, and choose) sin, separation from God occurs. You may not feel like you have chosen Satan but the side you're on is built into your decision. Your name adapts according to who you are. Your character becomes like that of your father.

We witness this when women attempt to deceive men. Their actions are no longer loving and trustworthy. They use calculated manipulating movement. You do whatever you think to do to solve your problem. Isn't that what Adam and Eve did? After they ate, they saw themselves as naked so they sewed fig leaves and hid themselves. What, did they not think God would see right through them? Well ladies, men of God see right through manipulation as well because of the God in them.

> **Exodus 20-1-8**
>
> And *God spake* all these words, saying, *I am the LORD thy God*, which have brought thee out of the land of Egypt, out of the house of bondage. *Thou shalt have no other gods before me.* Thou shalt not make unto thee any graven image, or any likeness of anything that is in heaven above, or that is in the earth beneath, or that is in the water under the earth: *Thou shalt not bow down thyself to them, nor serve them: for I the LORD thy God am a jealous God, visiting the iniquity of the fathers upon the children unto the third and fourth generation of them that hate me*; And shewing mercy unto thousands of them that love me, and keep my commandments. Thou shalt not take the *name of the LORD* thy God in vain; for the LORD will not hold him guiltless that taketh *his name* in vain.

Final note about names area about the connection to generations and inheritances. You're a daughter of the King of Kings and Lord of Lords. When you get married you do a name change. The man that marries you gives you his name but it's through the daughter he gains access to throne. Jesus is not a careless King of Kings. He's going to make sure that whoever carries his name must be of royal blood. That's why the man has to be born again as well. He needs to be born again for the blood (lineage) and marries for the kingdom (inheritance). The name gives him access to the kingdom, providing the privilege of being part of the inheritance, lifestyle, status and wealth. While he's single he serves as son, but when he marries rules as a King.

That's one reason why God says "he that find a wife, find a good thing *and obtains favor*. Our Heavenly Father obviously has the most because he owns everything, so the man benefits more than the wife because for him, the union solidifies a seat on the throne. Note: this is king with a small "k", God is King of Kings. I'm referring to the territory that God has given man dominion over on the earth to subdue and rule in his stead.

Your Purpose Part 1

How do I find my purpose?

Have you ever asked yourself, "What's the meaning of life" or "what's my purpose"? This is a poignant question we ask ourselves in the quest to live the life we believe we're ordained to live.

But how do you find this purpose? People have traveled far and wide, tried different subjects in school, various careers, all in an attempt to find their purpose. Many have gone as far as experimentation with same sex relationships in a heartfelt passion to find their purpose.

Believe it or not the solution is simpler than you think. The answer not only encompasses your purpose while single, it also pertains to your overall life purpose.

It's not about, nor has it ever been… about *you*. It has and always will be, *to do the will of God!*

⁂ Purpose Principle #28 ⁂

Your purpose in life always has been and always will be to do the will of God.

> **Ephesians 1:11**
>
> In him we were also chosen, having been predestined according to the *plan of him* who *works out everything* in conformity with the purpose of *his will*.

Therefore, in order to discover your individual purpose, you must seek the word to learn what his *will is for you. As you begin to renew your mind and conform to his character, you'll begin to see things the way God intended.

Example: Imagine if you will, before giving your life to Christ, you used to be a pimp. In that realm you manipulated the minds of women convincing them to sell their body for money. Obviously, in order to dominate and control these women you had to have courage, charisma and seductive power. Knowledge of the street life, and understanding how to navigate it, was vital to survive competition.

Although this is an extremely negative lifestyle, it eludes hints to the gifts and talents God gave that were abnormally used. Once converted, the Holy Spirit enlightens your mind. Now you take that same gifting; courage, charisma and influence to minister to the very people/community you abused.

Since you're already familiar with the streets and they know you, you have access and credibility in the realm many would not have. Because people knew who you used to be, they could readily see the change in you without having to utter a single word.

Ultimately, what the devil meant for evil, God turned it around for good which was his purpose all along.

> ***Matthew 6:10**
>
> Your kingdom come, *your will be done on earth* as it is in heaven.

All you've been through in life and relationships; struggles, trials, tears, and victories store glimpses of your purpose through gifts and talents. These were markers to lead you to the place where you discover God and your reason for being.

God is your creator. He's the only one who can tell you who you are. The bible is his will and testament for you; it's your manual. The old and new testament *is a will*. You know the phrase "last will and testament". History is not about your story. It's about *His-story*!

A will reveals in detail what the deceased person left to his children for an inheritance like land, property, money etc. Oftentimes, the will contains contingencies.

For instance, the heir will receive the entire estate upon completion of their master's degree or when they get married. If neither obligation if fulfilled, they become ineligible to receive the inheritance. You are a legitimate heir of Christ. This is why you must *seek him (the word) first*.

God left instructions for you to obtain rights, privileges, property, wealth and benefits in his will. All of the benefits are yours as his children but there are contingencies like faith, obedience and righteousness.

MANIPULATION IS A FORM OF WITCHCRAFT

All these books on "How to make a man fall in love with you", "how to find, seduce a keep the man you want" etc.. is glorified witchcraft.

The advice given in these type of books is in rebellion to God's way. The bible says that rebellion is a form of witchcraft. When you feel like you're tired of waiting and you decide to just go out there and find you a man, you're violating your name.

It is your Father's job to choose your husband for you and give you away, in due time. The husband God ordained for you has the SAME NAME!

Therefore the lineage continues along with the blessings. But when you formulate your own system for getting a man, you violate the system and it won't work for you.

You are in the will of God! In his will, he has ordained for you to be single at this time. Therefore, it is incumbent on you to read the will (the word) and receive his instructions for you in this position so that you may obtain your benefits.

❧ PURPOSE PRINCIPLE #29 ❧

YOUR FATHER HAS LEFT YOU AN INHERITANCE. READ THE WILL (THE BIBLE) TO LEARN HOW TO RECEIVE IT.

> **Matthew 6: 30-34 (Message version)**
>
> If God gives such attention to the appearance of wildflowers- most of which are never even seen-don't you think he'll attend to you, take pride in you, do his best for you? What I'm trying to do here is get you to relax, *not to be so preoccupied with getting*, so you can respond to God's *giving*. People who don't know God and the way he works fuss over these things, but you know both God and how he works. Steep your life in *God-reality, God initiative, God-provisions*. Don't worry about missing out. You'll find all your everyday human concerns met.

When you seek God's face, his way of doing things, your heart, mind and lifestyle will change. God given instructions will come to you daily. That's why he said seek ye first the kingdom of God and his righteousness and all these things will be added unto you. Your purpose is included in "*all* these things". Also included in "all these things" is your future spouse, career and whatever you should be doing while single.

This lifestyle, new kingdom mindset is completely different from the life you used to know. Thinking Kingdom thoughts may feel unorthodox in this day and time. It seems so dated. But that's the trick of the enemy. Truth is, no matter what position you find yourself in

Christ, it will be *easier than being in the world. I'm not saying that you will not suffer any uncomfortable trials and tribulation. What I'm saying is that when you operate within kingdom principles you'll always win. If you lack wisdom, he has a whole book on that specific subject (Proverbs). All of the provisions have already been met but you must have faith and be in your rightful position to obtain it. If your mind is stayed on Christ, you will always be at peace no matter what is going on around you. Even when you go through unhappy times, you will have joy. Your faith in the Lord will get you through anything!

> **Matthew 11:30**
>
> *For my yoke is easy and my burden is light.

Ponder this thought. Think of all of the men that you've been with in your life. Think about how many men you've slept with. In the beginning they made all sorts of promises, professed undying love, etc. yet look around, they're not here anymore. Consider time wasted on dates that went nowhere or of all the years wasted being with the wrong one.

Think about yourself or the women you who've had children out of wedlock and countless abortions. What about all of the times your feelings were hurt or your heart got broken.

Now, think about how much would have been avoided if you were faithful and obedient to God, focusing on him, letting him choose for you. What if you would have lived by his principles of no fornication, no adultery, no covetousness and no lasciviousness etc?

You would have saved yourself, heartache, misery and most of all time. It's God's word, his principles that makes the difference not worldly knowledge.

> **Proverbs 1:23**
>
> If you had *listened to my rebuke*, I would have poured out my heart to you and made *my thoughts known* to you.

Proverbs 1:23 gives us a wisdom key. He's saying that the Holy Spirit is speaking to you, correcting wrong behaviors and choices but we haven't been listening. However, if we did listen to him, he would make his thoughts known to us. You would have discovered your purpose a long time ago.

That's what we needed! No matter what relationship we're in, personal, business, married, single, family, we need to know God's thoughts so we can make the best decisions. As we continue to read God's word and learn his principles, we must remember that it's the Holy Spirit guiding us. If he tells you to do something you don't want to do, submit and do it anyway so you can hear God's thoughts.

On the forefront it may seem like what you want is getting farther and farther away but remember God is omnipotent and omniscient. He knows what's best for you. Yielding to the Lords rebuke is the beginning to having the desires of your heart.

~ Purpose Principle #30 ~

THE REVERENTIAL FEAR OF THE LORD TRULY IS THE BEGINNING OF WISDOM. FEAR DISAPPOINTING GOD MORE THAN MAN AND YOU WON'T END UP DISAPPOINTED.

Walking with God induces spiritual labor causing your true purpose to emerge. Character develops in you through faithfulness, righteousness and obedience. The direct result of this paradigm shift is your perception about love, self and people.

As your relationship with Love progresses, you'll find yourself at the right place, at the right time, doing the right things. When it all comes together, God gives you an aerial view of what's been going on all along.

Your Purpose Part 2

Hebrews 10:5-10

Therefore, when Christ came into the world, he said: "Sacrifice and offering you did not desire *but a body* you prepared for me; with burnt offerings and sin offerings you were not pleased. Then I said, "Here I am –IT IS WRITTEN about ME IN THE SCROLL have come *TO DO YOUR WILL*, O God."

⁸First he said, "Sacrifices and offerings, burnt offerings and sin offerings you did not desire, nor were you pleased with them" (although the law required them to be made).

⁹Then he said, "Here I am, I have come to do your will." He sets aside the first to establish the second. ¹⁰And by that will, we have been made holy through the sacrifice of the body of Jesus Christ once for all.

¹⁶"This is the covenant I will make with them after that time, says the Lord. I will put my laws in their hearts, and I will write them on their minds."[b]

¹⁷Then he adds: "Their sins and lawless acts I will remember no more." ¹⁸And where these have been forgiven, there is no longer any sacrifice for sin.

¹⁹Therefore, brothers, since we have confidence to enter the Most Holy Place by the blood of Jesus, ²⁰by a new and living way opened for us through the curtain, that is, his body,

²¹and since we have a great priest over the house of God, ²²let us *draw near to God* with a *sincere heart* in *full assurance of faith*, having our hearts sprinkled to cleanse us from a guilty conscience and having our bodies washed with pure water. ²³Let us hold unswervingly to the hope we profess, for he who promised is faithful. ²⁴And *let us consider how we may spur one another on toward love and good deeds.* ²⁵Let us not give up meeting together, as some are in the habit of doing, but let us encourage one another—and all the more as you see the Day approaching.

²⁶If we deliberately keep on sinning after we have received the knowledge of the truth, no sacrifice for sins is left, ²⁷*but only a fearful expectation of judgment and of raging fire that will consume the enemies of God.*

²⁸Anyone who rejected the law of Moses died without mercy on the testimony of two or three witnesses. ²⁹How much more severely do you think a man deserves to be punished who has trampled the Son of God under foot, who has treated as an unholy thing *the blood of the covenant that sanctified him*, and who has insulted the Spirit of grace?

³⁰For we know him who said, "It is mine to avenge; I will repay," and again, "The Lord will judge his people." ³¹It is a dreadful thing to fall into the hands of the living God.

³²Remember those earlier days after you had received the light, when you stood your ground in a great contest in the face of suffering. ³³Sometimes you were publicly exposed to insult and persecution; at other times you stood side by side with those who were so treated.

³⁴You sympathized with those in prison and joyfully accepted the confiscation of your property, because you knew that you yourselves had better and lasting possessions.

³⁵So *do not throw away your confidence*; it will be richly rewarded. ³⁶You need to persevere so that when you have done the will of God, you will receive what he has promised.

> ³⁷For in just a very little while, "He who is coming will come and will not delay.
>
> ³⁸But *my righteous one will live by faith*. And if he shrinks back, I will not be pleased with him."
>
> ³⁹But we are not of those who shrink back and are destroyed, but of those who believe and are saved.

Phew! Yes, it's long and I'm aware I was in jeopardy of losing your attention but this passage is so important and life changing it was worth the risk.

What makes this scripture so relevant is the person speaking. In Hebrews 10:5 Jesus, God in the flesh is speaking to God the father about the reason he came here. If you pay attention to the conversation, you'll hear Jesus establishing his purpose. Since Jesus lives in us, you just read *your purpose*.

Now that you've offered your body to God, your purpose is to do his will. Our natural physical body is controlled through the mind. The brain tells your body what to do and the body obeys. Since you *offered* your body to the Lord, the Holy Spirit will be in control. Therefore, you do what God wants you to do not because you *have to* but because you *want to*. THAT'S YOUR PURPOSE, to surrender your entire *body and spirit* to the will of God. "I have come TO DO YOUR WILL, O God." –Jesus

✌ PURPOSE PRINCIPLE #31 ✌

WILLINGLY SURRENDER YOUR BODY AND SPIRIT TO DO THE WILL OF GOD. THAT'S YOUR PURPOSE!!!

> **THERE ARE THREE TYPES OF PURPOSES:**
>
> - Individual purpose
> - Corporate purpose
> - Divine purpose

Divine Purpose

First and foremost, you'll never find your purpose in another human being. However, our purposes are intertwined with other people in God's divine plan. This is why it's so important we come to the realization of why we're here. The divine purpose incorporates everybody and everything. We all work together, voluntarily and involuntarily with each other in the grand scheme of things. Nothing just happens; there's a system in place.

Because God is a God of order, his systems are designed to get us to an expected end. The mind of God is a mystery to the world. But the mystery is revealed to his children when we seek *him.

What you do, who you do it with divinely affects other people. Our primary example of divine purpose is in the lineage of Christ. People were born, married, died, produced offspring at specific times and places over the span of 2000 years to produce a royal bloodline.

In the beginning I'm sure few people involved in that lineage had any idea how significant they were!

> ***Deuteronomy 29:29**
>
> The secret *things belong* unto the LORD our God: but those *things which are* revealed *belong* unto us and to our children for ever, that we may do all the words of this law.

> Please understand that you are VERY SIGNIFICANT! Although it may not look or feel like it right now, it's true. From this point on, you're responsible for what you know. Your purpose is connected to God's will. He is strategic; at times we're not privileged to understand what he's doing until the end. But you must have faith that he knows what he's doing with you. If you've been single for a long time, THAT *IS* PART OF HIS STRATEGY! It is part of your purpose. The manifestation of bitterness simply means you don't understand your purpose. Keep *feelings* and *flesh* in line because it will attempt to contradict the word of God and your purpose. No matter what, remember your will should always be to do God's will.

Therefore, it should come as no surprise to you if you're single at this time. Especially, if you really got it going on!

It's been divinely arranged for it to be so for now (that doesn't mean it's a permanent position).

> **Romans 8:30**
>
> And those *he predestined*, he also called; those he called, he also justified; those he justified, he also glorified.

Corporate Purpose

Your corporate purpose is your assignment in the body of Christ.

> **Romans 12:5**
>
> So in Christ we who are many form one body, and each member belongs to all the others.

> **1 Corinthians 12:26**
>
> If one part suffers, every part suffers with it; if one part is honored, every part rejoices with it.

This realm of purpose is where you make your contribution to the edification of the body of Christ. As with the physical body, they are many parts. Although one member may be small, it doesn't quantify them as insignificant.

Likewise, if a branch of the body appears larger in stature, it doesn't make it greater. The key while you're single is to identify you own gifts then present them back to the Lord in ministry. For the body of Christ to function normally, every joint must supply. God has given the body of Christ various gifts for the edification of the church.

~ PURPOSE PRINCIPLE #32 ~

LIKE IT OR NOT, YOUR LIFE IS A MINISTRY.

The church has work to do and you're assigned to participate. This doesn't mean you have to constantly work within a church building.

Your *life* is a ministry. Utilization of your gifts and talents on a daily basis are ministry. Active participation in the divine mission of the church to win souls is your corporate purpose.

> **NOTE:**
>
> All that "free time" spent crying, trying to figure out "where all the good men are",
> should be used more constructively by operating in your corporate purpose.

> **1 Corinthians 14:1-5**
>
> *Follow the way of love* and eagerly desire *spiritual gifts*, especially the gift of prophecy. ²For anyone who speaks in a tongue does not speak to men but to God. Indeed, no one understands him; he utters mysteries with his spirit. ³But everyone who prophesies speaks to men for their strengthening, encouragement and comfort. ⁴He who speaks in a tongue edifies himself, but he who prophesies *edifies the church*. ⁵I would like every one of you to speak in tongues, but I would rather have you prophesy. He who prophesies is greater than one who speaks in tongues, unless he interprets, *so that the church may be edified.*

Individual Purpose

Most of the time when we're considering our purpose, we look at our life as a whole. Questions like, "why am I here?", "Why was I born", "what is the meaning of life", is generally the overall scope for purpose. Inquiry of that nature falls more or less under the category of divine purpose. I say that loosely because divine purpose encompasses all purposes. But for the sake of my point, I'm going to adjust the lenses a bit, focusing on individual purpose.

Individual purpose is the assignment God *specifically* intended for you to do. On the journey of discovery to finding your own purpose, every aspect of your life should be explored. First, look within yourself through the eyes of the Holy Spirit (Proverbs 20:27 the spirit of man is the lamp of the Lord, searching all the inner depths of the heart). Since the Holy Spirit is the spirit of truth, you can trust that he'll reveal to you who you are and what you should be doing. Second, look without, into the physical environment around you. What's the reoccurring theme in your life? Who is and have been around you? And finally look above to the heavenly Father/Jesus.

Our Lord and savior Jesus Christ has created all things and the Father has put everything under his feet. The Father created the divine master plan and knows your individual role. You see, God has placed within you gifts and talents reserved for your contribution to the kingdom, not just personal endeavors. Remember, it's always been and will be about God's will. The enemy has brain washed people through the world system to believe in *self*. That vantage point is false and distracts you from identifying what's truly real. If all of your attention is centered on self, it's impossible to be focusing on God. The error in "self help" is that you did not create yourself. You cannot find your purpose through self and the world system. That system is based on senses, self and knowledge. When your born again, you are no longer your own. You're a spirit wearing a body. The body is not wearing the spirit. To learn the purpose of that body and spirit, you must go to the father of creation. He left his will (the word) for you to explain his intentions and instructions for you.

> **Jeremiah 29:11**
>
> For I know the thoughts that I think toward you, saith the LORD, thoughts of peace, and not of evil, to give you an expected end.

The thing is God does not want us to be ignorant about *his purpose* for our individual lives. Notice, until now you probably never thought about God's will for you in this single position. Most singles are always in a rush to get a relationship with a man...but not with God. Consider yourself blessed. He has selected you on purpose! There's nothing wrong with healthy relationships with people but he desires for us to have an active, personal, loving relationship with him *first*.

The Strategy of Purpose

There are laws to every kingdom. For example, the oceanic kingdom has laws that must be obeyed in order for us to exist in it. God made it that way. If I want to go into the ocean for an extended period of time, I need a wet suit, oxygen tank and understanding of how to dive etc... In the earth realm, they are laws as well. In order for a spirit to be tangible on earth, it needs a body.

> **Romans 8:3,4**
>
> For what *the law* could not do, in that *it was weak through the flesh*, God sending his own Son in the likeness of sinful flesh, and for sin, condemned sin in the flesh: ⁴*That the righteousness of the law might be fulfilled in us*, who walk not after the flesh, *but after the Spirit.*

God created those laws as well. Since God is true to his word and cannot lie; he cannot go against his own laws. Therefore, in order for him (a spirit) to inhabit the earth where we can see him, he needed a body. Adam failed at this because of sin. Jesus the Holy Lamb understood God needed a body and became the perfect sacrifice. When he gave his body, it was a template for us to identify God in relation to our body. Christ/the Holy Spirit lives within us and wears our body. God exist in the flesh on earth through you!

> **Ephesians 5:31**
>
> For this reason a man will leave his father and mother and be united to his wife, and the two will become one flesh.

That's one reason why God doesn't want us to do drugs, alcohol, cigarettes, fornication and adultery and the like because of the effect it has on the body. God will not reside in a contaminated body, it's against the law (he is Holy). He doesn't ask you to kill the flesh to deprive you, he requires it so that he can have a real love relationship with you.

Contrary to the laws of the earth, the laws of the spirit realm require you to *take off the body* in order for you to inhabit it. Jesus laid down his life (body), no man took it. He voluntarily laid it down so that we may access the Father in the spirit. Your individual purpose is found through your relationship with Christ.

In the beginning was the word, and the word was with God and the word was God. He was with God in the beginning. Through him all things were made; without him nothing was made that has been made. In him was life, and that life was the light of men. The light shines in the darkness, but the darkness has not understood it.-John 1:1-5 The secret lies in who you really are. This scripture, which has been here all along, reveals this to you.

The scripture says, "Through him all things were made", "in him was life and that life was the light of men". Now what does this have to do with being *single on purpose*? Everything. This is the rock that we will build our foundation.

When you were born, whether you knew it or not, you were born in sin. We all were. That's why when people say to me, "I was born gay"; I say "you're probably right". That was the particular sin you were born into. The key is to be born again and not *remain* in sin. You may ask how is all this possible? When I was a baby, I was innocent and pure. The explanation I'm about to give you is the first key to unlock the secrets you need for the loving relationships that seem to keep slipping through your grasp.

First, let's talk about God. The Lord is perfect and in John 1 he says that in him was life and that life was the light of men, the light shines in the darkness but the darkness understood it not. When God created man, he did it in his own image. Although, Adam and Eve were pure in the beginning, *their decision to disobey* made them flawed. The reason their choice changed things was simple mathematics.

> ### KNOWLEDGE DEFINED:
>
> **1.** The state or fact of knowing.
> **2.** Familiarity, awareness, or understanding gained through experience or study.
> **3.** The sum or range of what has been perceived, discovered, or learned.
> **4.** Learning; erudition: *teachers of great knowledge.*
> **5.** Specific information about something.
> **6.** *Carnal knowledge.*
>
> Knowledge can be good or evil information. Sometimes its knowledge that gets us in trouble because we think we know better than God. It's best to learn from Adam and Eve. Listen to and obey God's instructions, it will always be "good". What satan has to offer will *appear* good and always end bad.

If you add, subtract, multiply or divide any number with another number the original sum will change. They added disobedience.

Remember, in the beginning Adam and Eve had no evil in them. They were all good before they ate of that fruit. But let me show you something:

> ### Genesis 1:29
>
> I give *you* every *seed-bearing plant* on the face of the whole earth and every tree that has fruit with seed in it. *They will be yours for food.*

> ### Genesis 2:8,9
>
> ⁸Now the Lord God had planted a garden in the east, in Eden; and there he put the man he had formed. ⁹And *the Lord God* made *all kinds of trees* grow out of the ground— *trees that were pleasing to the eye and good for food.* In the middle of the garden were the tree of life and the tree of the knowledge of good and evil.
> And *the Lord God commanded the man, "You are free to eat from any tree* in the garden; ¹⁷*but you must not eat from the tree of the knowledge of good and evil,* for when *you eat of it you will surely die."*

First, God says I have given you every *seed bearing plant* and fruit with *seed in it*; this will be yours for food. But then we see God made all kinds of trees grow and they looked good for food. What was so different about the tree of the knowledge of good and evil? It was *not a seed bearing* plant. This revelation is so relevant because remember… *the spirit is in the seed!* Without seed there is no reproduction. That's why God said "they will surely die".

Since God is perfect and pure, the addition of sin broke the covenant. Now they possessed knowledge of good and evil. Think about it, why did they need knowledge of evil when everything was all good? That evil seed was like a drop of black ink on a white sheet of paper. Even though it's just a drop, it's there.

No longer is it a pure white sheet of paper. If you make copies of this piece of paper, no matter how many copies you make it will always have that spot on it. That's what sin did to mankind. We were reproduced with dead seeds (like weeds).

Naturally, the father produces the seed (sperm) and the mother carries the seed to term. When a child is born it possesses DNA characteristics of both parents. In the spiritual sense, your DNA would be knowledge of good and evil. So how do you change your DNA? How do you change your parents? You must be born again.

YOU MUST BE BORN AGAIN

This is not about religion. Religion has been the smoke screen that Satan has used to keep you from discovering the truth. The truth is Satan is the father of lies and if you're not born again he is your father too. If you notice, children usually have characteristics of both parents. Some children will be more like one parent than the other. We see this spiritually. Prior to being born again, you had the sin nature. Now that you've been born again, God is your father. You have the heart and mind of Christ, full of love, life and purpose!

Galatians 5:17-21

¹⁷For the sinful nature desire what is contrary to the Spirit, and the Spirit what is contrary to the sinful nature. They are in conflict with each other, so that you do not do what you want. ¹⁸But if you are led by the Spirit, you are not under law. ¹⁹The acts of the sinful nature are obvious: sexual immorality, impurity and debauchery; ²⁰idolatry and witchcraft; hatred, discord, jealousy, fits of rage, selfish ambition, dissensions, factions ²¹and envy; drunkenness, orgies, and the like. I warn you, as I did before, that those who live like this will not inherit the kingdom of God.

Colossians 3:5

Put to death, therefore, whatever belongs to your *earthly nature*: sexual immorality, impurity, lust, *evil desires* and greed, which is idolatry.

Mark 7:21

For from within, out of men's hearts, come *evil thoughts*, sexual immorality, theft, murder, adultery.

> **Romans 8:13**
>
> For if you live according to the *sinful nature, you will die*; but if by the Spirit you put to death the misdeeds of the body, you will live.

Sin is a major contributor to why many haven't found the love they desire, simple as that. We've been using the world system, which hates us, to obtain the things we want. If you're not born again, of course the sinful nature is natural to you!

If you're in sin, you're in darkness, which is why you keep making the same mistakes over and over. Darkness was in you and you couldn't even perceive it.

> **John 1:5**
>
> And the light shineth in darkness; and the darkness comprehended it not.

In order to get rid of this death cycle, you must be born again and live holy. Jesus is God in the flesh. The Holy Spirit came upon Mary and planted this new seed in her womb. After Jesus was born, he lived a sin free life. Therefore the seed remained pure. The seed is the Holy Spirit. The outer casing of our spirit is the flesh.

This flesh has been contaminated by sin. Jesus had to die on the cross to destroy the shell of our sinful flesh to get the Holy contents out. So when you give your life to Christ, you're not born again into the physical realm, you're born again in your spirit. This rebirth reveals who you really are. God is your new parent, which makes you pure. You now possess the DNA of your father. You are a God.

> **1 John 3:2**
>
> Beloved, now are we the sons of God, and it doth not yet appear what we shall be: but we know that, *when he shall appear, we shall be like him*; for we shall see him as he is.

❧ PURPOSE PRINCIPLE #33 ☙

THE SON OF GOD HAS APPEARED ALREADY. HE APPEARS IN THE BELIEVER.

1 John 3:2 says that we now are the sons of God, when he shall appear, we shall be like him. Jesus has already appeared. God revealed to me that when the bible says "when he shall appear" one dimension of this meaning is when he appears in us.

When someone describes you, they express your characteristics. Everything we know about Jesus character should be identical in our lives once we've given our life to Christ. The "you" that you knew your old nature/character is dead. Since Jesus lives inside of you, you should have the characteristics of Christ which is love. Jesus appears in you!

> **James 1:17**
>
> Every good gift and every perfect gift is from above and cometh down from the father of lights, with whom is no variableness neither shadow of turning.

When we walk in the character of Jesus, we shall be like him. This is key. Walking in righteousness is powerful. If you notice, the world punishes people who are righteous. I'm sure you've experienced this in your own relationships. You're too "nice" they say.

There was nothing wrong with you being "nice". The darkness in the world "comprehended it not". When you meet someone that doesn't love the God in you and respect you for it, run! Their spirit is in opposition to the light in you. And if they are not ready for the light to come on, they will try to put yours out or leave because their spirit is convicted by the light of God in you.

Righteousness may *appear* corny and unattractive. But I guarantee you; God's way is the answer to everything that is good.

Jesus is so powerful that the seas and the waves lay prostrate before him. Demons trembled begged him not to send them to the pit. He healed the sick, raised the dead, made the blind see, the lame walk, turned water into wine, walked on water and countless other miracles that was too much for them to record.

Why am I telling you all this? You may ask, again, what does this have to do with being single on purpose? It is because of your purpose I share this with you. All of this time you have been thinking, behaving, seeing like a human being seeking his/her own, when you should be living, behaving and operating like a god for God.

> **John 14:12**
>
> Verily, verily, I say unto you, He that believeth on me, the works that *I do shall he do also*; and *greater works* than these shall he do; because I go unto my Father.

> **Psalm 82**
>
> "I said, 'You are "gods"; you are all sons of the Most High.'

If you're a god, where's the fruit? Why are you not producing the success, love and prosperity that's right in front of you? Look at it from this perspective. When you have a child, you've produced another person. Obviously, just because you gave birth it doesn't mean the baby will come out walking and talking, ready to take care of itself. The baby has to be fed, nurtured, loved and taught in order for it to get stronger and grow.

We're no different in the spirit. In this new world, the kingdom of God, we have to learn how to live and operate in it. Once maturity is met then we can manifest the sons of God, which is our purpose.

> **Romans 8:19**
>
> The creation waits in eager expectation for the sons of God to be revealed.

> **John 12:24-25**
>
> Jesus said, "Verily, verily, I say unto you, except a corn of wheat fall into the ground and die, it abides alone: *but if it dies*, it brings forth much fruit. He that loves his life shall lose it; but he that hates his life in this world shall keep it unto life eternal."

Who we really are, is spirit. And the death Jesus is speaking of is the death of "self/flesh/carnality". Once you kill "self" motives, you'll bring forth much fruit. Commitment to live for the Lord requires you to make some tough decisions.

Example: You may be in love with a man that you know is no good for you but won't let go because you don't want to be alone. Holding on to something that you think you *want* is "loving your life" because you're avoiding the pain of disciplining (crucifying) the flesh. You will inevitably lose in this situation because the enemy will eventually kill your spirit.

Not letting go, because you don't want to be alone, shows lack of faith that God can replace him. Instead of leaving a dead situation with faith that God will not withhold any good thing from the upright (which is the word), you stay worshipping at the altar of relationships. Making your flesh acquiesce to the word, no matter what you think or feel is the killing of the flesh. Once the flesh is dead the power of Christ is manifested in you.

> **Romans 8:14**
>
> For as many as are *led by the Spirit of God*, they are the *sons of God.*

> **John 4:24**
>
> God *is* a Spirit: and they that worship him must worship him in spirit and in truth.

All of this leads to the reason why Satan is behind bad relationships. He wants you to focus on the self debilitating feelings of being single, causing you to implode being ineffective in ministry. He doesn't want you to walk, talk, love, live, fight like a God. He certainly doesn't want you to complete your assignment to be fruitful and multiply. Therefore, he implements the war tactic of "divide and conquer". Because he knows the word:

> **Matthew 18:20**
>
> For where two or three are gathered together in my name, there am I in the midst of them.

> **NOTE:**
>
> Single or not you always have 2 or 3 gathered in his name
>
> When you are born again, you have your spirit man and you have the Holy Spirit gathered in his name.

Section 2

Give me body.

"I" GIVE UP!

> **Ephesians 5:27**
>
> That he might present it to himself a glorious church, not having spot, or wrinkle, or any such thing; but that it should be holy and without blemish.

The eye "I" represents who you think you are; self perception. If you see yourself and the world with the eye of "I" that is the spot and wrinkle this scripture is speaking of. Your eye should be Holy without blemish.

Think about it. If your body is the temple for the Holy Spirit, your entire body belongs to God. The bible says that if your eyes (I/self) are evil, then your whole body is filled with darkness. This may be hard to understand at first, it was for me too. God, with his grace and mercy gave me natural illustrations to reveal this truth.

Notice how the earth is called "mother earth". The bible says that the earth is the Lord's and the fullness thereof. When Jesus comes back to earth, he's looking for his *bride*. When we truly devote our*selves* (our "I"/flesh) body and spirit, God covers our eyes "I" with his blood. Remember, God is looking for himself, in you. Ephesians 5:27 says that *he* might present *himself*. Yet Christ lives in us, we are the body of Christ. Therefore, we see God talking to himself through us.

Now take look at this picture of a natural water hole. If you take a step back and look at the image, it looks like a huge eye.

From another perspective, we see an entire body of water. The colors and depth match everywhere except for where the hole is.

That hole looks like the retina in the eye. A dark spot in the middle of what would have been consistent color. But if you fill that hole, the spot will no longer exist. Once that spot is gone, we see an infinite body. That's what God is looking for in us a church without a spot or a wrinkle, a flawless infinite body.

Humans do not have the capacity to fill a hole like this, only God can. The same is true with us. Only God can fill you with the Holy Spirit. When you try to do it with your "I" you make a mess of things. There is no way possible that you can fill this hole by your*self*.

Flesh wants to have a life without God. Therefore, your flesh sends messages to your heart and brain telling it what it wants, how it feels, and what to do. What does that sound like? It sounds to me like the flesh wants to be God.

When you obey the flesh, guess what, it becomes god in your life. This is idolatry. The "I" (self/flesh/pride/me) all must come down and be destroyed.

If you look at these illustrations of the eye and read how the eye works, it's easy to see why God tells us to pluck it out. It's not the literal eye that he's referring to. He's saying make sure you pluck out your "I", in other words, remove self. Use the eye of the Holy Spirit (which is the true right eye).

The Eye "I am"

Jesus says "why behold the speck in your brother's eye but not consider the beam in your own *eye"? He calls the person who does this a hypocrite.

My question here is, have you ever considered what the speck and the beam is? I did and I've discovered that the speck is... *self/I*.

It is self motives that clouds the eye (will/motives/plans) of God.

> **Matthew 7:3**
>
> *3And why behold you the speck that is in your brother's eye, but consider not the beam that is in your own eye? 4Or how will you say to your brother, Let me pull the speck out of your eye; and, behold, *a beam is in your own eye*? 5You hypocrite, first cast out the beam out of your own eye; and then shall you see clearly to cast out the speck out of your brother's eye.

This is what your eye looks like when you put your "self", the dark speck in front of God:

Looks normal to you right? But here's how the eye looks when you remove self, God's mind/spirit takes over the body (no spot or wrinkle):

"The beam" was very interesting to me when I researched it. There's a beam that's actually called an "I beam"! I swear I can't make this stuff up! Look at the beam, it literally looks like a capital I in 3D. In essence, Jesus was asking the hypocrites how can you see the flaws of everybody else but you can't see your*self*?! Your*self* (will, thoughts, motives, ideas, opinions, feelings) have become this gigantic *image in your own eyes*.

The "I beam":

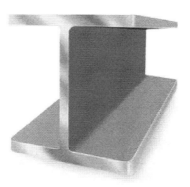

"I" is a symbol... the beam in your eye. It's a false "eye", an image of who you *think* "you" are. We're all created in his (God) image. The *image* is not God! Jesus, the Holy Spirit, The Father is the great "I am". The word said that when Moses asked God whom shall I say sent me, God told him to say "I am that I am" sent me.

Now your body is the temple for the Holy Spirit. God gave specific details for the design of the temple. Your hand and eyes are part of the body. Since God owns you and your body is the temple for the Holy Spirit, he should have full access to all of the faculties of the building. Therefore your eyes, hand, mouth, ears, nose are his. If your eye or hand offends you, cut it off.

What does all this mean? You and your senses are no longer *in charge*. If the body belongs to God for his use, then we release our authority, opinions and feelings. When you do so, the Holy Spirit fills the temple/body. Now the Holy Spirit tells you what to feel and reveals who you really are.

The "You or I" that you used to know is gone. That's when the veil is removed and the true you enters the Holy of Holies. This spiritual place is in the mind. Here is where you give God your (self/I) thoughts and he replaces them with his thoughts.

Once you've completely removed your "I" that false image, the fake you, God give s you his eye "I". Since you're in agreement with him you see people, places and things the way he intended. No longer do you have the weight of relying on "you". Nor do you carry the burden of people, rejection, loved ones, family, jobs, perceptions of others, status etc.. "YOU", your "I", "self", "your opinion", "your view", "perspective", "feelings" and "personality" has disappeared.

"You" were never the answer! Jesus is the answer. Therefore, when you put on Christ, everything changes for better.

~ PURPOSE PRINCIPLE #34 ~

WHEN YOU REMOVE THE BEAM OUT OF YOUR OWN EYE GOD WILL REALLY USE YOU.

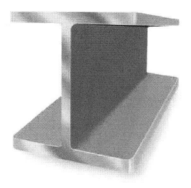

Until now, many of you were single as a result of operating independent of God. Your "I" was in the way. That "I" eye was fake, had no purpose, power or love. It's not attractive at all. Love is attractive because God is love. That self/flesh/I was a box that trapped you from seeing the blessings God has for you.

Once God gives you his eyes, pluck out the old one. The flesh wants what it *sees*. Ask yourself, what "I/eye" are I getting sight from? Here's how you know the difference, if what you see only appeals to the senses, that's you/self. Remember, God is a spirit. Inside, you're spirit too. You are not just a body. The body is literally a building that covers the *real* person. That's why the bible says that Jesus is the door, light, truth and the way. He is God and God is love. Therefore, in order to break through the flesh into our true nature we must love God more than ourselves. When we accept Jesus as our Lord and Savior, we surrender our "selves" and enter the Holy Place through him.

> ### INTERESTING FACT:
>
> The Cherubim's and Seraphim's have eyes all over their bodies, yet they cover them in the presence of God (reverencing him), following God crying out Holy, Holy, Holy is the Lamb of God. Although they have many eyes (and I'm sure there are wonderful things to see), they still humble themselves and cover their eyes and faces in awe of the presence of God.

The human eye

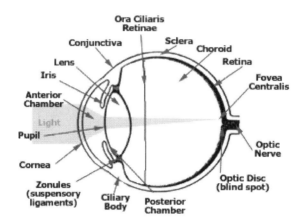

Take a look at the above illustration. When the physical eye "I" is present, it forms a mirrored wall over the true eye (your spiritual eye) like a cataract. Not only is it blocking accurate sight, when sun rays hit the wall of the eye/optic disk, it bends the light creating a beam, like a laser. We witness this in the physical, when we yell and treat badly the people who are close to us that really love us. Light shining from them to you, bounces off of your "I" and you end up hurting them.

Eye with a cataract:

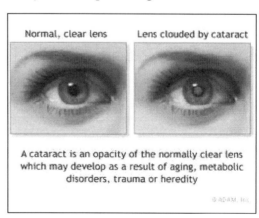

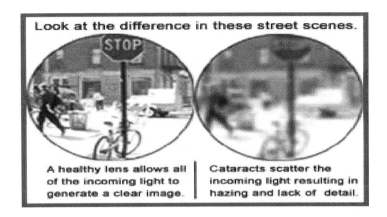

Double vision, also known as **Diplopia**, is the simultaneous perception of two images of a single object - the patient sees two images of a single thing either all the time, or some of the time. The displacement may be horizontally, vertically or diagonally. Diagonal double displacement (double vision) means both the horizontal lines and vertical lines are being perceived as doubled - also known as oblique separation.

Single binocular vision - each eye of the individual works independently, creating its own, faintly different image. The patient, however, only perceives one image because the brain is able to control the muscles of the eyes so that both of them point accurately at the object the person is looking at. The brain then joins the images produced by both eyes into one image - this is known as *single binocular vision*.

If, however, the eye muscles are damaged, or even the nerves, or if some health condition has weakened them, the muscles may not be able to control the eyes correctly, resulting in double vision.

Likewise, blurry vision caused by *double mindedness*, gives a distorted point of view as well. Faulty perception makes us fight those who really love us, thinking we're justified because of how we *feel*. Understanding this concept helps exposes the reason why you may not have received true love and why your relationships don't last. In the human eye diagram you see the optic disc. Ironically, it is called a blind spot. Double mindedness is a blind spot.

"I am" is always first!

> **Deuteronomy 9:3**
>
> But be assured today that the LORD your God is the one who goes across ahead of you like a devouring fire. He will destroy them; he will subdue them before you. And you will drive them out and annihilate them quickly, as the LORD has promised you.

"I" always wants to be first and walk ahead of God. This is out of order. You (self/I) must replace everything you say and do with Love. When you do so, God (I am) goes ahead of you like a devouring fire, annihilating the enemy. Single women need this protection. God sees the enemy before you do. He sees the liar, the cheater, the abuser, etc.. When you stop talking about "I want a man", "But I like him", God will go before you with his word by reminding you, "he's not a Christian", "he's not a tither", etc. In other words, when you *see* a man whose life is not in agreement with the word and you obey God instead of indulging in your flesh, you have just allowed God's "I/eye" go before you.

We're created in the image of God who is spirit. Therefore, the true image of God is in your spirit man, not what's visibly seen in the flesh. Your face, body, how you look in the physical, is just your earth clothes. You must remove *self image* so God's image is seen on earth.

> **Luke 11:34, 35**
>
> The light of the body is *the eye*: therefore when *thine eye is single*, thy whole body also is full of light; but when *thine eye is evil*, thy body also is full of darkness. The light of the body is the eye: therefore *when thine eye is single*, thy whole body also is full of light; but *when thine eye is evil*, thy body also is full of darkness. *See to it, then, that the light within you is not darkness*

Many women fail to identify the right man and true love because of their evil eye (self/I). The bible says if your eye is evil, the body also is full of darkness. That eye was you and you're wants/will. As a result, you were "a light that is darkness". What do I mean by that? The moon provides a great example of a light being darkness. In the evening, it *appears* as if the moon is genuinely producing marvelous light like the sun. However, the truth is the moon doesn't produce light at all. It's the sun that shines *on* the moon which gives it that luminescent quality. Not only that, research says if you were to actually land on the moon, there's no life and it's either extremely cold or hot. In other words, up close, it's nothing like it appeared.

God told me, you think men are attracted to you, but the reality is men are attracted to *me* in you. Men are attracted to the light. You have the light of God *on you* because you are in my presence. But when your eye is dark (selfish/carnal/fleshly), your whole body becomes dark.

Therefore men/people came to you for the light of God only to find out that you were a fraud.

Yes, you go to church faithfully, probably can quote scriptures, maybe even serve in the church. All of that is the light *on you*. Some women are so selfish and self centered that men are confused and turned off. When they met you, you professed to be Christian but the drinking, cursing, having sex and doing all of the things worldly women do, contradicted your *image*. Men came to you looking for love (not eros love but agape love), and for the light of God in you but what they found was a light that is darkness.

God requires *you* to sacrifice your *"I"* at the brazen altar, in the outer court, through the blood of Jesus. He's our perfect sacrifice, our High Priest. Through Jesus, is how we get to the Holy Spirit and the Father. You cannot go to the altar in flesh. What I mean by that is you have to put yourself out there…everything. Totally give up your I. Too many women are living double lives, going to church but refusing to *be* the church.

Malachi 1:6-8

[6]A son honoureth *his* father, and a servant his master: *if then I be a father, where is mine honour?* and if I *be* a master, where *is* my fear? saith the LORD of hosts unto you, O priests, that despise my name. And ye say, Wherein have we despised thy name? [7]*Ye offer polluted bread upon mine altar; and ye say, Wherein have we polluted thee?* In that ye say, The table of the LORD *is* contemptible. [8]*And if ye offer the blind for sacrifice, is it not evil?*

Return unto me and I will return unto you. Malachi 3:7. When you return back to God, his will returns revealing the *real you. You* don't have to do anything but obey the word. If it's God's will for you to have a husband, it's a done deal because God's word will not return unto him void. The will of the Lord does the work and his will/word always prevails. Like a literal will, our inheritance is written in the word.

Since we're his children, we shall have, receive, be and do whatever his will (the word) says. With that in mind, allow God to govern your thoughts and give you the correct perception of things. When you *think like God* you get God results. When you pray "the will of God" and not your own, his thoughts will be your thoughts and when you speak, it will be God speaking (pause. really think about that, powerful). Whatever *he* says, will accomplish that which it was *sent* to do.

Malachi 3:16-18

Those who fear the Lord spoke to one another, and the *Lord listened to them and heard them.* He listened and heard his word/himself in "them". So a book of remembrance was written before Him (God/the Word) for those who fear the Lord and meditate on his name (Jesus, the Word)

Jeremiah 31:3,4

Restore me and *I* will (God) return. For you are the Lord my God.

> **Jeremiah 31:18-20**
>
> Surely after my turning, "*I*" repented.

❧ PURPOSE PRINCIPLE #35 ❧

"HUMBLE YOUR SELVES UNDER THE MIGHTY HAND OF GOD"

> **Genesis 2:9**
>
> And out of the earth the Lord made every tree come delighting the eye and good for food; and in the middle of the garden, the tree of life and the tree of the knowledge of good and evil.

Your Father is always watching you. He wants you to be aware of who you really are. Check which eye is in control. If you find yourself manifesting things in your life that are not of God, you've been focusing on your own eye "I" instead of the will of God. "I need a man", "I'm lonely", "I'm depressed"… I, I, I! When these thoughts and feelings begin to take preeminence in your heart and mind, simply change your eye/I.

How do you pluck out that eye? Start by being grateful. Saying "thank you" changes your eye/perspective. Giving thanks, takes you outside of your*self* and gives honor where honor is due. Remember, you reap what you sow, when you sow gratitude, you reap honor because people will acknowledge you. The real *you*, may not be seen by people/men because you have been hidden in *self*. You've sow into self, "what about me", "what about my feelings", "my needs", "I've been hurt before", etc.. Those are empty seeds that reap nothing. This is part of the reason some of you have been single, with no purpose. But you can turn it around. STOP FOCUSING ON YOUR*SELF*. Care for the things of the Lord (think about someone else). GIVE UP YOUR SELF.

What you see in the mirror is not your true self it's an *image* of you. So don't focus as much on what you look like, take the focus off of *you*. I cannot emphasize this enough. Many are trying to devote their body to God and men with an evil eye "I". That's out of order and God will not accept this.

Your fabulous eye "I"

Imagine if you will, God made a movie and decided to let you be an extra. While the movies playing, people are trying to watch and enjoy it. They came to see God, the star of the movie. But the physically attractive extra, decides to stand in front of the screen while the movie is playing (the extra that nobody knows, nor came to see) and proceeds to *tell* people about the movie (God). Christians, women in particular, do this all the time. Men are attracted to the God *in you*. But you take your I/eye (body, education, money, thoughts, feelings) and stand in front of God dictating the movie instead of simply allowing men to find you *in* the movie! Let people watch the movie (your life ministry) for themselves.

If you notice, most of the images portrayed on TV, film and magazines are telling you what to do, how to be and what to think. Most of you obey without question. Television (tell-a-vision) are telling you to be independent, focus on self, be competitive, focus on your looks, talk about how you feel. Think about it, this false idol never satisfies you. Fashion never remains the same; they keep raising the bar on luxury and the standard of success according to world. Society never says "you've officially arrived". God is not behind that, satan is. He's the false eye controlling your eye "I". That's why you have to *give* God your entire body which includes your eyes (all of your "I", self thoughts).

Your eye "I" will have you in relationships that you don't really want to be in. Since you don't have the faith to trust in God's will, you trust in "your" will. But when you finally get tired of your*self* and take "I" out, you will leave the things that offend your father, relationships that God did not ordain….*happily*. Why? You'll finally see yourself and the entire situation differently.

You keep asking the man that won't marry you…When? You let him into your house because *you* just can't be alone, *you* couldn't *wait. The bible says "weak willed women" do this. Carnal will is weak and fragile. Strength is built into your obedience to the word of God because you become one with God. It's the weak-willed eye "I" that invited the *thief. If you want the blessing your father has for you and you desire for things to go well with you, the "I/eye" has to die! Give God what belongs to him and that would be ALL OF YOU!

> ***2 Timothy 3:2**
>
> People will be lovers of themselves, lovers of money, boastful, proud, abusive, disobedient to their parents, ungrateful, unholy, [3]without love, unforgiving, slanderous, without self-control, brutal, not lovers of the good, [4]treacherous, rash, conceited, lovers of pleasure rather than lovers of God— [5]*having a form of godliness but denying its power. Have nothing to do with them.*
>
> *Continued …*

> 6They are the kind who worm their way into homes and *gain control over weak-willed women*, who are loaded down with sins and are swayed by all kinds of *evil desires,* 7always learning but never able to acknowledge the truth.

> ***John 10:1**
>
> *"I tell you the truth*, the man who does not enter the sheep pen by the gate, but climbs in by some other way, is a thief and a robber.

The war over your "I"(eye)

Five senses; sight, touch, taste, smell, hearing are not controlled by the appendages of the body. In other words, your eyes do not see, your nose doesn't smell, your tongue doesn't taste, you don't feel with your hand and you don't hear with an ear.

All of those *senses* are controlled and defined by the mind. It's your brain that sends the messages and transcribes what is going on with the body. Considering that information, it's easy to realize that the battle is over the mind.

> ### MANIFESTATION OF *I AM THAT I AM*
>
> - Love
> - Fruit of the spirit
> - Blessings
> - Peace
> - Correct vision/perception
> - Righteous thoughts
> - Divine revelation
> - Success
> - Perfect timing

When you were in the world, Satan controlled your mind. You believed your thoughts were your thoughts. But they were influenced or controlled by the enemy.

However, once born again, Jesus became the rightful owner of you and your thoughts. Here's where the confusion comes in. Although,

> ### MANIFESTATION OF *SELF EYES/I/FLESH*
>
> - Bad relationships
> - Wrong perceptions
> - Wrong decisions
> - Wrong thinking
> - Wrong feelings
> - Wrong hearing
> - Curses
> - INSANITY/going in circles (different man, same

your spirit has been renewed, your body is used to obeying its former owner. Satan understands that you're no longer his and has no authority over you. Therefore he attempts to trick you into believing that Jesus is *not* Lord over your mind… *you are* (that's how he fooled Eve). He seduces your senses sending old signals to your brain, so you could think the thoughts he wants you to think because he understands whoever controls the mind is Lord over the body.

God will only speak Love and righteousness into your spirit. Loving people who refuse to reciprocate, can *feel* horrible. Loving God more than your self doesn't feel good to the flesh either. When operating in the flesh, if you don't feel good, a message is sent to your brain signaling something must be wrong. So the flesh tells the mind, you need to go do something to make your*self* feel better. The flesh is influenced by the devil, always telling you to do something disobedient to God so that you can sin. Remember Satan *needs* you to sin so *you* can separate from God.

God is not *emotional*, he's a *spirit. You shouldn't be emotional either, following your *senses*. Flesh follows sensuality, spirit follows *Spirit. God's word is black and white, not grey. There is only one way and that is his way. He paid the price to be the boss of your mind and body. And when you get married, your husband does the same thing. He pays the price for your body with his life and his name.

> ***John 4:2**
>
> God is spirit, and his worshipers must worship in spirit and in truth.

> ***Galatians 6:8**
>
> Whoever sows to please their flesh, from the flesh will reap destruction; whoever sows to please the Spirit, from the Spirit will reap eternal life.

CHICKEN HEAD: GET YOUR MIND RIGHT

Throughout the bible, you'll never see a woman referenced as the head. She's always identified as the *body. In essence, the woman is the womb of the body of Christ, designed to carry seed (the Holy Spirit). We also know that God made us wives through covenant with him. That makes God your spiritual head and when you get married, God the father gives you away to your husband who then he takes over as head (because you both become one, God remains head over both of you).

> **1 Corinthians 7:4**
>
> *The wife's body does not belong to her alone* but also to her husband. In the same way, the husband's body does not belong to him alone but also to his wife.

> **Ephesians 5:3**
>
> For the husband is the head of the wife *as* Christ is the head of the church, *his body*, of which he is the Savior.

Carnal minded women reject this divine patriarchal system because they're in rebellion of the idea of submission. Consequently, women often accept the Matriarchal system because it empowers them and emasculates men. This feminist mindset leads disobedient women to the misconception that they lose something of value when they come under the authority of a man. Part of this misunderstanding spawned from women submitting to boyfriends (who have abused the misplaced privilege), instead of their "own husband". This rebellious attitude have caused women to forfeit their own benefits reserved for them under the patriarchal order because either they want to be the head or have taken care of themselves so long they feel like the head themselves. We observe the unfortunate consequence for headless women everyday; bitterness, loneliness, baggage and oftentimes bastard children.

The underlying tone for this rebellious nature is fear. Women in general crave safety and security even if it's a false. Without a sense of security, women simply run amuck with emotions and feelings with no guidance. This is a very scary place for a single woman. It's impossible to have faith and fear at the same time. If you pursue faith, then you must abandon fear. If you chase after fear, you're going to lose faith. If you don't have a father, a head to protect and guide you, how could you ever feel secure enough to have faith and not be afraid?

Consequently, we often see this fear factor in women as they sabotage one relationship after the other. They can't quite put their finger on why this keeps happening to them. They blame men, circumstances, other women and never realize that it was the spirit of fear that lead them in and out of those situations. They couldn't see it because a body without a head *has no vision*. That's why these women constantly need reassurance…"where is this relationship going", "do you love me", yadayadayada! They can't see their value or where their relationships are going because THE HEAD CONTAINS THE EYES!

Every woman has a paternal father regardless of the nature of their relationship. But spiritually, a lot of women make themselves *bastard children because they refuse to allow God their Father to make correction in their lives. They miss the opportunity to learn how to love through their father. He's supposed to be the first man you love. The father is the first man that love's you without having to earn it. He loves you for who you are, not because of what you have or what you can do for him. When the father/daughter relationship is non-existent in the developmental years, women tend to operate off of insecure feelings. The reason being, there was no brain/head that you could trust to help decipher your feelings. The father is the role model that shows you how to love, reverence, and submit to a man. But if your father wasn't there how can you be sure about the things you're experiencing as a woman? Or what if you had a father and he just didn't know how to be a good head? How do you discover who you are? How do you learn to love and be loved?

Mistakenly, headless women often think it's a good idea to seek counsel from other beheaded women. The results are generally a compilation of rational scenarios from former experiences loaded with emotion and speculation. Don't get me wrong, there are many women who are wise with great counsel. But women are not men. God has an order and the wisdom is built into his way. The father is the brains of the operation. The brain has thinking capability that's influenced by the spirit *not emotions*. For women to digest this truth it requires death to the ego. Once that happens you'll notice emotions are connected to the senses making it subject to change depending on how you *feel*. Spirit is eternal and immutable. It is sure and stable, not subject to feelings.

If your father has been unavailable in the natural sense, you're especially susceptible to headless behavior. No matter how it came about that your father wasn't around during the developmental years of your life (he left, divorce, died...etc), it still had conscious, unconscious, psychological ramifications. Lack of guidance, disappointment, loss, hurt pain and ignorance have women running around like chickens with their heads cut off trying to find love and security (often through multiple men and relationships).

Although "Running around like a chicken with his head cut off" is a common phrase, I mean it literally. Let's examine what happens when a chicken is amputated. First let's address the obvious; it no longer has a head. That means no brain, eyes, nose, ears or mouth, no personality. Yet once the head has been removed, the chicken's body has the ability to continue to run around in circles anywhere from a few minutes to a couple of months. The reason the body is able to continue to wander around is because of the place where the head was severed. The spinal cord was cut just above the *medulla oblongata leaving a portion of the brainstem. That part of the brain controls heartbeat, respiration and the most basic of functions. Since the nerves are still active, the body continues to perform but the movement *is not conscious* but rather "knee jerk" reactions. There is no cognitive thought, control or feeling in the body, just aimless movement.

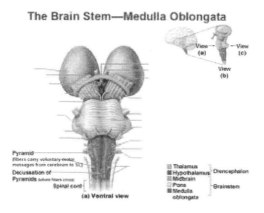

CHAPTER 10 – CHICKEN HEAD: GET YOUR MIND RIGHT

> ### WHAT IS A "KNEE-JERK" REACTION?
>
> an immediate unthinking emotional reaction produced by an event or statement to which the reacting person is highly sensitive; - in persons with strong feelings on a topic, it may be very predictable

Medulla Oblongata/Brainstem (doesn't this look like the same shape as a woman without a head?)

Headless dummies

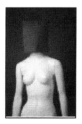

A real man of God cannot marry a headless dummy. To be honest, no man will. How can he?

Look at the illustrations above. If you don't have the head of your father, which is your very spirit and life, all you have to offer is a body. Your personality doesn't amount to anything without the spirit of God because you are lacking love for yourself.

When you're in the chicken head state of being, this is what you look like to a man:

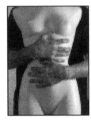 

If this man took this mannequin home to his family they would think he was crazy. Well, that's you in the spirit and this is how he sees you…an inanimate object with little to no value. Just like a mannequin, all its good for it to be used up and thrown away.

The minute you have determined to "do what *I want* to do", you have severed your head. You made the executive decision to take control of your life and your relationships (Nimrod). But in reality you had no purpose, identity or *vision*. Nor do you have the power or capacity to be the head.

Your behavior has been insanity (doing the same thing, expecting different results). Going in circles from one relationship to another, different men but the same situations because you have been functioning like a chicken with its head cut off!

Self without God in control is a false identity and false sense of security. When you've been hurt by people your *natural* tendency is to block them out.

How do you do that? You tell yourself…"*I'm* going to be successful", "*I'm* going to have my own money", "*I'm* not going to let nobody use me", "no man can tell me what to do", "*I'm* going to be selective of the friends I choose etc…" There's nothing wrong with desiring loving caring, nurturing reciprocal relationships. But you cannot have it without God. He is your head and *He is Love*. He's the one who should be in control over all of your body, thoughts and feelings.

Put on the mind of Christ

Why do you need to *put on the mind of Christ? A woman without a head will always be lead by her emotions. It is only through the brain/mind that your emotions are deciphered. Example, you may initially *feel* afraid of roller coasters. Your emotions say, "If you get on this ride you're gonna die,"; but your mind tells you, "Although it appears scary, it's safe and fun, you can get on".

Another example would be like if you had a hot cup of coffee. When you receive the coffee it's hot. *You feel* the heat, but your brain tells you, "*the truth* is, even though it feels hot, let it cool down and it will be safe to drink".

If you didn't have a brain, your emotions will have you afraid of everything because you'll have feeling with no instruction or direction.

*Put Off the Old Man and Put On Love

> **Colossians 3:5-17**
>
> ⁵Mortify therefore your members which are upon the earth; fornication, uncleanness, inordinate affection, evil desire, and covetousness, which is idolatry:
> ⁶For which things' sake the wrath of God comes on the children of disobedience:
> ⁷In which you also once walked, when you lived in them.
> ⁸But now you also *put off all these; anger, wrath, malice, blasphemy, filthy talk out of your mouth.*

> ⁹*Lie not one to another*, seeing that you have put off the old man with his deeds;
> ¹⁰And have put on the new man, that is renewed in knowledge after the image of him that created him:
> ¹¹Where there is neither Greek nor Jew, circumcision nor uncircumcision, Barbarian, Scythian, bond nor free: but Christ is all, and in all.
> ¹²*Put on therefore, as the elect of God, holy and beloved, compassion, kindness, humbleness of mind, meekness, longsuffering*;
> ¹³Forbearing one another, and forgiving one another, if any man have a quarrel against any: even as Christ forgave you, so also do you.
> ¹⁴*And above all these things put on love, which is the bond of perfection.*
> ¹⁵And let the peace of God *rule in your hearts*, to which also you are called in one body; and be thankful.

Prior to marriage your head should be your father. When you get married, your husband assumes the head position. Your father not only serves the purpose as protector, guardian, teacher and disciplinarian, he's also the first to teach you how to love without having to earn it.

You may or may not have had a father that covered all of these bases but your heavenly Father can. As his daughter, while caring for the things of the Lord, he takes the time to teach you how to receive love without effort. He loves you just because, he doesn't need a reason and we don't have to work for it. As you walk with him he'll translate, what you're feeling. He'll tell you if you're being selfish, unreasonable or if there is a reason for concern.

Your father deciphers your feelings because he is the brain/mind. His love reminds you that you're worthy of love. Most of us weren't taught by our fathers how to receive love "just because". That's why headless women give too much, too soon, for too little. Their emotions told them a lie and they believed it.

When you put on the mind of Christ, you allow your father to tell you the truth about who you are, corrects your behavior and provides discernment regarding people trying to enter your life.

Imagine a teenage girl bringing a guy home to meet her father. All it takes is one look from the dad and he knows if the guy is worthy of his daughter or not.

The majority of the time, whether we heed his advice or not, his opinion is right on point! God the father is perfect so when he exposes the true character of a man, we can trust his judgment and avoid the chicken run.

Putting on the mind of Christ removes you from the "chicken head syndrome". With God the Father as your head you're whole. He's the aspect of your life you've been missing. Your "knee jerk" reactions were the sensual impulses of the world/flesh without the head of God.

Every time you put your wants/will a-head of God, you cut your own head off! Whenever you get out of the mind of Christ and go get you some sex, curse people out, lie, manipulate, hate, etc.., get ready to run in circles like a chicken with its head cut off!

The mind of the flesh has 2 sides. In the world this is natural. You're either a right brain thinker or a left brain thinker. If you split your brain in half you will see the limbic system in the brain (which ironically looks like the eye of Ra a demonic Egyptian deity) *see addendum.

But when you bring the two sides of the brain together, it no longer have that resemblance. We're not always privileged to *see* how God operates. Let me show you what this means to you and why it's relevant to you being single on purpose.

The Eye of Ra/Horus:

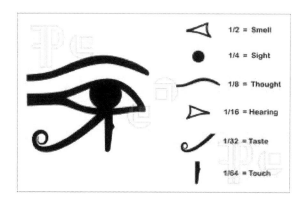

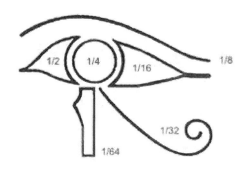

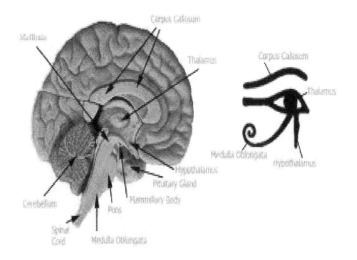

The limbic system is responsible for controlling various operations in the body. Some of these functions include interpreting emotional responses, storing memories, and regulating hormones. The limbic system is also involved with sensory perception, motor function, and olfaction.

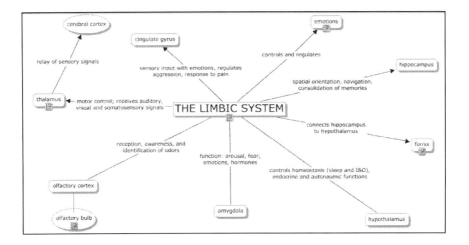

You see, the enemy is well aware of the significance of the eye. He understands sight doesn't come from the natural eye but in the mind (brain/head/spirit). When we were in sin, satan had control of our minds. But when we got born again, Jesus bought us with a price. That includes our eye "I".

The enemy wants you to believe it's more normal to *think* about self. As long as you operate in the "self" satan can control/influence your perception of how you feel and think.

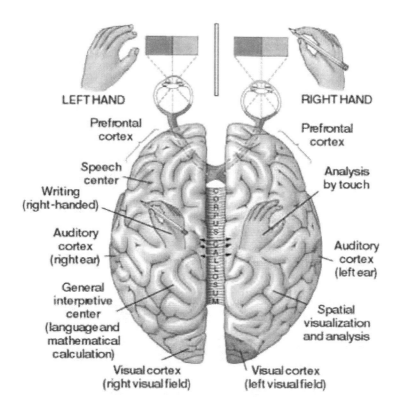

If you had to choose between being right or left brain that would mean you would be lacking qualities. When you're *double minded, you alternate between your right or left brain.

There are 12 intelligences and you waver between them. God is not dual he is singular; one mind, eye, hand, mouth, ear and body.

The enemy has been very effective at convincing people that the thoughts and feelings they've been experiencing are real and true. But when you put on the mind of Christ, God combines all of your intelligences and gives them to you along with his wisdom making you limitless.

No longer do you have to feed off the tree of the knowledge of good and evil. Everything will be all good. Therefore it is imperative that our mind is one in Christ to make better choices not only with the opposite sex but in all situations.

> ***James 1:8 KJV**
>
> A *double minded* man *is* unstable in all his ways.

> ***James 1:8**
>
> Their loyalty is *divided* between God and the world, and *they are unstable in everything they do.*

Left and right brain

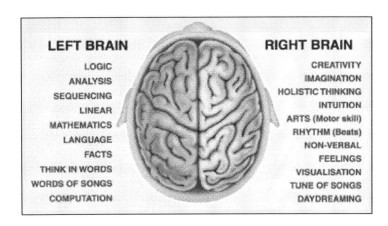

Your thinking doesn't make *sense*

God is perfect, therefore he continues to be perfect *in you*, settling your mind, controlling your senses. Senses cannot be controlled for long, within your own ability. Look at the Limbic System and the Eye of Ra, you'll not only see the biological connection to your senses, you also see how the enemy has positioned itself as God over this area. On our own, we do not have the power to defeat satan and his demons. It's only through the blood of Jesus that we gain control over our mind and feelings.

Why am I talking about the brain, satan and his demons when we're supposed to be talking about being single on purpose? I'm explaining in detail to help you understand that the answer to our dilemma is only through the *mind* of Christ. Without God, we are women without a head.

If you remain slave to the world system, which is a decapitated state, your thoughts will be solely based on emotions and feeling. Since our hormones fluctuate, moods and seasons change, you'll never find stability within yourself. It is only done through the mind of Christ.

The limbic system in the brain is the area that controls your senses, what you feel. If you studied this system and how it affects people, you would find that the body can unconsciously produce chemical imbalances (i.e., hormones) which trigger sensations causing you to literally, feel, see, smell and hear things that either doesn't exist or have in the past feel very present.

Sadly, these emotions only *feel* real to you, but in reality it's an apparition, an illusion…a lie. Unruly senses *gives* the enemy power to keep you in the holding pattern of the past. This holds especially true when you esteem ex-boyfriends who weren't good to you. Women find it hard to move on with their life because they keep reliving old memories.

These sensations *feel real and present* but the fact is it's an imagination. In order to have the correct perception of what's true, your mind has to confirm what you experience is really accurate. Remember, you're *actual* sense of taste, touch, smell, hearing and sight comes from the mind. If the devil is influencing your mind/senses, he's lying to you about what you're feeling because *he IS a liar*!

Only through the Holy Spirit can you know if what you *feel, hear and see* is real. It's through the mind of Christ that you find the wisdom and correct way of doing things. The head (which contains the eye) provides you with vision. The head does of all of the *thinking* for the body.

What this means for you is that no matter what your status is, age or stage in life, God can and will use you. You will go as far as you let him. If God doesn't use you a man will! God will use you like the golden vessel you are but a man will exploit you like a mindless dummy.

The Holy Spirit is your counselor. He reminds the old "you" that it's no longer in charge. He tells you how you should feel about things because he is going to tell you the truth. The Holy Spirit *is the truth*. Ever been with a man and right away *something* tells you that he's not for you or he's crazy, married, has kids, felon or abusive…etc.

Although you've heard this voice in your spirit, you ignored it just to find out that *something* was right! That voice was God (your head) warning you, telling you the truth of pending danger. Your flesh, your "I" wants what it wants. It will always guide you to pleasure, things that feel good to the senses. Ironically, most of the time when we do that, we lose our senses! In essence, God the father controls the mind and God in the form of the Holy Spirit takes over your soul (self/flesh/I) and gives you *his* feelings.

Love cast out all fear because God isn't afraid anything! There's no failure in him so when you think like him, you'll see success, a way out and the answers for your life. His thoughts are higher than your thoughts. Read, study the word, and know it. These are God thoughts. You really *can do* all things through Christ who strengthens you.

If you desire something, think about how God would feel about it. Whatever you think *HE* feels about it, *you* should feel about it. For instance, you're home feeling lonely and horny, you think about calling someone to come over to sleep with you. If you're operating with your own eyes (I), you will have a man (that doesn't want you but wants your body), come have sex with you, eat *your* food, take *your* money, leave and make a fool out you. Or you can think about what God wants. If he is Lord over your life, his will supersedes your *wants and feelings*.

Jesus gives us an example with him in the Garden of Gethsemane. He was tempted to give into the flesh and let the cup pass him, but he told the Father, not my will but thine will be done.

If you desire money, think about what God would do. He said give and it shall be given unto you, pressed down, shaken together and running over shall *men give* unto your bosom. Therefore, think about *giving* money, then expect God to give it back to you through men. When you did that, you just obeyed *his* word, *his* thoughts. This is so important because it's a law.

Remember, *God's word* will not return unto him void. When you *think* like God, you *see* like God, which makes you become like God. The word says if *the eye* is filled with light the entire body is filled with light (God) *Sight comes from the mind*! The mind/thoughts are spirit. God is a spirit. Changing your "I" for his eyes is changing your mind.

Mary, mother of Jesus exercised these principles when Jesus turned water into wine. When she and Jesus were at a wedding, they ran out of wine. Mary goes to Jesus and tells him that they ran out of wine. The first step she did was go to Jesus. Then she told the servant to DO WHATEVER HE SAYS!

Jesus instructed the servants to get pots and fill them with water. They did *exactly* what he told them to do. They never saw with their natural eyes *how* the water turned into wine. As the servants filled the pots with water and brought them to Jesus, he never told them what he was doing. Nevertheless, in the end, Mary and the rest of the wedding party were able to partake and enjoy the wine (the miracle).

Again we witness the phenomena of thinking God thoughts and receiving God answers/results with the boy with 5 fish and 2 loaves. The problem was a multitude of people needed to be fed but they didn't have enough food or money. The boy gave Jesus what he had in his hand. Jesus (God) took it, broke it, gave thanks and gave to the disciples. Then the disciples gave to the people. By the end of it all, they had 12 baskets left over.

Look at the process, the boy decided (thought) to offer his food (sacrificed self) to Jesus. That's when God took over, multiplied and blessed everyone. The point is you must give God ALL OF YOU. Remember, when you give God all of you, God gives you ALL of HIM, unlimited love, wisdom, peace, wealth and riches. All of you includes your "I" (physical eyes/thinking)

Do you hear the words that are coming out of my mouth?!

He that has an ear let him hear. Faith comes by hearing and "hearing" by the word of God. In other words, how you hear is determined by the ear you use. Your physical ear receives sound from the carnal mind. But once you've given your eyes to God, he now has your whole body. Therefore your "hearing" doesn't come from sound, senses and vibrations.

Hearing comes from the word of God (His spirit). If you haven't given all of yourself you won't hear him (God/love) when he is speaking to you.

In relationships today people are constantly thinking about themselves and their needs. Women in particular tend to be more emotional, so they may talk more and are sensitive to things they see and hear. Therefore, it's imperative the Holy Spirit take over your *heart.

---

*Matthew 13

He replied, *"The knowledge of the secrets of the kingdom of heaven has been given to you*, but not to them. [12]Whoever has will be given more, and he will have abundance. Whoever does not have, even what he has will be taken from him. [13]This is why I speak to them in parables:
"Though seeing, they do not see;
though hearing, *they do not hear or understand.*
[14]In them is fulfilled the prophecy of Isaiah:
"'You will be ever hearing but never understanding;
you will be ever seeing but never perceiving.
[15]*For this people's heart has become calloused;*
they hardly hear with their ears,
and they have closed their eyes.
Otherwise they might see with their eyes,

> hear with their ears,
> understand with their hearts
> and turn, and I would heal them.
> ¹⁶But *blessed are your eyes because they see, and your ears because they hear.*

The heart has a mind of its own. It holds on to memories, feelings, emotions and that contribute to your personality. This area is so sensitive and volatile that you cannot afford to be in self mode. You need the Holy Spirit to take over in order for him to give you a new heart.

Why do you need a new heart? Feelings, emotions, memories stored in your old heart can be deceptive. If unchecked, the heart can make you feel sensitive to the present with the past. The most dangerous factor is that which you believe in your heart, your mouth will proclaim.

> **Matthew 15:18**
>
> But the things that come out of the mouth come from the heart, and these make a man 'unclean.'

Therefore, a new heart from the Holy Spirit produces a new ear, perspective, loving feelings and loving words. The manifestation of that new heart, eye and ear is righteousness, love and *fruit of the spirit.

> ***Galatians 5:22-23**
>
> But the fruit of the Spirit is love, joy, peace, patience, kindness, goodness, faithfulness, 23gentleness and self-control

> **John 8:47**
>
> 47He who belongs to God *hears* what God says. The reason you do not hear is that you do not belong to God."

> **John 8:31-32**
>
> 31To the Jews who had believed him, Jesus said, "If you hold to my teaching, you are really my disciples. *32Then you will know the truth, and the truth will set you free.*"

Your Body *Is* The Temple

When we look at our lives, we tend to feel like we own it. Partially, because we've been in our own skin since birth and know no other existence. You get up in the morning, bathe, get dressed with whatever you want to wear, eat, then out the door. There you just took care of the physical body for "yourself". It probably never dawned on you, when you woke up, that your body is the temple for the Holy Spirit. With your mouth, did you give praise? Did you feed your spirit bread (the word)? Did you anoint your head with oil (the anointing of the Holy Spirit)? Did you cleanse yourself with the word? Did you put on the garment of praise and righteousness?

As Christians we need to understand our bodies are designed to serve a purpose. The purpose is the will of God, to serve as a temple for him. When you live your life day to day, remember how sacred your body is. You don't have the authority to just give your body away or sell it because you want to. It's not yours to give.

With that concept in mind, as single women of God, we need to recognize the significant purpose of our bodies. Aside from being the temple for the Holy Spirit, the bible refers to women as "vessels". There are a few interesting things going on here. First, let's dig into what it means to be a *vessel*.

The first miracle Jesus performed was turning water into wine at a wedding. It was ironic that his first miracle was at a wedding because marriage is symbolic of the covenant between Jesus Christ and the church. In this story, Jesus told the servant to get 6 pots made of stone. The pots were made of stoneware, which is strong clay that's fired at high temperatures, over a thousand degrees higher than *earthen*ware. The stone pots are symbolic of our bodies. Jesus also told them to fill the pots with water (this represents the in filling of the Holy Spirit into our bodies). After they filled the pots to the brim, he told them to *draw out now! What happened? He turned water into wine. The blood of Jesus is the wine, the Holy Spirit is the water and our bodies are the pots. It was the word (Jesus) that changed the water into wine in the pots.

> ***John 2:7**
>
> 8And he saith unto them, *Draw out now*, and bear unto the governor of the feast. *And they bare it.* 9When the ruler of the feast had tasted the water that was made wine, and knew not whence it was: (but the servants which drew the water knew;) the governor of the feast called the bridegroom, 10And saith unto him, Every man at the beginning doth set forth good wine; and when men have well drunk, then that which is worse: but thou hast kept the good wine until now.

You and I represent a variety of vessels. The design and function of the container is usually an indication of how it should be used. For instance, if you were having a birthday party for child, you wouldn't use fine baccarat crystal stemware, you would use paper cups. Although they're both vessels used for drinking, fine crystal wouldn't be appropriate for the occasion because the children will mishandle it, or get hurt if someone breaks it. Therefore, the project at hand would be better suited with paper cups. Likewise, God uses us at different times for different purposes according to how he made us.

The bible instructs husbands to deal with the wife as the weaker "vessel". Why is that? In caring for the things of the Lord, one of the "things" is the temple of the Lord, which is your body. One of the functions of the body as pertaining to the vessel is the capacity to carry things. Men are depositors and we are receptors. If you're depositing something, let's say into a bag, you don't feel the pressure of the bag. If the bag doesn't bust or show signs of severe stretching, you probably would continue to dump more things into the bag because you're oblivious to the pressure. Men sometimes do this to women because they are depositors and are not cognizant of the fact that we are the receptors (the weaker vessel). Therefore, it is incumbent on us as women to remember we're vessels and consciously monitor what we allow people to deposit into our spirit.

Definition of vessel:

- A hollow utensil, such as a cup, vase, or pitcher used as a container, especially for liquids.
- A nautical craft, especially one larger than a rowboat, designed to navigate water
- An airship
- Anatomy, a duct, canal, or other tube that contains or conveys body fluid.
- A person seen as the agent or embodiment, as of a quality: *a vessel of mercy*.

The vessel defined further reveals God's intention for our bodies. You're so much more than just a suit of flesh. When you meet a man you like and just give your body away, without thinking, you totally violate God's objective. In this definition you can see the specific purpose of a vessel. The interesting thing is the very first definition. It describes the vessel as "a hollow utensil". I believe God wants us to be a "hallow utensil", which is to make or set apart as holy.

The vessel could also be a nautical craft, designed to navigate water. In the bible water represents truth. Women are designed to navigate the truth. I find this especially funny because as a woman, (and I'm sure you can relate) when something seems fishy we cannot rest until it is well with our soul!

We will persistently seek answers to get to the bottom of the matter. It is not until our spirit agrees (the Holy Spirit, the spirit of truth) that we can rest. I literally *navigate* through what is being said until I find the truth! Wow, glad to know that God put that there!

Another interesting description of a vessel is a duct, canal, or other tube that contains or conveys body fluid. We just learned that to be adequately equipped for our assignments, God gave us the ability to navigate on water.

But now we're seeing another purpose. We are the vehicle used to convey body fluid! That body fluid is blood and water! The blood of Jesus and the water of the Holy Spirit.

> **John 2:7**
>
> Jesus saith unto them, fill the *water pots* (you the earthen vessel) with water (the Holy Spirit). And they filled them up to the brim.

> **2 Timothy 2:21**
>
> In a large house there are articles not only of *gold and silver*, but also of *wood and clay*; some are for *noble purposes* and some for ignoble purposes. Therefore if anyone cleanses *himself* from what is dishonorable, he will be a *vessel* of honorable use, *set apart* as holy, *useful to the master of the house*, ready for every *good work.*

In these scriptures, God is talking to us about our purpose *according to* the construction of the vessel and the condition of it. Obviously gold and silver will be used more often for noble purposes because of their value.

As believers, we are living, breathing "arks of the covenant". The ark was made of shiddum wood (which represents mankind) and the entire outside was laid with pure solid gold (this represents the deity of God over us).

Whatever material the vessel is, it's no good for use if it's dirty. If you're unclean, God cannot use you the way he intended. Unfortunately, in the body of Christ, too many women find themselves in this situation.

Yes, you're born again, and go to church but your vessel is unclean! 2 Tim 2:23 plainly tells us if you want to be an honorable vessel, you must "cleanse yourself".

> **FYI, GOLD REPRESENTS:**
>
> 1. Kingship
> 2. Purification process
> 1. Gold is the only metals that when heated with fire will not lose anything of its nature, weight, color, or any other property. Genuine faith is the same way. Gold is used in scripture when talking about the strength of someone's faith. Job refers to gold after he has been through all his trials. Job 23:10, Job says, "But he knows where I am going. And when he tests me, I will come out as pure gold."
> 3. the divine nature
>
> As gold is the highest, most precious metal, so the divine nature is the highest nature, the only nature having immortality.
>
> **Silver: represents truth**
>
> "The words of the Lord are pure words: as silver tried in a furnace of earth, purified seven times." Psalm 12:6

The Temple of the Holy Spirit

> **Matthew 7:6**
>
> Give not *that which is holy* unto the dogs, neither cast ye your pearls before swine, lest they trample them under their feet, and turn again and rend you.

When the scriptures remind us not to give that which is holy unto the dogs, one of the "Holy" things is your body. Matthew 7:6 holds so true. I'm sure plenty single women have found themselves in situations where they're trying to wait to have sex before marriage then meet a man they're physically attracted to who doesn't have the same Christian values. Of course this man turns you on because we all know the devil sends what we like. So you try to remain strong, know that you shouldn't, but end up succumbing to his seductive words. Next thing you know, you've given that which was holy to the dogs! Before you know it, things change. They become mean, cold and distant. They trample the sacred expression of love you gave them under their feet then turn again and rend you. This is real folks. The bible is trying to warn and protect us from the enemy by teaching us how to reverence God with our bodies.

God has made you pure and a virgin through the blood of Christ. This put you in alignment with his divine order. Your purification process begins before you meet your high priest (the future husband God has ordained for you). It has to be this way. The High Priest is anointed and ordained to care for the temple (your body). He cannot touch an unclean thing and serve in the temple. If you are not clean by the washing of the word, your garment is defiled. Before entering the temple, the High Priest must cleanse himself.

> ### Leviticus 21:10
>
> *The high priest,* the one *among his brothers* who has had the *anointing oil* poured on *his head* and who *has been ordained* to wear the *priestly garments*, must not let his hair become unkempt or tear his clothes. 11. He must not enter a place where there is a dead body. He must not make himself unclean, even for his father or mother [12]*nor leave the sanctuary of his God or desecrate it,* because he has been dedicated by the anointing oil of his God. I am the lord. [13]*The woman that marries must be a virgin.*

Carnal, worldly people are living out of order. When you fornicate, (this goes for both men and women), you defile the temple of the Lord. A sinner's body is dead in the spirit. Therefore, when a Christian man fornicates with a woman, he just entered a place where there's a dead body which makes him unclean!

God the Holy Spirit is in the sanctuary, which is your body. He will not share space with sin. God set the priest aside by anointing him for *his purpose*. When we violate the laws of the kingdom by operating in the flesh we distort the divine order.

Disobedient Christian women are sleeping with the dogs. The bible says, "don't to give what is sacred to the dogs". So, who are the dogs? The dogs are the unbelievers.

> **Revelation 22:15**
>
> *Outside are the dogs* and sorcerers and the sexually immoral and murderers and idolaters, and everyone who loves and practices falsehood.

> **Matthew 7:6**
>
> Give not *that which is holy unto the dogs*, neither cast ye your pearls before swine, lest they trample them under their feet, and turn again and rend you.

> **Leviticus 11:27-28**
>
> Of all the animals that *walk on all fours*, those that *walk on their paws* are unclean for you; whoever touches their *carcasses* will be unclean til evening. ²⁸Anyone who picks up their carcasses must wash *his clothes*, and he will be unclean til evening. *They are unclean for **you**.*

> **Matthew 15:26**
>
> He replied, "It is not right to take the children's bread and toss it to their dogs".

Even in the world system, bad men are called dogs. In the kingdom of God, the dogs are men that are outside of the covenant. These ravenous animals want to destroy the body.

When a man doesn't love and care about you, he's totally ok taking everything from you. He doesn't mind using you up and wearing down your body. The man outside of the covenant of God is self serving.

And the bible tells us that if you give that which is holy to the dogs, they will trample you and rend you! They don't value and appreciate what's sacred, they're dogs!

As it is written in Leviticus 11:27, they are unclean for you:

> **Leviticus 11:27-28**
>
> And whatsoever *goeth upon his paws*, among all manner of beasts that *go on all four*, those are unclean unto you: whoso *toucheth their carcass* shall be unclean until the evening. ²⁸And he that beareth the carcass of them shall wash his clothes, and be unclean until the evening: *they are unclean unto you.*

Even if you don't know the bible, I'm sure you've heard of Jezebel. As a result of her wickedness, she was thrown out a window and left dead on the ground. I'm pointing her out because of what happened to her *body* afterwards:

> **2 Kings 9:34**
>
> Jehu went in and ate and drank. "Take care of that *cursed woman*," he said, "and bury her, for *she was a king's daughter.* But when they went out to bury her, they found nothing except her skull, her feet and her hands. ³⁶They went back and told Jehu, who said, "this is the word of the Lord that he spoke through his servant Elijah the Tishbite: On the plot of ground at Jezreel *dogs will devour Jezebel's flesh.*

> **Revelation 2:20**
>
> But I have this against you, that you *tolerate that woman, Jezebel*, who calls herself a prophetess. She teaches and seduces my servants to commit sexual immorality and to eat things sacrificed to idols.

Jezebel was a cursed woman because of sin. As a result, her body was eaten by the dogs. How many times have you been bit by a dog? They had sex with you, broke your heart and left? The dogs are after your body! The enemy's goal is to defile and destroy the temple. When you voluntarily allow this to happen you're operating under the spirit of Jezebel and the result of your body will be the same.

In Revelation 2:20, God said men *tolerated* Jezebel. Jezebel had a controlling spirit, where she would do whatever she had to do to get what she wanted. If you adopt this kind of spirit, you may end up getting what you want but you won't want what you got.

Shacking up with a man and fornicating is a manifestation of the Jezebel spirit. Men don't love Jezebel, they tolerate her. You don't want to be tolerated for years and years.

Women wonder all the time how they can be in a relationship with a man for 3, 5, 10, 20+ years and they never marry them. Then after wearing your body out all of those years, robbing you of your youthful essence, they marry someone younger in less than six months. While you thought you were keeping your man happy by sacrificing your body to him, he tolerated you.

God knew there were dogs out there. That's why he's telling you not to give what is sacred to the them. Your body *is sacred*! He specifically instructs us to watch out for them. You must know how to identify them.

A dog cannot speak, understand, nor identify the things of God. All they can do is keep you company but they cannot be a priest over you and your home. They are unclean for you.

> **Philippians 3:2**
>
> *Look out for* the dogs, *look out* for the evildoers, *look out* for those who mutilate the flesh.

> **Isaiah 56:11**
>
> *The dogs have a mighty appetite*; they never have enough. But they are shepherds who have no understanding; they have all turned to *their own way*, each to *his own gain, one and all.*

Today, I hear people say more and more that the bible is dated. As a result of this mindset, they don't read or believe in the word. Dogs do not understand and they've all turned to their own way! They're not interested in the truth their only interest is selfish access to your temple and the treasures therein.

These are the men that constantly try to debate or dispel the validity of the word. To them the word is a book of nice concepts for people "back then". It feels that way to them because their goal is to satisfy the flesh and the word is standing in between them and your body.

They're so used to women indulging in their lust, that when you show up with discipline, order and structure it confuses them. Because of their nature, they will either attack you or reject you.

Don't be surprised by this behavior. Rather, resist and they will flee from you.

> **James 4:7**
>
> **Submit yourselves therefore to God. Resist the devil, and he will flee from you.**

What's important to understand is that the body/flesh represents the wall of the temple. The Holy Spirit resides within your flesh like a seed. When the outer casing of a seed dies, then and only then, will the plant within emerge. This is the mystery of the body and spirit. That's why you must crucify the flesh. Lustful whims of the flesh mean nothing. It's the Holy Spirit within you that's truly valuable.

To comprehend this truth and live in it, "you" have to die. This is the only one way. The bible says in Proverbs 14:12, "There is a way which seems right unto a man, but the end thereof is the ways of death". That way the word is referring to is "your own way". That's why in Isaiah 56:11 it says that the dogs have turned to their *own way*.

God has taken time in his word to warn us about the dogs of this world to protect us. You are valuable to him. You are a golden vessel! I cannot emphasize how important it is for you to grasp that. If you're cognizant of your worth you won't give yourself away so cheaply. Daughters of the Most High God are priceless.

Before giving your life to Christ you may have been a prostitute, drug addict, whore, liar, thief, you name it. You *were* a vessel of dishonor. But today you're part of the body of Christ, valuable and priceless!

Don't let anybody (including yourself) tell you otherwise. YOU ARE WORTHY OF TRUE LOVE. From now on maintain your golden vessel with honor.

Now, let's divert our attention back to the structure of the temple. Upon close examination you'll see the correlation of the body and the temple. In the Old Testament we see the tabernacle of Moses, the tabernacle of David, the temple of Solomon's structure and materials written in explicit detail. Every item in and around the tabernacle is relevant. It expresses a shadow and type of things to come.

The Ark of the Covenant was deep within the Holy of Holies in the tabernacle. The tabernacle is a pattern of you. *Our bodies are the new temple.*

> **Mark 14:58**
>
> We heard him say, I will destroy *this temple that is made with hands*, and within three days I will build another *made without hands.*

The Tabernacle

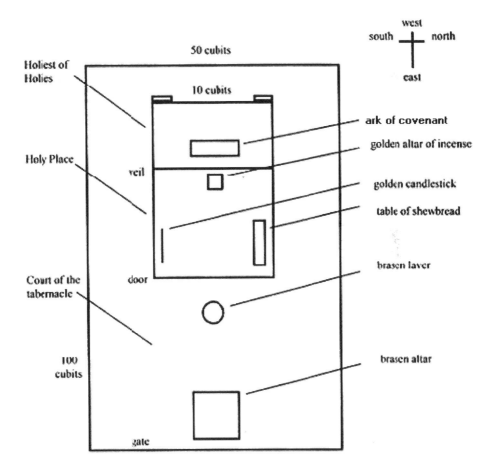

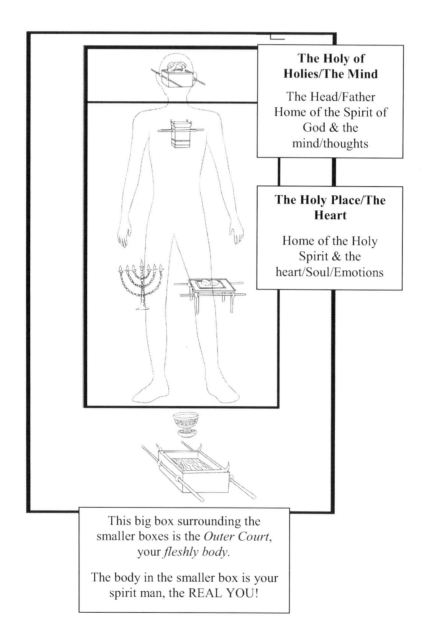

Basic understanding of the physical arrangement of the tabernacle structures and its function reveals knowledge of the sacred purpose of our bodies.

The white linen walls

First, the tabernacle exterior walls were surrounded by fine linen panels. The purpose of the linen was to divide/separate the outside world from the precious contents inside. This detail illustrates to us that we need to sanctify ourselves from the world.

The fact that those on the outside of the tabernacle cannot see inside, typifies that outsiders are blinded by the Holiness of God. The white color represents righteousness. We are to be righteous. Our righteousness stands as protection from unrighteous outsiders.

A man in the world cannot see the spiritual things of God, they are blind to righteousness. So when you meet a man that's worldly and you're living righteously, he will at some point reject you.

Stop thinking something is wrong with you, it's not. The righteousness of God protects you and sometimes he allows the enemy to reject you if you don't have the strength to leave. Unbelievers do not, cannot, see the true beauty in you because they are blinded by the righteous linen.

> **Leviticus 22:2**
>
> Speak unto Aaron and to his sons, that *they separate themselves* from the holy things of the children of Israel, and that they profane not my holy name in *those things* which they *hallow unto me: I am the LORD.*

> **1 Corinthians 2:14**
>
> But *the natural man receiveth not the things of the Spirit of God: for they are foolishness unto him*: neither can he know them, because they are spiritually discerned

> **Revelation 22:15**
>
> *Outside are the dogs* and sorcerers and the sexually immoral and murderers and idolaters, and everyone who loves and practices falsehood.

The one gate

In the tabernacle of Moses there was one gate that faced the east whereby the priest entered. This one entrance into the tabernacle represents Jesus, who is the only way to salvation. As it pertains to your physical body, it represents your private parts. The only one who is to enter the temple is the one approved to do so, which is the high priest. Your God ordained husband would be the high priest.

The word says that there is only one way and that is his way. Anybody that comes in other way, God is telling us right here in the word, are thieves and robbers. This is why you feel robbed after you've been intimate with someone and they leave you or cheat on you. You did get robbed! They illegally entered the temple and defiled it!

> **John 10:1**
>
> "I tell you *the truth*, the *man who does not enter the sheep pen by the gate*, but climbs in by some other way, is a *thief and a robber.*

The Brazen Altar

Inside the outer court is the Brazen Altar. Here's where the sacrifices were made. In order to move into the presence of God, atonement had to be made for our sins, something had to die. Today, we no longer have to make physical sacrifices of killing bulls and rams because Jesus Christ was the Holy sacrificial lamb that was slain for our sins. The shadow and type of this illustration of the sacrifice of blood in relation to our bodies would be when a marriage is consummated. In a perfect world, a man would be marrying a virgin.

In biblical times, a part of the marriage ceremony would be the consummation of the marriage. The entire tribe/family would wait outside the tent as the couple would go inside and consummate the marriage on white linen.

Afterwards the husband would come out and show the linen with the blood on it proving that his wife was pure. The husband, who represents the priest, made the sacrifice of matrimony to his bride. The intertwining of the blood made the covenant official.

This covenant is sacred and this sacrifice is a form of worship. This is one of the reasons why the union is called Holy Matrimony. Sex is not only for your pleasure to share with whomever you want. As you can see, in addition to being a covenant it is a Holy form of worship.

Also note; the priest who ministered on the Brazen Alter had to wear certain attire. They had to wear the uniform of the priest which was anointed (completely smeared with oil). All who touched the altar had to be holy and ceremonially clean. Therefore, you should take note of the characteristics your future husband should have. He should be anointed to serve in your temple, clean and obedient the word of God, respecting his own body as well as yours. This is an absolute must because in the future he'll be going before the Lord on your behalf.

> **2 Timothy 4:5**
>
> But you, be sober in all things, endure hardship, do the work of an evangelist, fulfill your ministry.

Another key note is the altar had to be sanctified and anointed before use. As a woman, your body, your intimate parts should be sanctified and anointed before use. Sanctified means to be set apart. You also have to be anointed. To "anoint" in Greek means "Crio" to smear with oil and "Aleipho" means to anoint. In other words you were set apart for service to the Lord. The oil represents the Holy Spirit. Ultimately, we are to constantly be filled with the Holy Spirit and in service to the Lord.

The brazen laver

This item in the temple was where the priests would wash their hands and their feet. It was made out of brass. The brazen laver was located in the outer court. The brazen laver is known to be symbolic of baptism and washing of the water by the word. Here is also where the priest would check themselves as a in a mirror through the reflection of the water in the brass.

Today, we reflect through the water of the word. While still in the outer court, you cleanse yourself before coming into the presence of the Lord. This preparation is designed for you to get your spirit in order.

Seeing yourself through the reflection of the word helps you to perceive the filthy things on you and around you that you need to get rid of.

> **Acts 22:16**
>
> And now why tarriest thou? arise, and *be baptized, and wash away thy sins*, calling on the name of the Lord.

> **1 Peter 3:20-21**
>
> Which sometime were disobedient, when once the longsuffering of God waited in the days of Noah, *while the ark was a preparing*, wherein few, that is, eight souls were *saved by water.* [21]The like figure whereunto even baptism doth also now save us (not the putting away of the filth of the flesh, but the answer of a good conscience toward God,) by the resurrection of Jesus Christ.

The Golden Lampstand

This particular item is very special indeed. It is located in the Holy Place. The Golden Lamp stand is made from one piece of pure gold, beaten into shape.

Gold is symbolic of the Divine character of God. This beautiful lamp stand has 7 stems. The center stem is higher than the three on the left and on the right. The oil that fuels the lamp is poured into the center stem and flows throughout to the other six stems.

This light was to be kept burning perpetually. By now I'm sure you realize that we are talking about the infilling of the Holy Spirit. Your power comes from the center branch. It is only through the center branch you can be filled. I can't over emphasize how important this information is.

A lot of our losses, heartbreaks and disappointments are caused by having an expectation from men/people to fuel this fire. That is too much to demand from anybody and impossible for them to accomplish. This fuel in your spirit is found only in the Holy Place, in the word, in your prayer time, through the Holy Spirit. It is a continuous process that you must do alone.

Another important note about the golden lamp stand is that it was the only light in the tabernacle. The light of the word reveals what was once hid in darkness.

> **2 Corinthians 4:6**
>
> For God, who *commanded the light to shine out of darkness*, hath shined in our hearts, to give the light of the knowledge of the glory of God in the face of Jesus Christ.

> **Ephesians 3:5**
>
> Which in other ages was not made known unto the sons of men, as it is now revealed unto his holy apostles and prophets by the *Spirit.*

> **Matthew 5:16**
>
> *Let your light so shine* before men, that they may see your good works, and glorify your Father which is in heaven.

The Table of Shewbread

This table that is located in the Holy place. There were 12 loaves of bread prepared and placed on this table daily by the priest. The bread for us today would be the word of God. Every day, as a priest (and yes, you are a priest through Jesus Christ), you must place the word within your spirit daily for your sustenance.

The bible tells us that man cannot live by bread alone but by every word that proceeds out of the word of God. You see, it's not enough that you feed your body natural food every day. You must also feed your spirit man.

The materials used for the table of showbread were shittum wood on the inside and gold on the outside. The wood represents the humility of Jesus and the gold represents the divinity of God. All of these things about the temple are symbolic of your relationship to God today!

Another interesting thing about the table of shewbread was the children of Israel would bring the table of shewbread and the Ark of the covenant with them to battle. These are hints to how and why we must know what God has put in us.

It wasn't the table or the ark itself that had the power. It was the presence of God that made the difference. The presence of God resides within your body! You need to eat the word, your bread daily! You are what you eat!

The Altar of Incense

This is the place where you draw near to the Lord, pray, make your petitions made known and intercede for people. All of these things are happening in the spirit, in your body. You must enter into Gods presence with praise and thanksgiving. Your prayer, praise and thanksgiving are the fragrant incense that you offer to the Lord.

The altar is strategically positioned at the entrance of the Holy of Holies. The altar was made of shiddum wood and gold, with 4 horns, one on each corner with blood on it. This is the place where you offer up the sacrifice of praise to the Lord in order to enter into his presence.

The blood on the horns represents the blood of Jesus. We are able to enter into the Holy of Holies through the eternal sacrifice Jesus made for us on Calvary.

The Veil

The veil in the temple separated and shielded our eyes from the divine presence of God. The veil itself represents the flesh of Jesus Christ.

When he died the veil was torn from the top to the bottom. This symbolizes how we are now given access into the presence of God through him. In those days, if an unauthorized person or unclean priest entered into the Holies of Holies, he would drop dead.

Today, when you allow someone to enter your body, they are illegally passing through the veil, into the Holy of Holies in your temple!

What I'm saying is a hard thing to conceive but it is truth. The dogs of this world will not understand, receive nor respect this. That's why God said that if anyone enters any other way, they're a thief and a robber.

What you experience in the Holy of Holies is a personal intimate time in the presence of God. Only a high priest can enter the Holy of Holies.

When you get married, the two of you shall become one flesh. Both of you should be believers. Which means the two of you through Jesus our high priest, can legally go through the veil into the presence of the Lord. Now that is making love!

The Ark of The Covenant

This piece is the most important item in the tabernacle. The Ark of the covenant represents the presence of God. Without the ark, the temple means nothing.

Obviously, there is a direct correlation with our bodies. If you don't have the presence of the Lord residing in you, you're just a body of flesh.

Unfortunately, people today feel free to be promiscuous because they think that they're just a body of flesh. They have no idea that they're a living temple. You are born again; God the Holy Spirit resides within you! *Never forget that*!

Within the ark were several items: The 10 commandments, a pot of manna and Aaron's budded rod.

1. The two tablets containing the 10 commandments: represents God's covenant with Israel.
2. The pot of manna: represents the provision of God; Bread from heaven.
3. 3. Aarons rod: this represents God's chosen priesthood.

Today, God has written his law/commandments in our hearts. The manna is symbolic of the word of God, our bread from heaven. Aarons rod represents us, God's chosen priesthood.

There is another significant piece to the ark; the mercy seat. The mercy seat covered the contents within the ark. This piece was made of solid gold, which is symbolic of the deity of God and his throne.

This seat was protected by two cherubims whose angel wings touch each over, covering the mercy seat. Thank God for the mercy seat! When we fall short, we know that God mercifully covers us with his blood and forgive us our sins.

It is so important that we understand what the temple is all about and why we need to regard our bodies as sacred. For this reason, we cannot give what is sacred to the dogs.

Revelation 2:7

He that hath an ear, let him hear what the Spirit saith unto the churches; To him that overcometh will I give to eat of the tree of life, which is in the midst of the paradise of God.

Section 3

Want him to put a ring on it?

Read this...

God's System: matchmadeinheaven.com

In God's divine system he doesn't position his daughter to date, he *arranges* her marriage. Your heavenly Father appointed a husband for you before the beginning of time. God is your heavenly Father.

In the physical world, when a woman is about to wed, her father gives her away. A good father will not readily walk his daughter down the aisle if he felt the man she was about to marry was a bad choice or if she were too immature. Now God, being the best father anyone could have, selects a husband for you.

God's choice will be a *priest* over you and your home. Therefore your future husband has to go through a process in his life to be worthy and prepared to cover you. In order to see get a sneak peek into the temple to see who your husband is (your high priest) you must *be a priest*. Meaning, you must seek the Lord in your spirit so that God can reveal things to you.

Women are part of the royal priesthood through the blood of Jesus Christ. Now that you're in Christ you can boldly go through the veil to the throne of grace and make your petition made known unto God to see what he has in store for you. If you ask him, the Holy Spirit will reveal to you who your husband is.

Remember, God himself will arrange your marriage and he doesn't need your help to do that.

Before you see your high priest (future husband), you must prepare yourself. In the Old Testament, a priest could not touch an unclean thing. If they did they were not permitted to enter the Holy of Holies where the spirit of God dwells. You must cleanse yourself through the word and get into the Holy Place to get the answers you need.

We mistakenly think we could just sin, do what we want to do, go before God filthy and get the desired results. Not so. Never forget that God is sovereign. If you've been seeking the Lord about your future husband and have not heard anything yet, check to see if you are clean.

✥ Purpose Principle #36 ✥

Never forget that God is sovereign. If you have been living in sin, before you go to the Lord repent. Humble yourself before him.

Know ye not that you are the temple for the Holy Spirit? This knowledge is critical in understanding the divine order of things. There is divine order in place for the tabernacle (your body). We know that after Jesus died and was resurrected, he went and sat at the right hand of the Father.

But did you know that Jesus still serves in the sanctuary?

> **Hebrews 8:1-2**
>
> The point we are saying is this: We do have such a high priest, who sat down at the right hand of the throne of the Majesty in heaven ²*and who serves in the sanctuary, the true tabernacle set up by the Lord.*

That sanctuary is within your body! So the priest (man) that desires to enter within the tabernacle (your body) has to be *in the order* of Melchizedek. God said that Jesus is forever established in the order of Melchizedek, so there is no other way. You and your future husband must be in this order. Well, how can this be if Jesus has been made High Priest in the order of Melchizedek and this cannot be changed? And what does it mean to be in the order of Melchizedek?

The man who is to be your husband must to be *born again*, which means he's in Jesus. Therefore he is *in the order* of Melchizedek. His decision to be born again cancels the worldly laws he used to live by. This is great news for you because the change of the priesthood ushers into your husband the heart and mind of Christ.

> **Hebrews 8:10**
>
> This is the *new covenant* I will make with the house of Israel after that time, declares the Lord. I will put *my laws in their minds* and write them on *their hearts*. I will be their God and they will be my people.

How can two walk together except they agree? Agreement is a form of order. A covenant is a lifelong agreement that is bound by blood. When two believers come together, they remain under the same agreement, sealed by the blood of Christ.

Once you get married, the two of you enter into a legal covenant in writing and sealed with an oath. The bible says, "the two shall become one flesh". So, both of you are one high priest *in the order* of Melchizedek. This new covenant with Christ was sealed by an oath from God.

> The emphasis of the order of Melchizedek is to illustrate how NOTHING is happening accidentally.
>
> This order reveals why relationships with some men will NEVER work. And why some men would NEVER marry you. They're not in the divine order.

Hebrews 7:20-21

And it was not without an oath! Others became priests without an oath [21] but he became a priest with an oath when God said to him: "The Lord has sworn and will not change his mind: You are a priest forever".

In our old way of doing things, we allowed boyfriends to become high priests in our lives without an oath! We've been intimate with people who are not in agreement with the order God has ordained. This explains why sinful relationships do not work. You cannot dethrone God! Remember I told you singlehood is an office and marriage is an office? This is what the word says about why lustful, worldly relationships fail and why his system works:

> **Hebrews 7:22**
>
> Because of this oath, Jesus has become the guarantee of a better covenant. ²³Now there have been *many priests, since death prevented them from continuing in office* ²⁴but because Jesus lives forever, he has a permanent priesthood.

> **Hebrews 7:28**
>
> For the law appoints as high priest men who are weak: but the oath, which came after the law, appointed the Son, who has been made perfect forever.

Death=Sin. Hebrews 7:22 says that death/sin, prevented those men from continuing in office. God is Holy and does not tolerate sin. He doesn't want us to tolerate it either. His system is designed to keep men with the sin nature out.

The Lord knows how devastating relationships are when joined to someone with the sin nature. Being involved with someone like that is like being married to Dr. Jekyll and Mr. Hyde! When someone has a sinful nature, even if they're aware of what's right, their very nature forces them to do wrong. Disorder is natural to the sinner.

❧ Purpose Principle #40 ☙

When you connect with a person with a sin nature, they may know the right thing to do, want to do right by you but in the end their *nature* will prevent them from actually doing it.

Galatians 6:8

The one who sows to please his sinful nature, from that nature will reap destruction; the one who sows to please the spirit, from the Spirit will reap eternal life.

Romans 7:20

Now if I do what I do not want to do, it is no longer I who do it, but it is sin living in me that does it.

God is a God of purpose. He arranges a priest to be over you and your home for the purpose that he has ordained for your family. Not just your immediate family today but for generations to come.

A house divided cannot stand. You can't be as effective life ministry if you're constantly battling within your home because you're unequally yoked!

The High Priest God selects to cover you and your family will have the spirit and character of Christ. You need this type of man to be over your household for divine purpose.

Oh, so you thought that you were just going to find a man, get married and live happily ever after? What is all this ministry talk anyway, I'm not a minister. Oh, yes you are!

You may not be a preacher on the pulpit but your life is most definitely a ministry. And when you do get married, the ministry will continue. That's the purpose of your union in the first place.

~ PURPOSE PRINCIPLE #41 ~

THE MAN GOD PLACES IN YOUR LIFE TO BE YOUR HUSBAND WILL BE THE HIGH PRIEST OVER YOUR HOME.

> **Hebrews 7:26**
>
> Such a high priest *meets our needs*-one who is holy, blameless, pure, set apart from sinners, exalted above the heavens.

The order is established. There is no other way. If anyone comes any other way, the bible calls them a thief and a robber. Just "liking" or being attracted someone is not a secure foundation to build your future. You cannot join with unbelievers, men from other religions, etc and think it's going to work, it won't.

Trust me, God's system is not designed to rob or deprive you. It's for purpose and protection. That's why I keep reiterating biblical principles regarding your singlehood. This is not a bunch of religious rhetoric! You must understand it's not a numbers game of how many men are interested in, or how old you are etc. It's a waiting game…waiting on the Lord in service.

God's divine system for husband and wife is a patriarchal order. God the Father is over the husband, the husband is over the wife and parents are over the children.

Patriarchal Order

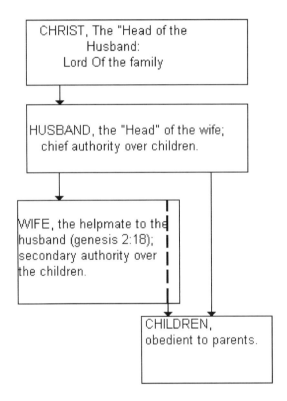

1 Corinthians 11:3

But I want you to realize that the head of every man is Christ, and the head of the woman is man, and the head of Christ is God.

God's Prenuptial Agreements

Oftentimes when a wealthy person gets married, the first thing we say is, "Did they sign a prenup?" In a lot of high society arenas that's a no brainer.

Why? Most people who have millions and billions of dollars are not interested in putting half of their empire in jeopardy because of "feelings". "Yes honey, we can get married but … I'm gonna need you to sign this first"!

Now we all know that God owns everything. If the world is smart enough to protect their assets, what makes you think God doesn't protect his? Well, he does. The terms of his agreement is sorted out in the betrothal (engagement) period.

When you get engaged you pledge to enter into the covenant. During this preparation period, both sides of the family discuss the terms of the covenant until an agreement is reached. The entire time and process of engagement is one of planning.

All questions of the terms and conditions must be resolved *before* the wedding ceremony. After the covenant ceremony, the agreement in no way may be altered or nullified.

> **NOTES ABOUT MARRIAGE/COVENANT:**
>
> - Covenant in Hebrew means, a cut where blood flows. The purpose of covenant was to create a binding agreement, more powerful than a contract agreement. This was to be forever-the life span of the participants, it was to be Holy, sacred, and to violate the covenant would mean death. The blood covenant was the ultimate insurance of loyalty and fidelity.
> - Wedding rings are symbolic of the scars that would have been part of the ceremony.
> - Marriage is the closest agreement to the blood covenant in modern society. However, marriage today is closer to a contract than a covenant.
> - Covenant is a permanent lifelong agreement with no escape clause. Covenant is used to join people, families and tribes to each other with terms that cannot be altered or nullified.

Covenant Stage 1

You're a believer now, therefore your old way of doing things are over. This may be uncomfortable at first because the part of you that has been born again is your spirit not your body/flesh. It's the fleshy part of you that's still in the natural state; it hasn't changed and continues to crave the things of the world.

Although the flesh wars against the spirit, your spirit will win because the flesh was defeated at the cross, through the blood of Jesus Christ. With that said, it is incumbent on you to understand your divine nature.

I know, I know, I really would like to make this a typical relationship book with 10 easy steps to make someone fall in love with you. Well, I can't because that's manipulation/witchcraft. It's the truth that destroys yokes and makes a difference. A difference, is what God is about to do in your life.

Remember, God is one with 3 persons, the Father, the Son and the Holy Spirit. All three are one God but serve different purposes and operate in different realms.

This information is vital in discovering our purpose in the single position.

In the system God has ordained, it shows how we indeed were created in his image and likeness and that we are to mirror the divine nature of the trinity.

God the Father: God of your Soul
God the Son: God of the Body
God the Holy Spirit: God of the Mind

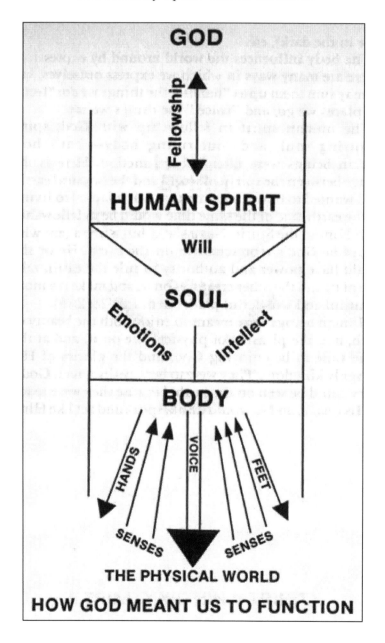

We are made 3 in one as well:

> Mind=your thoughts, imagination
> Body=your physical existence
> Soul=who you really are

In order to comprehend how our covenant relationship relates to us today, for simplicity I arranged 3 covenant stages. Each phase explains how our walk as Christian single women should evolve. The divinity of the trinity remains intact; I have listed them as stages to illustrate how we go from faith to faith and *glory to glory.

> ***Romans 1:17**
>
> 17For in it is the righteousness of God *revealed from faith to faith*: as it is written, the just shall live by faith.

Covenant Stage 1 Outer court.

- Transformation
- The Holy Spirit (The mind of Christ)
- Sons & Daughter of God

> **2 Corinthians 6:18**
>
> I will be to you a Father. You will be to me sons and *daughters*, says the Lord Almighty.

> **John 15:26, 27**
>
> When the Counselor comes, whom I will send to you *from the Father*, the *Spirit of truth* who goes out from the Father, he will testify about me. ²⁷*And you also must testify, for you have been with me from the beginning.*

Stage one of your covenant is where you take the first step into the Kingdom of God and the body of Christ. *Disciplining your thoughts* to be subject to the will of God begins here.

The Holy Spirit, as your guide, divinely speaks to you and leads you to all truths. He's also the confirmation, (your birth certificate if you will) of who we are in Christ. His presence is necessary to lead us from the mind of a bastard child to a daughter of the King.

The word tells us:

> **1 Corinthians 7:34**
>
> There is a difference also between a wife and a virgin. The unmarried woman *cares for the things of the Lord, that she may be holy both in body and in spirit*: but she that is married cares for the things of the world, how she may please her husband.

First thing, you must develop the mind of Christ to obey. Second, you have to be a child of God for him to share his plans to you. The most important thing that occurs in this process is a change of heart. A servant will obey a command but his heart is one of hired help, not an heir. The heart of a son or daughter is totally different. A son or daughter will have a deeper sense of loyalty and commitment pertaining to the property of the parent/family because of their vested interest. It's equally true that a Father will share more information and secrets to his children than he would a servant. An heir is more inclined to die trying to protect the family legacy from attack than a servant. When you were in the world you were just a servant but now you have the love, connection, commitment, heart and loyalty as a daughter.

> **John 10:11-14**
>
> "I am the good shepherd. The good shepherd *lays down his life for the sheep.* [12]The hired hand is not the shepherd who owns the sheep. So when he sees the wolf coming, he abandons the sheep and runs away. Then the wolf attacks the flock and scatters it. [13]*The man runs away because he is a hired hand and cares nothing for the sheep.*

> ¹⁴"I am the good shepherd; I know my sheep and my sheep know me - just as the Father knows me and I know the Father - and I lay down my life for the sheep.
> ¹⁵I no longer call you servants, because a servant does not know his master's business. Instead, I have called you friends, for everything that I learned from my Father I have made known to you. ¹⁶You did not choose me, but I chose you and appointed you to go and bear fruit - fruit that will last. Then the Father will give you whatever you ask in my name.

Renewal of the mind is necessary so that you to line up with the will of God because you're caring for the things of the Lord. Why? God needed a body in the earth realm to carry out his business. Therefore, single people have the task of caring for the things of the Lord in order to execute *his plans*, not ours. As an ambassador for Christ, you have the Holy Spirit and the word guiding you through life and training you to comprehend what the will of the Father is and how to complete your assignment.

When God created woman, he created her to be a suitable *helper. Many feminist of today scorn the idea of being used but the fact of the matter is, that's what women were made for! Of course, when you think about getting married, you visualize being this perfect wife, prepared to please her husband. However, what you actually *do* when you have a husband in reality may be not be as pleasing as you intended because you weren't prepared. In regards to our relationship with the Father, he created you to be a suitable helper for him first. God gets EVERYTHING FIRST! Rehabilitation of our mind to the will of God through the Holy Spirit teaches us how to serve the Lord the way we were created to, proving we are daughters worthy of his son. When you finally do get married, *you will be ready* because God himself trained you to be a suitable helper for your own husband (not boyfriends).

> ***Genesis 2:18**
>
> The LORD God said, "It is not good for the man to be alone. I will make a helper suitable *for him.*"

> The idea of being *used* is unattractive because you think so highly of yourself (pride). If you follow God's system (humble yourself), you will be helping people and in doing so you'll feel real good being used! For a lot of women, the reason they have a problem with submission and being used is they have given up too much or all to *boyfriends*. Give your best to God and he will give his best to you. Then, when your husband finally does come, you won't be all used up.

Your assignment to care for the things of the Lord requires an ear to hear, understanding, obedience and sacrifice. In phase 1 you learn the voice of the Holy Spirit who will be speaking to you guiding you to all truths. He reveals truths about himself (the word), you, your assignment and future.

Caring for the things of the Lord simply consist of being available to be used by God, on earth, performing his will.

Re-discovering your identity...

Prior to being born again, God gave you the breath of life from the spirit realm through the vehicle of a seed in your father. That seed was conceived in your mother and through her body you were birthed, becoming a living being with a body made of flesh. Intercourse is a transaction between spirit and blood. The seed contains the spirit but life is in the blood. The two shall become one, spirit and flesh, heaven and earth.

We inhabit the earth following the laws of the body, i.e., needing oxygen, eating, sleeping, breathing, etc and the laws of the earth such as, gravity and physics, etc applied. All the things of this natural world that we have come to know are temporary. People, animals, plants, they all die. Buildings, cars, and material things eventually corrode and disappear. This temporary kingdom is the world as we know it.

> **1 Corinthians 15:42**
>
> So will it be with the resurrection of the dead. *The body that is sown is perishable*, it is raised imperishable;

> **1 Corinthians 15:54**
>
> But when this corruptible will have put on incorruption, and this mortal will have put on immortality, then what is written will happen: "Death is swallowed up in victory."

> **Galatians 6:8**
>
> For he who sows to his own flesh will from the flesh *reap* corruption. But he who sows to the Spirit will from the Spirit reap eternal life.

When you get born again, there's a transfer that occurs. In other words, on earth you were a spirit born into a body. But when you enter the spirit realm, you lose the physical body and the seed of the Holy Spirit that was planted in you is birthed into that domain. The baby (you) entered through the body of Jesus. We come through the blood of Jesus into his kingdom, the kingdom of heaven. This transaction gives you an instant status change. Simultaneously, you become a wife because of your covenant with Christ and a daughter of the King of Kings and the Lord of Lord because you are birthed through the blood of Jesus. God is your father, your King and he is your God.

Now that you understand that you're a daughter of the King, a princess, you have royal obligations. This assignment is part of your purpose. We were created for the use of the Father for the Kingdom. This explains why there may be long periods of you being single and why most men *cannot* be the one for you.

As a daughter of the king, the bible tells single women, to care for the things of the Lord. Obedience to this instruction places you in proper position. Once you devote yourself body and spirit, you have officially ignited your faith. Faith in God confirms who you are to him and who he is to you. The husband that he sends to you will be the evidence of the relationship that you truly have with him.

In any kingdom, the consideration of who marries the daughter of the King is serious business. *She cannot just marry who she wants,* *because the kingdom is at stake*. The King selects someone worthy to rule in his stead on earth, one who observes, obey and executes his will. He selects the one who is worthy of the crown, willing to defend the kingdom to the death. It's the character, a man after God's own heart that the King of Kings is looking for. Not looks, financial status, education etc., it's the *heart.

Understand every man aspires to be king but most are not willing to lay down their life. Although the past men in your life appeared to be the one, they were not. They came for the benefits of the gift instead of relationship with the giver, the King of Kings. The only man God will have on the throne is his son, which means the man must be born again (the order of Melchizedek). If a man will not lay down his life for God, he's not worthy to be crowned and placed on the throne of your heart.

> ***Samuel 16:7**
>
> Do not consider his appearance or his height, for I have rejected him. The LORD does not look at the things man looks at. Man looks at the outward appearance, but the LORD looks at the heart."

The daughter of a king has duties in the kingdom. God, our king, has kingdom business that he positioned us to fulfill. It shouldn't feel like a chore to serve God with your life. As a privileged daughter, you should reciprocate with a loving heart, and serve her father in whatever he requires. Sacrifices you make in order to serve him are *reasonable* *service. The Lord will do his part, as he always does and take good care of you. When you complete your assignment, you'll receive the promise.

> ***Romans 12**
>
> 1 I beseech you therefore, brethren, by the mercies of God, that ye present your bodies a living sacrifice, holy, acceptable unto God, *which is* your reasonable service.

> **Hebrews 11:1**
>
> ¹Now faith is the substance of things hoped for, the *evidence* of things not seen.
> ³Through faith we understand that the worlds were framed by the word of God, so that *things which are seen were not made of things which do appear.*

The fact of the matter is most single Christian women have allowed themselves to be used by men and have not allowed themselves to be used by God. Women have a natural proclivity to assist, nurture and support, which often gets abused. This happens because of the disorder in your life. You are to be devoted to God first, then to your *own* husband, *not boyfriends*! Single women have wasted too much valuable time and resources trying to get a man. Royal princesses don't pursue men, that wouldn't be proper. The beautiful, precious resources God gave us were to be used for the sole purpose of doing *his will*, not our own. Resources include your beauty, body, money, mind, social connections etc. The reward for allowing God to use you is a relationship with him. When you sincerely please him, he *gives you* the desires of your heart. If you desire to get married, he will arrange *the best* for you!

Just going to church and hearing the word is not enough. All that I'm talking about in this book is not religious rhetoric. You must make these adjustments in your life. Have you noticed that I'm not discussing much about men, their flaws and shortcomings? I specifically avoided going down that road because if you change you, you change your surroundings. You cannot make concrete changes within without God, there's no love without God! A relationship with God is not about going to church. It is about *being the church*; reading, studying, speaking and living the word. I cannot emphasize this enough. When you do this, you'll witness immediate changes in your life. Stop living like the world expecting God results.

Manifestation of the sons and daughters of God comes when the seed (the word) is planted and conceived. In other words, you will not receive what God has for you if you don't understand what he's telling you. You must study the word for yourself by reading, listening to preaching, fasting and praying. By singing praise and worship you are inviting Gods presence. He's trying to get us to know that he *really is* who he says he is. The only way for that to be proven in your life is for you to make the transfer from flesh to spirit. Transference (an exchange) has to be made between the earth realm and the spirit realm.

> **John 4:24**
>
> God is a Spirit: and they that worship him must worship him in spirit and in truth.

Chapter 13 – God's Prenuptial Agreements

RECAP

1. God is God, he is King of Kings and Lord of Lords.
2. God the Father, Jesus the son, the Holy Spirit is one in three persons.
3. Each have a function; God and Jesus are in heaven. God the Father is the Father. Jesus came to earth as a son and redeemed us (re claimed us for his father, because we already belonged to him) The Holy Spirit is the spirit of God living in us.
4. In the spirit realm, there are no limits. You can do anything through Christ because he is God. This is so important to know and understand! This is why you need faith.
5. Once born again you become indoctrinated into the family of The Most High God. We become the body of Christ. Therefore, we're sons and daughters that have the same privileges and authority as Jesus because Jesus is the son. We come in his name.
6. The sons of God have a purpose to serve God and please him.
7. The daughters of God serve God through devotion.
8. Prayer is how we talk to God.
9. Your belief that God is who he says he is and your faith that he can do what he says he will do is the transfer needed to make things appear on earth.
10. We are a spirit living in a body. In order for there to be a transfer of things you desire between you and God, heaven and earth, there has to be an exchange. Just like exchanging currency in another country. You give God your faith in exchange for your request. That is the transfer policy for heaven. It is against the law of heaven to just ask and not believe. The belief is the conversion. The answer is the receipt of faith, plus proof that you are a believer/daughter and God is your Father.
11. The tithe is set aside as divine portion for God. It is a devoted thing.
12. First fruits from you are set aside for divine portion. It is a devoted thing.
13. Vessels of the Lord are set aside for use in the temple, in our Fathers house. It is a devoted thing.
14. Daughters *are vessels and devoted things* that belong to God.

Covenant Stage 2 - The Holy Place

In stage 2 of the covenant, we enter into the phase of devotion to the royal priesthood. This is where we begin to come out of our comfort zones and get busy! In this place we lay down our lives.

Jesus had the daunting task of surrendering his body to the affliction and pain of the cross in order to do God's will. We're not exempt. We must crucify our flesh in order to fulfill the will of the father.

As single women, we do this by devoting ourselves body and spirit. Your devotion is mandatory, not an option. God has things that are exclusively his. The tithe is a prime example of divine portion.

When God created woman, he removed the rib (a portion) from the man. This portion should be devoted unto God. Yes, that means all single women of God.

Why is it so important that we give God his portion? The first reason is there must be a divine transfer. Anything that remains in the natural state will eventually die. God takes the divine portion, transfers it from the natural to the spiritual making it blessed.

Secondly, the woman *is the vessel* used to carry seed. Anything devoted to God must be Holy because he is Holy. Our heavenly Father has special vessels in his kingdom ordained for his use. God in his infinite wisdom decided to allow you to be single at this time to use you for his glory.

Yes, GOD IS GOING TO USE YOU! This is the very essence of being *single on purpose*! Therefore your vessel (you) must be Holy, clean and pure. The only way to accomplish Holiness is through righteousness; you have to kill the flesh. Walking in righteousness is the process and the function of the royal priesthood.

> **1 Peter 3:9**
>
> But ye *are* a chosen generation, a royal priesthood, a holy nation, a peculiar people; that ye should shew forth the praises of him who hath called you out of darkness into his marvelous light.

In 1Peter 3:9, it's clear God has selected you not only to be a daughter in the kingdom but to be part of the royal priesthood. You *should be different* and stand out! This is why my book sounds and feels so different. I'm not talking about how to get a man because that's not the point. The point is the assignment God has given you. As a daughter, you're royalty entitled to the inheritance of the kingdom. However, your inheritance is conditional; you must serve as a priest and ambassador between kingdoms.

How do you serve in the temple? On this level, you serve by sacrificing yourself. In order to be worthy of the next phase, it will cost you your life. When you decide to devote yourself and help the body of Christ, you're laying down your *life. I mean, you could be doing anything with your time but you have devoted it to helping others. Service as a priest, is not limited to working at a church facility. It could be helping family, a friend, philanthropy, ministering to people at your job or in public, etc. Selfless activities inspired by the Holy Spirit is an act of service in the temple because your body *is the temple* for the Most High God!

> ***John 12:24**
>
> I tell you the truth, unless a kernel of wheat falls to the ground and dies, it remains only a single seed. But if it dies, it produces many seeds.

Speaking of which, the sacrifice of your body is of high value. I truly understand if you've already been sexually active it's extremely difficult to turn celibate. Even after you've come to terms with doing so, most men today do not have the discipline or fortitude to hold out for you. When you take the stance of obedience to Christ by offering your body as a living sacrifice, God says, "it's your reasonable service". It's what you are supposed to do because you're part of the royal priesthood. Although it's hard, requiring strict discipline, the laying down of your life is how you worship God. Not only does he honor what you do, he'll reward you! When you lay down your life, you've just made a divine transfer from an ordinary vessel to a Holy one.

The woman (the vessel) is designed to carry, house and nurture the seed. Part of the purpose of marriage is to produce godly offspring. If the seed is Holy and the vessel is not, it contaminates the seed. This is why the priesthood in you must rise up and consecrate the body to be a living sacrifice.

If you're not living a righteous lifestyle, it contaminates your ministry making you appear fraudulent. People won't listen to you because they don't believe you. They're not stupid… they know that if you genuinely believe the word, you would follow it. How can you expect others to lay down their lives by dying to self when you can't kill your own flesh?

This portion of the covenant is so important! Here's why many Christian women are in a holding pattern. You're so close to God releasing his blessing upon you but you won't crucify your flesh. You will lay down your life for a man but not for God! Have you noticed that? It's absolutely imperative you realize *you're already betrothed*! God has already destined a husband for you, his daughter. You were the rib taken from the man's side. The man that you were taken from *exists*!

CHAPTER 13 – GOD'S PRENUPTIAL AGREEMENTS

> **Proverbs 19:14**
>
> House and riches *are* the inheritance of fathers: and a prudent wife *is* from the LORD.

A woman doesn't receive a wife from the Lord, the man does. So, how can God give what he doesn't have? You devote yourself to God body and spirit in order for him to give *you* away! *You* are the prudent wife! He's also your father; therefore both you and your husband inherit houses and riches from God when we do things his way. This is his divine system! You cannot plant an orange seed and reap an apple. Kind produces kind.

If you want a husband, God's system requires that you sow yourself. *You* (the wife) are the seed deposited into the kingdom to reap your own husband. Remember, when you plant a seed you don't get a seed back, you get a plant. The latter will be greater. The woman was made from the rib of a man (the seed), that was the divine portion (which is why God tells the woman to "devote herself body and spirit). The man is the rest of the body (the plant). Ironically, the same system works for the man. When he lays down his life for God and sows himself, he reaps his wife and gets the rest of his glorified body.

A great illustration about stage 2 in the covenant is explained in the process of the old traditional Jewish wedding. In biblical times, Jewish marriages were arranged. The fathers from each party would come together and discuss the potential joining of their son and daughter in marriage. At this juncture the children are not part of the negotiations.

After the informal arrangements has been made, the potential bride and groom along with their family have dinner together. A cup would be placed in front of the woman and in front of the man. If the woman is willing to marry the man, she would drink from the cup then the man would do the same. From that moment on the two are considered married. They're now betrothed.

Even though technically they're married, the couple doesn't interact until the wedding. The groom goes back to his home where he begins to prepare a home for his future bride. The bride to be then goes to her residence and prepares *herself*.

*Side note: This is where you are once you decide to devote yourself body and spirit. You're officially betrothed and now you must prepare yourself for the arrival of your future husband.

During the betrothal period the bride wears a veil on her face so that other men will not look at her because she is taken. This preparation process usually continues for about a year. What's interesting about this *is neither the groom nor the bride knows when the actual wedding will be…* only the father does.

The father of the bride is the one who approves the date and time of the wedding. Periodically the father inspects the place the groom is building. When the father concurs that the living conditions are right for his daughter, then he informs the groom he can go get his bride. The bride to be has no idea when the groom is going to come, *she simply has to be ready*.

So how does a woman of God prepare for her husband? Devoting yourself body and spirit *is the preparation*! Aside from being a daughter of the King, you are also the royal priesthood of the Most High God.

In the first covenant stage we understand God renews our mind and introduce us to the kingdom. He assures us that he is our father and we are his daughters. As you step into this second phase of the covenant, you completely lose yourself. As a priest, you go into the temple and prepare the sacrifice (yourself). Phase one you surrendered your will, in Phase two you surrender your body.

When the daughter is at the table and the cup is placed in front of her, she has a decision to make. She can either choose to drink from the cup, accept the terms of the agreement and *consecrate herself* or she can decline and continue to be by herself.

We're faced with the same decision. You're already in the Christian family, but if you want to get married you have to drink of the cup like Jesus did. Once you drink and tell God yes I will obey, I will care for the things of the Lord and I will *devote myself body and spirit*, you've agreed to the terms and are officially betrothed.

In the Jewish tradition, although the couple technically was married, they were not physically joined together yet because the groom had to prepare a place for his bride. Sounds familiar? This is the same as Jesus, how he has gone to prepare a place for us. As the betrothed, we're waiting for the Father to tell the groom, OK the place is ready, go get your bride.

The key for women of God who are betrothed through devotion is to prepare. The betrothed woman in the Jewish wedding had to cover her face so that no other man would look upon her while she was waiting on her husband. This is exactly what you do when you decide to devote yourself to God body and spirit.

You have taken yourself off of the market. No longer are you spending time, money, and resources soliciting attention from men. You're not looking for a man anymore because you know that you are *already* betrothed.

How do you know that you are betrothed? In order to walk in obedience to Gods will and match making system, you'll need "now faith". That level of faith makes you a wife in the *present*. Women of

God are the "PRESENT" their husband receives from God after he pleases him with *his* faith.

Anything in a natural/worldly state will eventually die; it has an inevitable shelf life. This is why past relationships didn't work. Our Heavenly Father is an eternal spirit therefore everything that belongs to him is blessed and eternal. God is also Holy, perfect and pure. Anything that is devoted to him must be Holy, pure and unblemished. You may say, "I have done this or I have done that; I can never be without blemish" but when you get born again, God washes all of your sins away.

Once born again if you sin, you cleanse yourself through repentance and the washing of the word. The reason why you absolutely have to be Holy is because you cannot make a divine transfer until you do. When you devote yourself as a living sacrifice Holy and acceptable in his sight, your Father can use you. He uses you, to give your future husband the rest of himself.

> **Romans 12:1**
>
> I beseech you therefore, brethren, by the mercies of God, that you present your bodies a living sacrifice, holy, acceptable unto God, which is your reasonable service.

Let me explain what I mean by that last statement. It's like the tithe, when you give God 10% of your money, you are giving God money by "now faith". You expect God to bless the remainder of what you have. However, in actuality God never touched your money. He simply gave you his currency on top of yours.

OK, let me explain it like this, when Peter saw Jesus walking on the water, Peter basically was saying to Jesus, "if you are who you say you are tell me to come". Then Jesus said "come".

Peter didn't just walk on water; he walked on the word "come". You cannot violate the laws of the kingdom. If you are in the earth, you have to obey the laws of the earth, i.e. gravity. But when you step into another kingdom, you enter a higher authority. That's what happened with Peter; he stepped into the kingdom of God for a minute and walked on the water of the word. In the kingdom of God, the word says "I can do all things through Christ that strengthens me".

Since the wife is a portion of a man, when she presents her body and spirit to God he holds her like a ransom in the temple of the Lord. She's a priceless golden vessel. When the man pleases the Lord (like in the Jewish wedding, the groom must please the Father) he gives him permission to go and have his daughter.

How does the man please God? Through faith. Faith is the substance of things hoped for the evidence of things not seen. When the man lays down his life for God, gives up the flesh (love of self) it requires faith. Faith is the substance, the body or the thing that makes what you believing for in the spirit world visible and tangible in the earth realm. The manifestation of faith is the evidence of what you saw in the spirit realm (the heavenlies), made tangible on earth which simultaneously confirms your acknowledgement of God, his presence, power and glory.

Now you have to really pay attention here. The man surrenders his life to Christ in order to find God (love). In essence, he sows his body into the kingdom of God like a seed. The woman also has sown her life already into the kingdom of God through devotion, because she is the first fruit of man. She was the devoted thing (the vessel). However, the word tells us that the woman is the body and the man is the head.

So what happened? A divine transfer was made. When the man laid down his life, he got a new body, his wife. It's the same as the tithe. You gave God 10% so that he can give you his blessed 90%. The man gave his life to find God and found himself in him. He found the part of him that was missing ... you. You were his rib (10%), when you return to him you are a blessed 90%! You devoted your body and spirit (10%) and received your blessed head 90%. In the end, you both have a 100% blessed body (family, marriage, home, children, etc.).

Consequently, when you give a man your body outside of marriage, you've just given him your tenth (10%). As a result, you both get a cursed 90%. In other words, that relationship is cursed because you used the 10% for yourself (the devoted thing).

When Adam sinned, God said that the ground was cursed for his sake and he will work to the sweat of his brow. Notice, when you fornicate and try to maintain a relationship outside the will of God, it's difficult. It's because you gave away the devoted thing.

For that relationship, you'll work to the sweat of your brow. The only way to end this curse is to repent, stop sinning and give God the devoted thing… *you*!

Genesis 3:14-19

To the woman he said, "I will make your pains in childbearing very severe;
with painful labor you will give birth to children.
Your desire will be for your husband,
and *he will rule over you.*"
To Adam he said, *"Because you listened to your wife* and ate fruit from the tree about which I commanded you,
'You must not eat from it,'

> "Cursed is the ground because of you;
> through painful toil you will eat food from it
> all the days of your life.
> ¹⁸It will produce thorns and thistles for you,
> and you will eat the plants of the field.
> ¹⁹By the sweat of your brow
> you will eat your food
> until you return to the ground,
> since from it you were taken;
> for dust you are
> and to dust you will return."

When you honor God by giving him the tithe, he tells you to prove him. He's guaranteeing you a blessing that you can call him on! Not only that, he said he'll rebuke the devourer for your sake. He didn't say he will send an angel or you'll have to fight for yourself, God said *HE* will rebuke the devourer for your sake!

So when someone comes to threaten what God has joined together (your future marriage) you don't have to fight to keep it together, all you have to do is remind God that he told you to PROVE HIM! He said he would rebuke the devourer and I promise you, the enemy will have to take his hand off of you and yours! This is the benefit of completely obeying God through devotion.

Why am I saying all this? Once you've purified yourself through sacrificial righteous living, and by faith devoted yourself to God, he can use you as a divine vessel. The plan is for God to reunite you with your betrothed husband. He's not holding you hostage.

Two cannot become one if they are not of the same kind. A man that is Holy and righteous cannot join with a woman who is not. God prepares you through devotion to him so that you'll be ready when your own husband comes for you.

> **Leviticus 27:28**
>
> Nevertheless no devoted thing, that a man shall devote unto the LORD of all that he has, both of man and animal, and of the field of his possession, shall be sold or redeemed: *every devoted thing is most holy unto the LORD.*

Another important note about being a devoted vessel; the woman prepares the body with the oil of the anointing. In the Old Testament the anointing oil was poured onto *the High Priest* and the oil flowed down to his descendents.

Then the priest would sprinkle this anointing oil on the tabernacle and its furnishings *to consecrate them Holy*. The priest was in charge of making the anointing oil with specific ingredients that could not be duplicated for personal use.

～ PURPOSE PRINCIPLE #42 ～

THE ALABASTER JAR IS LINKED TO THE IMAGE OF THE GRAIL. IT IS THE RECEIVING VESSEL, INTO WHICH THE HOLY SPIRIT POURS AND THE INDIVIDUAL CAN BE TRANSFORMED.

> **THE GRAIL:**
>
> 1. The cup or platter used by Jesus at the Last Supper, and in which Joseph of Arimathea received Christ's blood at...
>
> 2. A thing that is earnestly pursued or sought after.

Mark 14:3

³While he was in Bethany, reclining at the table in the home of a man known as Simon the Leper, a woman came with an alabaster jar of very expensive perfume, made of pure nard. *She broke the jar and poured the perfume on his head.*

Mark 14:6-8

"Leave her alone," said Jesus. "Why are you bothering her? She has done a beautiful thing to me.
⁷The poor you will always have with you and you can help them any time you want. But you will not always have me.
⁸She did what she could. *She poured perfume on my body beforehand to prepare for my burial.*

> **Exodus 30:25-33**
>
> Make these into sacred anointing oil, a fragrant blend, the work of a perfumer. It will be the sacred anointing oil. [26]Then use it to anoint the Tent of Meeting, the ark of the Testimony, [27]the table and all its articles, the lamp stand and its accessories, the altar of incense, [28]the altar of burnt offering and all its utensils, and the basin with its stand. [29]*You shall consecrate them so they will be most holy, and whatever touches them will be holy.* [30]*"Anoint Aaron and his sons and consecrate them so they may serve me as priests.* [31]Say to the Israelites, 'This is to be my sacred anointing oil for the generations to come. [32]Do not pour it on men's bodies and do not make any oil with the same formula. It is sacred, and you are to consider it sacred. [33]whoever makes perfume like it and whoever puts it on anyone other than a priest must be cut off from his people.'"

To be anointed is to be set apart, made sacred to serve God. We understand that our bodies are the temple of the Living God. Therefore, we're consecrating our temple like the woman with the alabaster box did with Jesus. In order for the woman to access the precious oil to anoint Jesus, she had to break the jar. Today, our bodies represent the jar. Our flesh must be broken to get the anointing out of our spirit. It is the humbling, submission of our flesh in the presence of our Lord that makes our vessel Holy.

Heart and soul surrender should not be duplicated for personal use. That anointing oil stored away inside of you is Holy and sacred unto the Lord. For this reason many relationships break up. Women have given this costly perfume to someone other than our High Priest.

Covenant Stage 3 – Holy of Holies

In covenant stage 1 and 2, God introduced us to the kingdom to reminding us that we're his daughters, royal heirs and priest created to serve. The third stage is the part we've been waiting for and that's the marriage. Elements of this phase contain a few key components. First part is, "the two shall become one", and second would be "government" and third, "submission".

Never lose sight that every single aspect of the covenant pertains to God's will and purpose. It's his divine will for the church to eventually rejoin with Jesus. Not only does he want the church body reconciled with the head (Jesus Christ) he wants you (the rib, the body) to be reconciled with your husband (the man, head of the body). In both cases there's a uniting of kingdoms, a formation of government. God is the King of Kings and Lord or Lords, therefore the union of Jesus and the church solidify his sovereign rule over heaven and earth with Jesus at the helm.

In order for Jesus to reclaim his territory (the earth, church), he had to go through a similar process we're going through right now. Jesus, well aware of his assignment kept his purpose on the forefront of his mind, that's how he endured. Satan was the temporary ruler of this world; he gained authority through Adam's sin. Jesus being God had to come to the earth through a pure virgin (the vessel). Once birthed, he had the flesh of a man and the spirit of God. The reason Jesus had to lay down his life is because he was in the second phase of the covenant. As a high priest, he had to make a divine transfer. The only way he could do this is through a perfect blood sacrifice.

On the cross, Jesus gave his body. His body is the seed that God needed to plant into the earth in order to reap believers into the spirit realm by faith. Flesh is not allowed in the spirit realm. Our fleshly bodies cannot survive in the kingdom of God, no different from how we cannot survive in the ocean without oxygen. That would violate the law of the ocean kingdom. Therefore, Jesus for the sole purpose of redeeming us, laid down his life (like a seed) to kill the flesh so that mankind would be able to be born into the spirit realm.

> **The only way you can endure the process is to stay focused on God and his promises.**

Prior to Jesus' crucifixion, he had communion with his disciples. Like the Jewish wedding, Jesus placed the cup in front of his disciples at the last supper. Jesus drank and his disciples decided to drink as well. This communion signified the betrothal of Christ and the church (formation of government). Likewise, you and your future husband have decided to drink from this same cup when you agreed to obey God's will and devoted yourself to him. All of these events are leading up to the marriage. The husband goes away to prepare a place and the betrothed prepares for her husband. What does this have to do with you? You are the betrothed wife and daughter of the king. It's through you that your heavenly father's kingdom is able to join with another kingdom.

In the case of the union between Jesus and the church, God is Holy; therefore he can only be joined to that which is Holy. Jesus kingdom is the kingdom of heaven. The woman's kingdom is the earth. For the two to merge, a transaction had to be made to make it one kingdom. The woman needed to be born again to become Holy. Prior to, a woman born of man is a daughter of this kingdom (the world system ruled by satan). When she becomes born again, that spiritual covenant makes a divine transfer. Although she's still on earth, God became her new father, husband and king. God expanded his kingdom/government on earth through her.

This may sound confusing at first but when you get it, you'll begin to realize how precious you are to the God. Look at it this way you have two kings, each rule over their own territory. When a king wants to expand his kingdom it usually happens through hostile takeover in war or through marriage. Satan was the temporary ruler of this earth and you were his daughter. Your marriage covenant with Christ makes Jesus king over you and your inheritance which is the earth.

The daughter transfers the kingdom of the earth to spirit realm, making her betrothed and when Jesus Christ and the church marry they will be one, ruling heaven and earth. When you marry your husband, he becomes your king so that both of you can govern the earth for the King of Kings.

Are you starting to see why you're *single on purpose*? God needs to prepare and position you to carry out a mission that only a woman can do. Devotion of your body and spirit makes you a golden vessel, used to literally defeat satan's kingdom. That's why satan hates women so much. He wants you to defile, worship and defeat yourself because while you're doing all of that, you're not defeating him.

Genesis 3:15

And I will put enmity between you and the woman, and between *your seed* and *her seed*; he shall bruise *your head*, and you shall bruise his heel.

---

1 Corinthians 7:34

but she that is married careth for the things of the world, how she may please *her* husband.

> **Malachi 2:15**
>
> And did not he make them one? Yet had he the remnant of the spirit. And why one? *That he might seek a godly offspring.* Therefore take heed to your spirit, and let none deal treacherously against the wife of his youth.

The daughter's purpose of combining kingdoms are not limited to the spiritual realm. It's also parallel in the physical. Joining in marriage in the physical to your God-ordained husband is part of your assignment to care for the things of the world.

Caring for the things of the world pertains to family and government. Once married, you'll oversee, children, family, inheritance, property, land etc. One of God's purpose for marriage is to produce godly offspring. That means children in the physical and the spiritual. You and your husband's assignment will be to manage your part of the kingdom together.

In God's divine plan, marriage is one of the vehicles in which we execute his command to be fruitful, multiply, replenish and subdue. God is talking about making his kingdom come and will be done on earth through us.

> **Matthew 6:9**
>
> " 'Our Father in heaven,
> hallowed be your name,
> 10your kingdom come,
> your will be done,
> *on earth* as it is in heaven.

In order for this exquisite system to manifest and work, you must be ready, willing and obedient. Jesus laid down his life in order to be eligible of his kingship over the earth. We have to submit to the Father and king in order for his will to be carried out.

The order of submission as a daughter of the king is of optimum importance. If the daughter refuses to drink from the cup, then the wedding is off! Likewise, if the daughter agrees to drink from the cup, gets married and won't submit, it's a violation of the covenant and the marriage will be off!

Submission is a huge aspect of the covenant. It's your part of the agreement before and after marriage. Once married, you've entered a form of government. Government hierarchy that's implemented for order, not condescension. There should be one head and one body or else you'll have a two headed monster.

By design, there's a king and a queen; President and a vice President. For all practical purposes, you're the queen, VP. This important prestigious position you're ordained for is designed for access and support. Both you and your husband together as one to rule and oversee the government but *he is the king*.

So many single women desire to be married, call themselves a queen but do not have the proper spirit to rule. Nor do they understand what it means to be married. God knew that we would fall short due to disobedience and ignorance. Our society has lied to women convincing them that a matriarchal form of government works. This is a lie birthed from disobedient men and rebellious women who tried to fulfill their lust of having marriage privileges without responsibility. This lie spawned haughty stiff-necked women who have no respect for anyone including themselves and are absolutely unwilling to submit to any form of authority. These women birthed a generation of bastard children who were

compelled to live out of order in confusion. Men courted and abandoned these women because their *position* was taken. The matriarchal system has no rules, boundaries, or order that men are obligated to follow because it was out of order. There was no place for the man to rule because in that system the body rules the head.

Submission of the covenant wife to God has the power to help bring the body back into alignment. Devotion to God body and spirit is submission to God, in which he uses your body for his will. His will is to draw all men unto him. It's through your rejection of the world system that the man is reminded (through your actions) of righteousness. Although the man is the head, God is the head of the man. When he's out of order, makes a bad decision or does something wrong, you can petition God on his behalf. If you continue to faithfully submit, even when you husband acts a fool, God can correct him on your behalf. God *never* stops being a good Father.

While you're single, if you reject a man that you're attracted to for righteousness sake and he leaves you, you've planted a seed in him that he won't forget. If all women were to submit to the will of God, men *couldn't* cheat! There would be no one for him to cheat with! If all single women were to submit to the will of God there wouldn't be children birthed out of wedlock because no one will be fornicating.

I'm saying all of that to say, your submission to your covenant agreement with God prepares you for your role as a wife. As a team, you and your husband have to agree because you are one. When an issue comes up between you and God or you and your husband there has to be a bottom line. God implemented the wise strategy of submission by the wife to resolve disputes and restore order in the home. When you submit to your husband, you've agreed *with him*. You may not agree with his methods or his solution but you agree *with him*. You were taught this technique through submission to God.

There are times God told me to do things I didn't agree with but I submitted to his will anyway. In the end everything worked out and I had the opportunity to see why he did what he did, the way that he did it. If I hadn't submitted, I could have aborted the mission. Once you're married, this requirement doesn't change. You'll be obligated to continue to submit to your husband. I guarantee you there will be a time that your husband will do something or make a decision that you don't understand. He may be very vague expressing details which is extremely frustrating for any woman! But God is not going to leave you dangling out there alone. When this happens in your family, you'll have the wisdom and fortitude to get behind your husband and support his endeavors even when you don't understand what's going on. The only way to do that is by simultaneously putting your faith in God.

The irony I've noticed is when women submit on this level they take pressure off of themselves and put the burden of proof on the man which makes him *feel more masculine*. He now feels obligated to deliver, and even if he fails, he will try everything in his power to make it right. This is no fairy tale relationship. This is the *reality* of two people joined together. Nobody is perfect. Therefore God is preparing us to have the character needed to sustain a relationship through fear, moods, tempers, failures and disappointments.

If the government fails, so does the kingdom. And failure is not an option. It's real easy to say, "it's the man's fault" or "he's just doesn't do anything right" but if you have never fully submitted to anyone, you'll never know what God or your husband can do for you if you never shut your mouth and release control.

For these reasons, single women ought not rush to get married for the sake of getting married. What I just discussed is a reality that almost every married woman will face. We need God to arrange our marriages and teach us real love and faith. It's better to do the work of dealing with your "self" now then try to find yourself in a marriage later. This is why we see so many divorces today. They joined together for the wrong reasons. We're not getting married for sex although sex is a part of it. We get married to establish God's kingdom on earth and to produce Godly offspring. There are rules and we don't make them, we follow them. The rules are already written and established in the word and the covenant.

God is King of Kings. When he gives you, his daughter, away to her husband, that man becomes her king. Together you are to rule the world together as kings and queens under the authority and dominion of the King of Kings. This is your purpose.

> ### Matthew 6
>
> "Our Father in heaven, hallowed be your name, *your kingdom come*, your will be done, *on earth* as it is *in heaven*.

Section 4

Girl, you better work!

Your Assignment

For his own divine reason, God decided to select you for the task of being single at this time. Therefore, instead of being at home miserable having a pity party, getting drunk, high and fat, making phone calls you shouldn't make, out in the streets soliciting attention or online trying to get matched up, put the ice cream down and get to work!

What is your assignment?

- 1 Corinthians 7, care for the things of the Lord
- Be fruitful and multiply
- Care for the widow, those in prison, the sick and the shut in
- Isaiah 54, ¹Sing, O barren woman you who never bore a child; burst into song, shout for joy, you who were never in labor; because more are the children of the desolate woman than of her who has a husband says the Lord. ²*Enlarge the place of your tent, stretch your tent curtains wide, do not hold back; lengthen your cords, strengthen your stakes.* ³For you will spread out to the right and to the left; *your descendants will dispossess nations and settle into their desolate cities.*

Why you?

You were selected because God preordained you for this assignment. Your heavenly father is a master strategist. He knew you before you were even born in the flesh. Everything about you, all your trials, tribulations, short comings, successes and triumphs all contribute to qualifying you to do the job that he created you for. It doesn't matter how horrible your past experiences may have been, God can and will use it. For instance, if you were molested, you may have compassion for children who are or have been in that situation. Or, your testimony will minister to adults who are struggling to cope. Because you're anointed in that area, the precious ointment of your trial becomes the balm to help heal their wounds. Your ministry would be more effective than most because they'll be more susceptible to receiving a word from you because they know you truly understand.

In the position God assigned you of being single, you have a freedom that's not easily afforded married couples. You may say, I'm a single parent and I don't have a lot of freedom. It might not be about you or your freedom at all. It could be about the child you're raising. Just because you're a single parent, divorced or widowed doesn't mean God doesn't have plans for you. Your singlehood at this point could have a lot to do with the purpose of caring for your children or someone else's children, because they are going to be important to the kingdom. Or there may be a widow or elderly person that God assigned you to care for.

You are special. So special, that you're blessed to have God himself as your covering. Unlike the masses, you have been called *and* chosen! When Jesus placed the cup on the table, you accepted and drank. He picked you and you said yes! You belong to Jesus and he already knew you would say yes.

Purpose Principle #43

God knows *you*

> **Jeremiah 1:5**
>
> Before I formed you in the belly, *I knew thee.*

> **John 17:6**
>
> *"I have revealed you to those whom you gave me out of the world.* They were yours; you gave them to me and they have obeyed your word. 2. none has been lost except the one doomed to destruction so that scripture would be fulfilled.

> **John 18:9**
>
> This happened so that the words he had spoken would be fulfilled: *"have not lost one of those you gave me."*

Jesus knew you from the beginning. The above scripture reference says that God the father gave us to him and he in turn revealed the father to us. Jesus also adds that he has not lost one that the Father gave him. That means you were predestined to do what God purposed you to do, successfully. We're not of this world. Jesus desires for us to remember who we are and where we came from. The victory of the cross through the blood of Jesus makes us winners! God has invested in you. He's looking for a return on his investment. This is where your talents come in.

> ### Jeremiah 29:11 NIV
>
> For I know the *plans* I have for *you*, "declares the Lord, "plans to prosper you and not to harm you, plans to give you hope and a future.

> ### Jeremiah 29:11 KJ
>
> For I know the thoughts that I think towards you, saith the Lord, thoughts of peace and not of evil, to *give you an expected end*.

The job description

As with most jobs, your assignment has a description. Duties include: loving, fasting and praying, tithing, sowing and reaping, intercession, travel, being fruitful, multiplying, having dominion and replenishing the earth. The office of singlehood uses your previous experience, which was your on the job training. To further your growth potential, you must study to show thyself approved. In addition, you must clean and manage the temple.

Special note; applicant must have strong faith and obedience. The competition hates you and will constantly oppose you. They will stop at nothing to keep you from being the best you can be. Although the hours are long, Jesus offer excellent benefits, salary and the best retirement package, eternal life!

You're uniform

Your assignment is relegated to a distinct group. In one sector you have married people in the other you have singles. We're all part of the same organization, faith, and body, just different roles for different purposes.

> **Uniform:**
> 1. always the same, as in character or degree; unvarying
> 2. conforming to one principle, standard or rule; consistent.
> 3. being the same as or consonant with another or others
> 4. unvaried in texture, color or design
> 5. a distinctive outfit intended to identify those who wear it as members of a specific group.
> 6. One set of such an outfit.
>
> *clothes
> - Righteousness
> - Humility

Your uniform is one of character and order, whereas we the body of Christ are united as a single impenetrable unit. It is incumbent on us to be consistent with the word and the way of the Lord. There is a standard of faith and obedience that we must adhere to. Our walk with Christ, holiness and righteousness, is the uniform unsaved people look for when they're in trouble. When unsaved family and friends need a word from the Lord they may not go to church but they'll come to you (the temple of the Lord) seeking prayer when in trouble. Why? They know you know the Lord because they identify the uniform. The word and Holy Spirit within us is consistent, making the entire body uniform. But the uniform *we put on* is the armor of God.

> ### Ephesians 6:10-18
>
> Finally, be strong in the Lord and in his mighty power. ¹¹Put on the full armor of God, so *that you can take your stand against the devil's schemes.* ¹²For our struggle is not against flesh and blood but against the rulers, against the authorities, against the powers of this dark world and against the spiritual forces of evil in the heavenly realms. ¹³therefore *put on the armor of God so that* when the day of evil comes, you may be *able to stand* your ground and after you have done everything to stand ¹⁴stand firm then, with the *belt of truth* buckled around your waist, with the *breastplate of righteousness* in place, ¹⁵and with your *feet fitted with the readiness* that comes *from the gospel of peace* ¹⁶in addition to all of this take up the *shield of faith*, with which you can *extinguish all the flaming arrows of the evil one.* ¹⁷take the *helmet of salvation* and the *sword of the spirit, which is the word of God.* ¹⁸And pray in the spirit on all occasions with all kinds of prayers and requests. With this in mind, be alert and always keep on praying for all of the Lords people.

When something is uniformed, you're talking about structure. Since we know God is strategic, we must follow his divine orders. Obedience to the word puts us in uniform with his will and way. Not only to keep our assignment on schedule but it's also for protection. Don't think for one second because you're single on purpose that the enemy is not going to send his best, most handsome demon your way. The enemy devises "schemes" to come against you. So how do you stand against the enemy? Answer: by occupying your position, standing in uniform, the armor of God.

◈ PURPOSE PRINCIPLE #44 ◈

THE ENEMY WILL ALWAYS TEST THE UNIFORM OF RIGHTEOUSNESS
FOR AUTHENTICITY

You cannot beat the enemy in your own strength. The word said to be strong "in the Lord". Not only that, the word explains *why* we're putting this armor on. God knows that evil days come. While single, trust and believe the evil day comes! You may not feel like it's evil because it feels real good to the flesh. You know, when you have someone you're attracted to, all up on you but you know they're not a believer…how do you stand?

How do you stay faithful to God, when your flesh is reeling? This is an evil day! You put on the armor of God and stand! You stand on the word and take the shield of faith which extinguishes the flaming arrows of the evil one. Have faith that God has someone…the right one, for you. Stand on his word and speak it to the enemy. That word is a sword cutting the enemy asunder.

The uniform you're to clothe yourself with is righteousness. Your protection is the armor of God. Put on the whole armor of God.

The standard

In addition to the uniform, you must uphold the standard. In society today, a lot of women have so few boundaries, just about anything goes. This shouldn't be with a woman of God. Unfortunately, those who do try to have a standard still fall prey to the enemy because of their *own set of rules*. They go with whatever is right in their own eyes.

However, it's not about your list of what you think a man should do or what he has or how you decide to ration out your affections. The standard that we are to live by is the word of the Lord.

Let's look at this scripture:

> **Isaiah 59:19**
>
> When the enemy shall come in like a flood, *the Spirit of the LORD* shall lift up *a standard* against him.

The word says when the enemy comes in like a flood, the Spirit of the Lord lifts up a standard against him. He doesn't say that he's going to send an angel or a miracle, he said, "lifts up a standard". The standard is the word, God's way of doing things. If you don't have the word in you, there is no standard to lift. The bible says "The Spirit of the Lord shall lift up". God is a spirit and God is the word. Get *his standard* in your life. So when the enemy comes at you, you'll be able to look him in the eye and say "no" if he doesn't line up with the word. That's the standard, not your rules!

> **Psalm 119:11**
>
> I have hidden your word in my heart that I might not sin against you.

Upright / Righteous

As children of God, *we are the righteous*. Righteousness is a huge part of God's divine strategy. When you're righteous, no enemy, no weapon, no scheme, can prevail against you.

You literally have God on your side. Satan cannot snatch you from Gods protection. Only sin can remove you from behind the shield of the Lord.

Fruit

> **Romans 6:20-21**
>
> For when ye were the servants of sin, ye were free from righteousness. ²¹*What fruit* had ye then in those things whereof *ye are now ashamed*? for the end of those things is death.

In the vein of singlehood, again let's discuss the obvious. You've decided to obey the word imparted into you about living righteously. Other single people, who may not be as strong or faithful, will be watching you to see if you're truly going to walk this walk. Let's say they're your co-workers. So you start seeing a handsome new someone in the office all the women want. The ladies in the office know that you're the good Christian girl who is celibate, trying to live Holy. For that reason, they want to see if you're truly a believer or if you're a closet hypocrite that's only faithful because nobody wants you.

Every day, your coworkers watch…waiting to see if something is different about you. Did she crack? Will she? Yet you stick to your faith and maintain your composure. The new guy is attracted to you but refuses to have a relationship with you without sex. Although you really like him, you eventually cut him off because you chose to be faithful to God over lust. The whole office is stunned!

Then something strange happens…the new guy quits without notice. Later, the staff discovers this man had aids. Who knew? The Holy Spirit did. The word did. *Now* when you talk to the single ladies in the office about abstaining and being faithful to God they respect your words (seeds) because of your actions (fruit). As a result of your faithfulness, they can receive and obey the word *from you*.

For the believer being fruitful is not a gesture. It's the way of life for our assignments, protection and purpose. We have no idea what part we play in God's master strategy. People are always watching and you never know who's listening and paying attention.

> **Isaiah 57:19**
>
> I create the *fruit* of the lips; peace, peace to him that is afar off, and to him that is near, saith the Lord; and I will heal him.

> **Hebrews 13:15**
>
> Through Jesus, therefore, let us continually offer to God a sacrifice of praise—the *fruit of the lips* that confess his name.

The fruit of righteousness will be peace; the effect of righteousness will be quietness and confidence forever

> **Galatians 5:23**
>
> But the fruit of the spirit is love, joy, peace, long suffering, gentleness, faith, meekness, temperance: against such there is no law.

> **Proverbs 11:30**
>
> The fruit of the righteous is a tree of life; and he that wins souls is wise.

> **Isaiah 3:10**
>
> Say you to the righteous, that it shall be well with him: for they shall eat the fruit of their deeds.

> **Proverbs 13:2**
>
> From the fruit of their lips people enjoy good things, but the unfaithful have an appetite for violence.

Production of fruit also represents the outcome of your investments. The Lord is asking us about the fruits/results of our worldly living. For all of the pain and misery of that life we thought was so much, really...what did you get from it? Nothing. To top it off, the word says, "Ye are now ashamed". Isn't that how you feel when you look back and see how you violated God and yourself?

The reason you violated is because you had fruit with no seed in it. Fruit or plants with no seed do not have the ability to be reproduced. In the end it will die. But have no fear that's no longer the case! Today, you have the seed of the Holy Spirit within you. Because you have this seed in you, God expects production. He's expecting you to be fruitful and multiply. That's your assignment.

> **John 15:2**
>
> *Every* branch in me not bearing fruit, He doth take it away, and every one bearing fruit, He doth cleanse by pruning it, that it may bear more fruit;

No man is an island. As believers we're all connected to the body of Christ. The bible describes Jesus as the vine and we are the branches. In order for a plant to grow and thrive it needs to be in the right environment and receive the necessary nutrients of sun and water. The sun represents Jesus (the word) and the water represents (the Holy Spirit). You cannot survive without them! There is however, a more painful part of the process that no one wants to endure. That process is called pruning. When plants are pruned there's a cutting away or plucking of the dead leaves in order for the healthier parts to take over and grow.

While single, walking out your purpose, you'll experience pruning in your life. The dead leaves could be family, friends, and loved ones. This is the time that we truly have to have faith that God is in control and know he's only doing what's best for you to become more fruitful in your life. Sometimes, God removes people who have become dead weight in your life that you don't have the courage, strength or common sense to leave. Sometimes, you have outgrown the pot you started in so he removes you and replants you in an environment more conducive to your growth. God is looking for a return on his investment and he will not let you botch things up. Allow him to remove the dead leaves, and cut whatever needs to be cut so that you can fulfill your purpose.

> **John 15:16**
>
> It's not you who chose me, but it is I who chose you and *appointed* you that you might go and be *fruitful* and *that your fruit might remain*; so that whatever petition you present to the Father *in my name* He may give you.

In John 15:16 Jesus clarifies to his disciples their relationship to him, what their purpose and assignment is. He's telling them they're not an accident. He specifically chose them and appointed them to go and be fruitful. The same goes for you. You are chosen and appointed. It is our assignment to go and be diligent in the work of the Lord (not diligent in finding a rich husband). Then he says, "that your fruit might remain". The only way that your fruit will remain is if *his seed* is in it. That's why when you ignore your God given purpose and pursue the lust of the flesh, (a relationship of your own choosing) you get fruit (results) that doesn't last.

When you're in your rightful position, working on your assignment, you have the right to petition God for what you need and he'll give it to you because it's in line with his will.

Notice he said make your petition *"in my name"*. That means in his character. Jesus was always about his father's business and will, so should you.

> **Colossians 1:10**
>
> That ye might walk worthy of the Lord unto all pleasing, being *fruitful* in every good work, and increasing in the knowledge of God;

Again, the emphasis is being fruitful in your life (ministry). The more you operate in your divine purpose; you increase in the knowledge of God. That increase comes from seeing God's involvement in helping you accomplish your assignment.

Knowledge of God is your foundation. When you know that God is your source, it will help you avoid feeling trapped, controlled, manipulated or desperate. If you're fruitful inside you will manifest love, joy, peace, longsuffering, gentleness, goodness, faith gentleness and self-control.

The bible says that if we delight ourselves in the Lord *he will give us the desires of our heart*. In the spirit, God plants those desires, Gen 17:6 says, "*I will* make you exceedingly fruitful". The seed doesn't come from you, it comes from him. Studying, eating the word is a way of collecting seeds. The manifestations of those seeds appear when you obey the word through action. Eventually you'll notice you've become a better woman producing good fruit; right choices with your time, life, finances, friendships and relationships.

> **Genesis 17:6**
>
> I will make you exceedingly *fruitful*, and I will make nations of you. Kings will come out of you.

> **Genesis 28:3**
>
> May God Almighty bless you, and make you *fruitful*, and multiply you, that you may be a company of peoples.

The word is all powerful. The blessing of God is built into the word because God is the word. I'm sure you've heard the saying "you are what you eat". There's a purpose in everything God does. He wants us to understand that if you desire love, you have to *be love*. You have to put love inside of you in order to give it. You can't give what you don't have. Men are looking for love too. They're looking for it inside of you, not your body, but your spirit.

So step one is to get seed in you, then produce fruit in your own life. This is done through the study and obedience of the word. Under the revelation of the Lord, you will get the "seeds" (word) that you need for your assignment. God is sovereign so I cannot tell you all of the ways that he will impart seeds into your life. The obvious would be reading the word and hearing the word from ministers of the gospel. However, on a day to day basis, you may get random word "seeds" from the Lord through people, places and things. The Holy Spirit will guide you as to what the Lord wants you to do to produce fruit.

16

MULTIPLY: IF "I" DIE, YOU WILL MULTIPLY

It is absolutely amazing how much we invest in attracting the opposite sex! We've done it so instinctively that we don't even realize the cost. How many hours of thought time? How many hours in shopping to find the right outfit? How much money spent in clothes, makeup, shoes, hair, nails, jewelry, cars, homes, furniture, travel, etc.? In an adult lifetime it would add up to thousands and millions of dollars and hours of investments in your "find the one" campaign.

The time spent fantasizing, manipulating, contemplating, words expressed, money spent are all seeds. God has given you the instructions on what to do with these seeds but he gives you free will to decide if you will obey or not. Just think of how many needs would have been met in people lives if you would have applied your seed to the kingdom? I'm sure you probably weren't cognizant of your seeds or that you were wasting them. Eating your seed and planting them into self, is natural in the world system. Sowing and reaping, is the systematic order for the body of Christ. God strategically arranged for the body to sustain itself. Finances are sustained by tithes and offering, marriages are forged through sowing and reaping, Godly offspring is produced by sowing and reaping. Care for the body of Christ it is intimately supported by the saints through prayer and intervention.

God never intended for you to abuse your seed. Using what God has given you to sow into the kingdom for selfish gain is like a man spilling his seed on the ground.

The purpose of a seed is to reproduce. If a seed is not planted there's no multiplication. And God gives seed to the sower. Therefore, if you have seed and don't plant it, you're disobeying his law of multiplication. This is wicked in his sight.

> **Genesis 38:12**
>
> 9But Onan knew that the offspring *would not be his*; so whenever *he lay with his brother's wife, he spilled his semen on the ground to keep from producing* offspring for his brother. 10What he did was wicked in the Lord's sight; so he put him to death.

Everything you have to give is a seed. Are you eating your seeds or are you planting them? A Christian single should be working in the kingdom planting seeds like crazy! It may feel strange because the roots and tentacles of the world system are strong. But the word of God is stronger!

God has an assignment for you, and this is it. You must plant your seeds and have faith that God will provide for you. That means you have take the focus off of "self" and care for the things of the Lord. It is impossible to receive something in your hand if you already have something in it.

When you're cognizant of God's system of sowing and reaping, you'll realize there's no need to embark on a campaign to solicit attention from men. God never told you to do that. But he did instruct you to be fruitful and multiply. If you're full of fruit, then you are full of seed. Don't eat it by indulging in self to get what you want. The bible says:

> **2 Corinthians 9:10**
>
> Now may he who supplies seed to the sower and bread for food, supply and *multiply your seed for sowing, and increase the fruits of your righteousness;*

Our heavenly Father has provided seed for *sowing*! The seed is not for your personal gain, the fruit is. Basically, God rewards your investment with multiplication! You will *always* get more fruit when you plant seeds! In other words, the multiplication doesn't stop with you, it continues wherever you sowed!

Example: My mom and I were having a conversation where she mentioned a spiritual concept to me that I've never heard before. The concept was birthed out of one word. What she spoke took root and the Holy Spirit began to expound on it. Through scriptures, sermons, just about everywhere, the word was growing within me.

So one day I told her that I wanted to write a book about it and she said, "There you go stealing my idea". Actually, I asked her if she would mind if I did and at first she said she didn't mind, now she says I'm stealing her idea. Nevertheless, I told her there's no need to worry or envy.

This is a perfect example of multiplication. My mother has been in ministry for almost 40yrs. She's so full of the word that I told her just about every time she opens her mouth fruit pops out. I reminded her that in Genesis, God said that he gives us seed bearing plant and fruit with seed in it for food. When that word came out of her mouth and registered in my spirit, that seed began to multiply within me. Then I told her, "God multiplies *you* through the seed". Now if my book became a best seller, she'll benefit financially for her contribution without having to do the work that I had to do to produce and market the book. Everyone ... the readers, myself, and my Mom, gets blessed from one word she imparted, one seed without sweat and toil.

Money is not the only thing that can be sown and multiplied. God multiplied *himself* through Adam by making man in his image. Of course we know that Adam failed in his assignment through sin. Man continued to multiply but could not multiply the original pure image. Through Christ however, we multiply the pure image of God.

So how do we multiply God in the earth? Through the word. God gives seed to the sower and bread for food, (he gives the word to you). You plant the word in people and you live the word. Remember, you can't give what you don't have. You must be *filled* with the Holy Spirit, the Word.

> **Acts 6:7**
>
> And the *word of God did increase,* and the number of the *disciples did multiply* in Jerusalem exceedingly; a great multitude also of the priests were obedient to the faith.

> **Genesis 9:7**
>
> Be fruitful and *multiply*. Bring forth abundantly in the earth, and multiply in it."

If you're pursuing the futile quest of finding a man you're being disobedient and wasting seed. The seed wasted is time, energy, word and money. God will not increase you this way. You're operating out of order and if there's a body part not functioning properly, it slows down the entire body. The Lord assures us that we will reap what we sow, you lose nothing and gain everything when you do the work of the Lord.

> **Genesis 17:1,2**
>
> And when Abram was ninety years old and nine, the LORD appeared to Abram, and said unto him, I *am* the Almighty God; *walk before me*, and *be thou perfect.* ²*I will make my covenant between me and you*, and will *multiply you* exceedingly."

> **Deuteronomy 7:13**
>
> and he will love you, and bless you, and multiply you; he will also bless the fruit of your body and the fruit of your ground, your grain and your new wine and your oil, the increase of your livestock and the young of your flock, in the land which he swore to your fathers to give you.

❧ PURPOSE PRINCIPLE #45 ❧
NEVER FORGET THE LORD

When you have seed remember:

¹Be careful to follow every command I am giving you today, so that you may live and increase and may enter and possess the land that the Lord promised on oath to your forefathers. ²*Remember how the Lord your God led you all the way in the desert these forty years, to humble you and to test you in order to know what was in your heart, whether or not you would keep his commands.* ³*He humbled you, causing you to hunger and then feeding you with manna, which neither you nor your fathers had known, to teach you that man does not live on bread alone but on every word that comes from the mouth of the Lord.* ⁴Your clothes did not wear out and your feet did not swell during these forty years. ⁵Know then in your heart that as a man disciplines his son, so the Lord your God disciplines you.

⁶Observe the commands of the Lord your God, walking in his ways and revering him. ⁷For the Lord your God is bringing you into a good land—a land with streams and pools of water, with springs flowing in the valleys and hills; ⁸a land with wheat and barley, vines and fig trees, pomegranates, olive oil and honey; ⁹a land where bread will not be scarce and you will lack nothing; a land where the rocks are iron and you can dig copper out of the hills.

¹⁰When you have eaten and are satisfied, praise the Lord your God for the good land he has given you. ¹¹*Be careful that you do not forget the Lord your God, failing to observe his commands, his laws and his decrees that I am giving you this day.* ¹²Otherwise, when you eat and

are satisfied, when you build fine houses and settle down, ¹³and when your herds and flocks grow large and your silver and gold increase and all you have is multiplied, ¹⁴then your heart will become proud and you will forget the Lord your God, who brought you out of Egypt, out of the land of slavery.

Leviticus 26:9

"'I will look on you with favor and make you fruitful and increase your numbers, and I will keep my covenant with you.

Deuteronomy 6:3

And thou hast heard, O Israel, and observed to do, that it may be well with thee, and that thou mayest *multiply* exceedingly, as Jehovah, God of thy fathers, hath spoken to thee, 'in' the land flowing with milk and honey.

Deuteronomy 7:13

and he will love you, and bless you, and *multiply* you; he will also bless the fruit of your body and the fruit of your ground, your grain and your new wine and your oil, the increase of your livestock and the young of your flock, in the land which he swore to your fathers to give you.

> **Deuteronomy 8:1**
>
> You shall observe to do all the commandments which I command you this day, that you may live, and *multiply*, and go in and possess the land which Yahweh swore to your fathers.

Subdue

What's interesting to me about reading and researching the word of God is how easily a profound message could be missed due to its simplicity. While contemplating the scripture reference, "be fruitful, multiply, fill and subdue", it read like a cliché. But as I began to dissect each word according to its own implication, it began to take on a life of its own. Like when I got to "subdue", just the definition alone made me stand at attention!

SUBDUE DEFINED:

1. To bring under; to conquer by force or the exertion of superior power, and bring into permanent subjection; to reduce under dominion; to vanquish.

2. To overpower so as to disable from further resistance; to crush.

3. To destroy the force of; to overcome; as, medicines subdue a fever.

4. To render submissive; to bring under command; to reduce to mildness or obedience; to tame; as, to subdue a stubborn child; to subdue the temper or passions.

5. To overcome, as by persuasion or other mild means; as, to subdue opposition by argument or entreaties.

7. To make mellow; to break, as land; also, to destroy, as weeds.

8. To reduce the intensity or degree of; to tone down; to soften; as, to subdue the brilliancy of colors.

The irony here is that the word subdue was the main one I would surpass. Yet, it's one of the most significant aspects of our assignment. I say that because in order to subdue something, you have to conquer or over take it. You must possess authority and strength. And in the time of seizure, you better be sure of it!

The assignment of being fruitful, multiplying, reigning, subduing and filling, is applicable to all Christians not just the single ones. However, the way you maneuver as an unmarried woman in this regard is the difference.

Unfortunately, too many are draining their virtue and strength trying to subdue a husband. By now we know that's not the way to go. So what do you need to subdue and why? I'm glad you asked. The first thing that you need to subdue is your *own body*.

> **1 Corinthians 9:27**
>
> *I beat my body and bring it into submission*, lest by any means, after I have preached to others, I myself should be rejected.

Before you can be effective in ministry, you must bring your own flesh into submission. The scripture tells us that when you don't bring your body into submission, when you finish fixing everyone else, you can end up rejected.

Oftentimes, the flesh is strong and takes an effort to subdue. Understand you cannot overtake your body on your own, it can only be done through the power of Christ.

Chapter 17 – Subdue

> **Philippians 3:21**
>
> Who shall change our vile body, that it may be fashioned like unto his glorious body, according to the working whereby he is able even to *subdue* all things unto himself.

As born again believers we're able to subdue all things unto Christ. "All things", means just that "all things". As Christians we have been too passive; especially the young, physically attractive ones. God did not create your beauty only to promote you and the expensive name brands you wear. He didn't give you creative ability for you to sacrifice your gift to the world. No, he gave you these gifts, talents and power through faith and the word of God so that you can make a difference! You're supposed to use whatever God gives you to conquer the world…for him. Video vixens, rappers and worldly popular celebrities represent satan well. Why do you think that you have to look, live and operate like them? Think about that for a moment. If you behave and look just like them, then what's the difference? What… just because you're young you don't think you have worked to do for the Lord? Well, you do. God is expecting you and me to be his peculiar people and change the atmosphere wherever we go. We must subdue!

Open your eyes! What have you been doing with your time? What have you been doing with your resources? Has it been about you all this time? Well that's why you're single! You look like everybody else. If you take over territory for the Lord, I promise, you will stand out. This is part of God's system. Subduing, reclaiming your inheritance of the earth for the Lord is your duty as a daughter. This is caring for the things of the Lord. In the field is one of the places in the bible where the man finds his wife. Subdue!

> **Hebrews 11:33**
>
> who, through faith subdued kingdoms, worked out righteousness, obtained promises, stopped the mouths of lions,

We subdue mighty kingdoms through faith. You cannot take a stand for the Lord if you don't believe in him. If you truly believe that God will give you the desires of your heart and that you don't have to look for a man, then you are ready to subdue. Walk in your purpose by being fruitful, multiplying and subdue. Use your gifts, talents and resources to take over enemy territory. Be about your father's business and he will be about yours. While you're fighting for him, he will be fighting for you. Don't think that everything will be a field full of roses when you subdue/take over; expect resistance. By faith you will successfully subdue whatever God has called you to do.

> **Deuteronomy 9:3**
>
> Know therefore this day, that *Yahweh your God is he who goes over before you* as a devouring fire; he will destroy them, and he will bring them down before you: so you shall drive them out, and make them to perish quickly, as Yahweh has spoken to you.

> **Psalms 18:39**
>
> For you have girded me with strength to the battle. You have subdued under me those who rose up against me.

❧ PURPOSE PRINCIPLE #46 ❧

IF YOU TAKE THE STAND OF RIGHTEOUSNESS, GOD WILL GO BEFORE YOU AND DESTROY YOUR ENEMIES.

Psalms 47:3

He subdues nations under us, and peoples under our feet.

Isaiah 45:1

Thus says Yahweh to his anointed, to Cyrus, whose right hand I have held, to subdue nations before him, and strip kings of their armor; to open the doors before him, and the gates shall not be shut:

God's system is so thorough that he uses being fruitful, multiplication, and subdual as a strategic time management program. Since God already has a husband for you, he doesn't expect you to waste time trying to find one. Nor does he want you to try to live like a single woman once you're married like many wives do. Some wives crave to get out and utilize their gifts and talents without restriction because they didn't get it out of their system when they were single.

You now have the opportunity to follow the brilliant pattern God set for his daughters so you can have fulfilling lives while you are single as well as when you get married.

The way his plan works is this; spend time in his presence and in his word to become fruitful. In that time and space you're communing with the Lord.

To avoid complete isolation from the world, God has even gone through the trouble of showing you how to make friends. Multiplication of the love God gave you for people increases your network of friends because you're now interested in others instead of self, which makes them interested in you.

Finally, when you subdue the territory God has given you to conquer, you'll receive rewards of seeing the glory of God change you, the lives of others and the atmosphere.

Here's an example of what I mean. Let's say you're a singer and want to sing gospel music but you're not sure if you'll get far in that genre so you do R&B or Rock instead. The influence of *the world*, subdued *you* in this scenario where it should have been the other way around.

If you focus on what *you want*, you won't be able to take over the world because you'll be enticed by it. Remember, our will is to do the will of the Father and he says subdue! We have to change the world, not let it change us.

Go ahead and sing the gospel. Use your gifts and talents the best way you know how and let God come in and take over. Your gift will make room for you. He will make your ordinary extraordinary!

Gospel music sends messages of worship, praise, hope and love. It's designed to change lives. It's not about you becoming a famous pop star (although God may still make you one).

The assignment of utilizing your gifts and talents to assist the kingdom in getting people saved, keeping them edified and lifted in spirit is our job! As you subdue for God, you'll be fulfilled in your life and spirit because you'll be doing what you were born to do.

Do it now, while you have your freedom! This is the will of God for you while *single.

> *Yes, you can utilize your gifts and talents while married. But your assignment on *how to use* them will be different from when you're single.

This is the time to do you! Not when you're married! God's infinite wisdom incorporated everything you need to feel whole, have fun and find love while single through his instruction.

Women of God, use this time to subdue and take dominion over the area God has placed you in. Perhaps, your domain is your job, or your circle of friends/influence. Look around and ask God to show you your territory and enlarge it. Maybe God placed a business in your heart, if he did pursue it. His word says that he will go out before you. If he spoke it to you, his word will not return void. Subdue!

Section 5

Where did I go wrong?

DISCERNMENT: MR RIGHT FROM MR WRONG

The story of Saul and David is very interesting. Here you have two men who were anointed and *appointed* men of God. Both in their journey fell short in a major way. Saul disobeyed God to the point that he lost the kingdom, his sons and his life. David, who succeeded Saul, committed murder to cover his adulterous affair and even had a child out of the whole debacle.

Although both sinned, God had more mercy on David than Saul. Why? The answer to this question will help you in discerning between men who are God's choice or yours.

Of course, we all know that God's selection will always be better. God preferred David and was more merciful to him because he had a repentant heart. David truly loved God but struggled with his flesh like we all do.

Nevertheless, his *heart* was after God and for the most part, he obeyed the word of the Lord. Saul however was disobedient with a rebellious heart and *refused* to obey the word of the Lord.

❦ PURPOSE PRINCIPLE #48 ❦

WE ALL MAKE MISTAKES BUT GOD HONORS A REPENTANT HEART

In the story of Saul, you can see character traits that parallel lots of men today. You may have been with this caliber of man; you may *still* be with him (wondering why you're there). Saul is a Christian woman's nightmare. You see, the scary thing about Saul is he was *not* an imposter. *He was* anointed and appointed. Ultimately, he was a good man gone wrong.

❦ PURPOSE PRINCIPLE #48 ❦

DON'T WANT A GOOD MAN, DESIRE A GODLY MAN

God is so strategic that his system transcends generations to accomplish his purpose. Jesus is a perfect example of this. From the Old Testament to the new we see lives and generations intertwining to produce the royal bloodline that would birth Jesus. That strategy has not changed. The purpose of marriage is for us to produce godly offspring. In order to fulfill that obligation we must be of royal descent. The royal bloodline came through the lineage of David. His life was a shadow of things to come. Like David, we were not naturally born into royalty. He became royalty though the marriage covenant when he married Saul's daughter. For us, our covenant through the blood of Jesus makes us royalty.

✤ PURPOSE PRINCIPLE #49 ✤

YOU BECOME ROYALTY THROUGH THE BLOOD OF CHRIST

Contrary to David, Saul was the people's choice (the world's choice). He was tall and handsome, he *looked* like a king. But like the world, he did not choose God. He was so consumed with what people thought of him and the *benefits* of his position that he would not respect and honor it.

All of Saul's choices were for himself, he always had what he thought was a good reason to disobey God. He refused to take responsibility for his actions with a repentant heart. His *heart* was not in covenant and agreement with God.

> There are always signs in the beginning of a man's heart and character. If he's mean, disrespectful, selfish and doesn't love the Lord, don't ignore it! If the Holy Spirit says no. leave him alone.

The bible refers to David as being a man after God's own heart. David loved the Lord. He wasn't perfect; he had an adulterous affair and in an attempt to conceal the matter he committed murder. Although he sinned in a major way, whenever God confronted about him about his sin he repented and accepted punishment. Like any father, God respects the repentant heart. This is the character you'll find in a true man of God. Look out for the man that is after *God's heart*, not yours.

Please, don't confuse what I just said. You and God are one. Therefore, when a man pursues the heart of God he'll find your heart as well along with good intentions for you. But a man that's solely looking for *your heart* has selfish, carnal intentions.

❦ PURPOSE PRINCIPLE #50 ❧

DON'T BE ENSNARED BY A MAN'S APPEARANCE SO MUCH THAT YOU DON'T SEE HIS HEART

> **1 Kings 9:3**
>
> "I have heard the prayer and plea you have made before me; *I have consecrated this temple, which you have built, by putting my Name* there forever. *My eyes and my heart* will always be there.
> ⁴"*As for you, if you walk before me in integrity of heart and uprightness, as David your father did, and do all I command and observe my decrees and laws,* ⁵I will *establish your royal throne over Israel forever,* as I promised David your father when I said, 'You shall never fail to have a man on the throne of Israel.'
> ⁶"But *if you* or your sons *turn away from me* and *do not observe the commands and decrees* I have given you and go off to *serve other gods and worship them,* ⁷then *I will cut off* Israel from the land I have given them and will *reject this temple I have consecrated for my Name.* Israel will then become a byword and an object of ridicule among all peoples. ⁸And though this temple is now imposing, all who pass by will be appalled and will scoff and say, 'Why has the Lord done such a thing to this land and to this temple?' ⁹People will answer, 'Because *they have forsaken the Lord their God,* who brought their fathers out of Egypt, and have embraced other gods, worshiping and serving them—*that is why the Lord brought all this disaster on them.*'"

The fall of Saul

> **1Samuel 15:22**
>
> And Samuel said, Does Jehovah delight in burnt offerings and sacrifices as in obeying the voice of Jehovah? Behold! *Obeying is better than sacrifice; to give attention is better than the fat of rams.*

> **1Samuel 15:23**
>
> For the *sin of divination is rebellion; insolence is both iniquity and idolatry.* Because you have rejected the Word of Jehovah, so *He has rejected you from being king.*

> **1Samuel 15:24**
>
> And Saul said to Samuel, I have sinned, for *I have transgressed the mouth of Jehovah and your word, because I feared the people,* and *I listened to their voice.*

> **1Samuel 15:26**
>
> And Samuel said to Saul, I will not return with you, *for you have rejected the Word* of Jehovah and *Jehovah has rejected you from being king* over Israel.

Although Saul was anointed and appointed by God to be king, it was his obligation to obey the word of God. Saul lost everything because of fear, greed, and disobedience. In a nutshell, he simply rejected the word of God. The story of Saul reveal serious truths. First, we must remember Jesus is the word, the word was with God and the word was God. Also, Jesus is the way, the truth and the light. No man comes to the father except through him. What this means to you and I is that when you don't listen to the word of God, you reject Jesus. Ultimately, Saul disobeyed Jesus.

If you reject God's son, he will reject you from being king. This fact explains why a lot of men are not seeing the fruit of the spirit in their lives. It's also why you see people going to church every Sunday, function within the church but have no power. These people blame everyone and everything else but themselves for their failures. Yet, they remain clueless that they're failing because they've been rejected!

My sisters, this is why God won't allow you to be joined to a man like this. In the physical he *seems* like a good choice. He goes to church, looks good and *acts* like he has some sense. *But he is an unbeliever!* God says not to be unequally yoked with *unbelievers*.

✑ Purpose Principle #51 ✑

David made God's objective his objective. He looked for a place for God to reside before he looked for his own. He always desired the presence of the Lord. Saul never sought out God's presence, he never tried to retrieve the Arc. Watch out for men who never seek the Lord.

What do you *do* when God rejects your choice?

Saul was rejected by God. However, the word reveals that Saul was never Gods preference. He was the *people's choice*. Remember, God was their king. That wasn't good enough for the children of Israel because they wanted a king they could *see*. So God gave them Saul. You may say the fact that God approved the children of Israel to have a king that he chose Saul. No, God *gave the people what they wanted*. Saul looked the part but didn't possess a heart for the Lord. The children of Israel wanted to be like all of the surrounding nations. Those kingdoms came with pomp and circumstance but didn't acknowledge, love or serve the Lord. Therefore, God gave them the king they wanted.

> God is not going to force you to do the right thing or to make the right choice. The Holy Spirit is a *guide, the counselor*. He will *lead* you to the truth but you must choose it. If you insist on being with a man that God has rejected, he will take his hands off you and let you have what you *want*! (Shadow chasing) Believe me, you will **REGRET THAT CHOICE!**

In today's society, this scenario would be equivalent to Christians wanting to live like the world. People watch videos and reality shows and see all the flashy fashions with celebrities appearing to be enjoying these wild luxurious lives and desire to be just like them. The bible instructs women to abstain from sex, dress in modest apparel but society around us says that boring and old fashioned! Natural is unattractive; you have to have a weave, loads of makeup, lashes, butt injections, boob job, designer clothes and shoes etc. Images of grandeur bombard the minds of men and women of God influencing them to feel like less needs to be more.

Humility, meekness, a quiet spirit is extremely attractive to a man that's looking for a wife. I know because the word says so. Society tries to confuse you, like the children of Israel by telling you God's way doesn't work and it is not enough. So, does God stop us from doing what we want to do? No! Nor did he stop the children of Israel. The children were more interested in what the eyes can see…they were faithless. So he gave them Saul. *He looked like a king*. If you reject Gods way, you will get Saul when you could have gotten David.

❧ Purpose Principle #52 ❧

If you hold on to a man that God rejects from your life, it will never work in your favor.

God will reject any man that doesn't believe and receive his son. And you should too! The danger in keeping what God has rejected is that it will try to kill you. A man that has a "Saul like" spirit is a man that's dangerous, disobedient, disloyal, in denial and a liar. You have the spirit of truth residing in you therefore that Saul spirit will always be at war with yours. THIS RELATIONSHIP WILL NEVER WORK! This union will be a love hate relationship. Didn't we see this with Saul and David?

When the Spirit of the Lord left Saul, God sent an evil spirit to him. Saul heard that David was skilled in music, so he invited him to come over and play for him to soothe his depressed soul. At first, Saul loved David so much that he asked him to come live in the palace. Isn't this how it starts with us? First a man is attracted to you for how you make his disastrous life better. Next, he invites you to come live with him or commit to him. Then, out of nowhere, he changes.

One day, David was playing music for Saul like he normally does, (like he was invited to do) and out of nowhere Saul throws a javelin at him trying to kill him! Saul attempted to kill him because he knew that David was blessed and destined to rule in his stead. He thought if he could kill David, he would kill the prophecy and anointing. That's how a man with a Saul spirit will look at you. He will love your gifts and hate you for it because he selfishly wants the gift without responsibility. This type of man will try to kill your spirit, because he wants to prevent the maturation of the potential he sees in you which will inevitably surpass him! Not that you're better than him, rather because of the God in you.

Believe me women of God; the fight with the "Saul" spirit is not worth it. It's better to do things God's way and have a man after God's own heart. Let God choose for you, he knows the difference between Saul and David.

He That Finds a Wife ...

Here's a common area where single women go wrong…their appearance. It's so sad today in western culture how women are taught to epitomize outward beauty.

The cosmetic surgery industry is a multi-billion dollar industry built on the insecurity of people. We seem to think that we can control men by seductive measures. If I just had bigger breast, bigger butt, smaller breast, smaller butt, bigger lips, smaller lips...you fill in the blank!

Whatever external method that can be employed to get a man, women will readily, anxiously, adapt to it.

External extremes are not the answer to finding a husband because a husband cannot be found. American society sends the false message that a woman who is visually attractive has a better chance of finding a man and getting married.

Note, I said a man, not a priest. God arranges marriages and will present you to your husband in his divine timing. The husband God has for you will be a priest in spirit because he is a born again believer with Jesus, the High Priest living inside him. He will be attracted to the God *in you*.

> **Genesis 2:22**
>
> ²²Then the Lord God made a woman from the rib he had taken out of the man, and *he brought her to the man.*

> **Mark 10:9**
>
> *What therefore God hath joined together,* let no man put asunder.

> **1 Timothy 2:9**
>
> In like manner also, that women adorn themselves in modest apparel, with shamefacedness and sobriety; not with braided hair, or gold, or pearls or costly array ¹⁰but (which becometh women professing godliness) with good works).

The husband God has for you may initially be drawn to physical attributes. However, when it comes to finding a wife that will be the least of his concerns. God knows this, that's why he is guiding Christian women on what to do and how to be.

He's saying in 1 Timothy 2:9,10, to adorn yourself in modest apparel, with shamefacedness and sobriety; not with braided hair, or gold, or pearls or costly array.

You don't have to go on an all-out campaign to attract a man. The joining of you and your husband is way more significant than how you feel. Marriage is symbolic of the relationship between Christ and the church.

> Contrary to popular belief, all the cosmetic extras women adorn themselves with, most men do not find attractive for long term.
>
> Being overdone or fake can send the wrong message of who you are. The bible teaches women what a man is truly attracted to.
>
> You may have to tone it down a bit.

A man needs a wife that will help him do his job. The wife was created to be a helper. Are you helpful or are you self serving? Through God's system, you develop the heart of a servant because you're caring for the things of the Lord. You're a wife in the spirit already.

The bible says, "Through faith we understand that the worlds were framed by the word of God, so that things which are seen were not made of things which do appear".

In other words, you were a wife in the spirit made by God first before you were made a wife in the physical.

> **Genesis 2:24**
>
> It is for this reason, this purpose that a man shall leave his father and mother and be united to his wife, and they will become one flesh.

What reason is Genesis talking about? The answer is in Genesis 2:

> **Genesis 2:18**
>
> It is not good for the man to be alone. *I will make a helper suitable for him.*

> **Genesis 2:20**
>
> So the man gave names to all the livestock, the birds of the air and all the beast of the field. But for Adam no suitable helper was found.

> **Genesis 2:22**
>
> *Then the Lord God made a woman* from the rib he had taken out of the man and he *brought her to the man.*

> **Genesis 2:24**
>
> *For this reason* a man will leave his father and mother and be united to *his wife* and they will become one flesh.

The reason God will join you with your husband is to be a suitable helper. This is the reason a man leaves his parents to marry you. He's not leaving everything he knows and own to marry you because you "fine". Looking good is just icing on the cake but it's not the cake! Notice the scripture begins by stating, "The Lord made a woman" but later says, "for this reason..." Instead of saying he'll be united with a woman he said "united *to his wife"*.

Hidden within Genesis 2:18 is glimpse our purpose and process. God said "I will *create* for *him*". What that means to you and I is God has to "create" a suitable helper in us *for him*. The process of caring for the things of the Lord and our devotion makes us prudent, competent, suitable helpers. Service to the Lord develops in you the heart and mind of a wife.

After God "created" Eve he brought her to Adam and the word says he was "united to his wife". The purpose is for us to help him (your husband) with *his* assignment.

◈ PURPOSE PRINCIPLE #53 ◈

YOU HAVE TO BE READY, WILLING AND ABLE TO HELP SERVE YOUR HUSBAND AND FAMILY. MOST WOMEN *CAN* HELP, BUT ARE YOU *WILLING* TO?

This information answers why some of your former relationships did not result in marriage. It's a strong possibility that you weren't a "wife" at that time. Also, if you did get married and now find yourself divorced, consider what the bible says, "What God has joined together let no man put asunder".

Sometimes, we by our own devices have joined together something that God did not. One of the biggest hints to see if God joined you and another together is to ask yourself, is there a purpose of you two beyond sensuality? Are you unequally yoked? You cannot get any work done effectively and efficiently if you don't agree.

> **Leviticus 19:19**
>
> You shall keep my statutes. You shall not let your cattle breed with another kind: *you shall not sow your field with mixed seed*: neither shall a garment of mixed linen and wool come upon you.

> **Deuteronomy 22:9**
>
> *Do not plant two kinds of seed* in your vineyard; *if you do,* not only the crops you plant but also the fruit of the vineyard will be *defiled.*

Women of God should be found. The reason why you couldn't be found before is because you were out looking! Instead of being "hidden" you were out on the prowl.

Not only should you be found you should be a virgin (not necessarily a virgin in the physical but in the spirit). We're required to be a virgin in the spirit because we're pure vessels.

The Holy Spirit impregnated Mary to produce Jesus. It had to happen this way because the seed of man (Adam) was contaminated by sin. Mary, being clean, pure and untouched, had the capacity to be used by the Holy Spirit to produce a Holy being, (Jesus).

Even if you're a golden vessel in the kingdom, God cannot use you if you're not clean.

> **Leviticus 21:13**
>
> The woman he marries *must be a virgin*. 14. He must not marry a widow, a divorced woman, or a woman defiled by prostitution, but only a virgin *from his own people*, ¹⁵so he will not defile his offspring among his people. *I am the Lord who makes him holy*.

✂ PURPOSE PRINCIPLE #54 ✂

LEVITICUS 21:13 SAYS FOR THE PRIEST TO MARRY FROM HIS OWN PEOPLE. THAT MEANS A PRIEST (MAN OF GOD) CAN ONLY MARRY A BORN AGAIN BELIEVER FROM THE BODY OF CHRIST.

Preparation

There is a very popular passage of scripture that many women refer to regarding how a man should pursue them. This scripture is found in Proverbs 18:22:

> **Proverbs 18:22**
>
> He who finds a wife finds what is good and receives favor from the Lord.

As with many scriptures, there are many ways to look at it. The perspective I'm coming from is how the word says, "He who finds a wife". Interestingly, the writer uses the word *"wife"* instead of simply saying, "He who finds a *woman*".

What's so profound about that scripture is in order for a man to find a wife she would have be married *already*. Or else the word "woman" would've been used. A woman could be any female.

Why did God make this distinction? I'm glad you asked. Prior to being born again, you were just a woman. When you entered into covenant with God, you became a wife in the spirit. "The wife" that's to be found is you. You should already be married to God. Married to God?!

Yes, although this sounds strange it is true. That's why God says, "He who finds a wife finds what is good and receives favor from the Lord". To be sure that this is not just my opinion, let's go to the word:

> ### Isaiah 54:3
>
> *For your Maker is your husband* - the Lord Almighty is his name-the Holy One of Israel is your Redeemer, he is called the God of all the earth. [6]The Lord will call you back as if you were a wife deserted and distressed in spirit-a wife who married young, only to be rejected, "says your God. "For a brief moment I abandoned you, but with deep compassion I will bring you back.

> **Hosea 2:16**
>
> "In that day," declares the Lord *"You will call me 'my husband'*; you will no longer call me 'my master'.

✌ PURPOSE PRINCIPLE #55 ✌

YOUR COVENANT RELATIONSHIP WITH CHRIST IS WHAT MAKES YOU A WIFE INSTEAD OF JUST A "WOMAN".

When you were connected to the world you were committing spiritual adultery. You were just a woman, not a wife. God redeemed you from the world where you were a servant and made you a wife. Therefore the word establishes where your focus and loyalty should be.

Again, your relationship with the Lord prepares you for relationships here in the physical world.. It's wrong for a wife to commit adultery. It is inappropriate for a wife to neglect or deprive her husband.

A good wife is faithful, loving, attentive, strong and caring. These characteristics are exercised and developed through your devotion to God while single.

When you think of being a wife, what does it mean to you? Think about that for a moment. I cannot answer that for you. What I will do is let you in on a little secret. Part of the purpose is ministry. When you're single in the physical world, you're a wife in the spiritual.

God gave me a revelation about the result of ministry from being a wife of God. People are led to Christ through observing your day to day life. As a result of your submission to the Lord, they're won over *without words*. This is the same effect wives have on their husbands according to the word. Look at the formation of ministry:

> **1 Peter 3:1**
>
> Wives, in the same way *be submissive to your husbands* so that, *if any of them do not believe the word, they may be won over without words by the behavior of their wives,* ²when they see the purity and reverence of your lives.

~ PURPOSE PRINCIPLE #56 ~

DON'T MINISTRY DATE

Let me clarify a few things, because this is where a lot of women trap themselves off. I'm not talking about the deceit of ministry dating where you lie to yourself and become unequally yoked with an unbeliever, because you're trying to convert them. No, what I'm showing you here is the system God has in place, along with our purpose.

People will notice something special and different about you because you have love, peace and grace in and around you. Why isn't she clubbing anymore? I don't see her out all the time anymore. She even took down all those half naked posts on all those social media sites! Her style used to be so overdone and now she looks naturally beautiful. Even her countenance is brighter. What happened? She is so…different.

They'll want to know…what it is about you that changed? You won't have to wear a T-shirt that says "I'm saved", they'll know.

This is one of the ways God draws the man that will be your husband to you. Your spirit will be more attractive than how you actually look. I don't care if you're a supermodel; a beautiful spirit is much more attractive.

I noticed with myself prior to giving my life to God, my attitude wasn't as pleasant as it is now. Today things that bothered me before doesn't anymore. Since I became more loving in my spirit, God gave me a meek spirit. My entire demeanor, tone of voice, everything, became calmer. I became... sweet. Is your spirit disturbed by bitterness, unforgiveness and vanity?

Let the Holy Spirit give you the kind of makeover that's going to make you beautiful for real. God says so, look:

---

1 Peter 3:3-4

Your beauty should not come from outward adornment, such as braided hair and the wearing of gold jewelry and fine clothes.
4Instead, it should be that of your *inner self*, the unfading beauty of a gentle and quiet spirit, which is of great worth in God's sight.

~ PURPOSE PRINCIPLE #57 ~

IT'S THE ANOINTING THAT MAKES YOU EXCEPTIONALLY ATTRACTIVE NO MATTER YOUR AGE, STAGE, WEIGHT, HEIGHT OR FEATURES.

God has called you to be a wife, not just a woman. All throughout the word, the Lord teaches you how to Love and how to be. Seeking out the word to know what his way is spiritually cleanses and enlightens you. It also strengthens the bond between you and the Father because you'll begin to see his truth *as the truth*. Proverbs 31 shows the characteristics of a wife:

> **Proverbs 31:10-31**
>
> ¹⁰A *wife* of noble character who can find? She is worth far more than rubies.
> ¹¹Her husband has full confidence in her and lacks nothing of value.
> ¹²She brings him good, not harm, all the days of her life.
> ¹³She selects wool and flax and works with eager hands.
> ¹⁴She is like the merchant ships, bringing food from afar.
> ¹⁵She gets up while it is still dark
> ¹⁶She considers a field and buys it; out of her earnings she plants a vineyard.
> ¹⁷She sets about her work vigorously; her arms are strong for her tasks.
> ¹⁸She sees that her trading is profitable, and her lamp does not go out at night.
> ¹⁹In her hand she holds the distaff and grasps the spindle with her fingers.

> ²⁰She opens her arms to the poor and extends her hands to the needy.
> ²¹when it snows, she has no fear for her household; for all of them are clothed in scarlet.
> ²²She makes coverings for her bed; she is clothed with fine linen and purple.
> ²³Her husband is respected at the city gate, where he takes his seat among the elders of the land.
> ²⁴She makes linen garments and sells them, and supplies the merchants with sashes.
> ²⁵she is clothed with strength and dignity; she can laugh at days to come.
> ²⁶She speaks with wisdom, and faithful instruction is on her tongue.
> ²⁷She watches over the affairs of her household and does not eat the bread of idleness.
> ²⁸Her children arise and call her blessed; her husband also, and he praises her:
> ²⁹"many women do noble things, but you surpass them all."
> ³⁰Charm is deceptive, and beauty is fleeting; but a woman who fears the Lord is to be praised.
> ³¹Give her the reward she has earned, and let her works bring her praise in the city gate.

Oh, my goodness! There is so much in this passage; I barely know where to start! I'm going to take my time with this because you need to see this. While becoming *single on purpose*, you need to know what the purpose is. The purpose is for character building, ministry, relationship, preparation for relations with your future spouse and family. But let's get to the meat of this passage.

The scripture starts off saying "a wife of noble character is hard to find". Funny, because so many women walk around with a sense of entitlement to have a good husband just because they're a woman. But what those women have forgotten is God is a Father to his sons as well. He's not going to send unprepared women to one of his well prepared sons. It's obvious that God *and* man are interested in your character. Conversely, it's interesting that the word says it's hard to find a wife with noble character.

❧ PURPOSE PRINCIPLE #58 ❧

GOD WILL NOT GIVE AN UNPREPARED WOMAN TO HIS WELL PREPARED SONS.

WHAT IS NOBLE CHARACTER?

Noble:
a: possessing outstanding qualities : ILLUSTRIOUS
    b: FAMOUS, NOTABLE <*noble* deeds>
    2: of high birth or exalted rank : ARISTOCRATIC
3*a*: possessing very high or excellent qualities or properties <*noble* wine>
    b: very good or excellent
4: grand or impressive especially in appearance <*noble* edifice>
5: possessing, characterized by, or arising from superiority of mind or character or of ideals or morals : LOFTY <a *noble* ambition.

Character; the combination of qualities or features that distinguishes one person, group or thing from another. ²A distinguishing feature or attribute, as of an individual, group or category. ³Genetics- a structure, function, or attribute determined by a gene or group of genes ⁴Moral or ethical strength. ⁵A description of a person's attributes, traits, or abilities. A formal written statement as to competency and dependability, given by an employer to a former employee; a recommendation. ⁷Public estimation of someone; reputation 8. Status or role; capacity: in his character of father

Once we grasp the crux of what noble character really is you can understand the depth of what the rest of the chapter is saying.

When a wife has noble character, she has established competency in life and relationships. She knows who she is. She is aware of her surroundings, and her responsibilities. She also knows that she is a representation of her husband and doesn't take it lightly. Her character is established through consistent honest behavior *before* marriage.

✌ PURPOSE PRINCIPLE #59 ✌

GOOD CHARACTER IS DEVELOPED BY CONSISTENT "CHRIST LIKE" BEHAVIOR

One way this pattern of consistency is established is by concerning yourself with the affairs of the Lord. The devotion of your body and spirit to God produces godly character. This Godly character is trustworthy. Men see this. This is what they're looking for. Yes, men are initially attracted to physical things.

But have you ever noticed men don't usually marry the prettiest girl they've dated? No, they marry the one they felt in their spirit was the right one. Ask any man, and they'll tell you one of the biggest things to them is to find a woman they can trust.

A man doesn't trust a woman because she *tells him* that she's trust worthy. No, they're looking at a consistent pattern of trustworthiness in your walk. Not only are they searching for that pattern in how you deal with them, they're looking and listening to your behavior with other people.

> **Proverbs 31:11-12**
>
> Her husband has full confidence in her and lacks nothing of value.
> ¹²She brings him good all the days of her life.

> **Proverbs 31:23**
>
> Her husband is respected at the city gate, where he takes his seat among the elders of the land.

Trust is so important in relationships because if you have it you can rest. God wants you to trust him so that you can rest in him. When God is your source while you're single, he won't stop being your source when you get married. Established trust in him overflows into your marriage, enabling you with the grace to submit and have faith in your husband without saying a word.

That's what God is training you to do. It won't be a hard thing to submit to your husband when you trust the Lord.

Ironically, your trust in the Lord makes it easy for your husband to trust you as well. Also, your trustworthy behavior and faithfulness makes your husband look good in public. Men love this!

◈ PURPOSE PRINCIPLE #60 ◈

AN AMAZING THING OCCURS WHEN YOU TRUST IN THE LORD. WHEN YOU KNOW HIS VOICE AND FOLLOW HIS INSTRUCTION, YOU WON'T BE AFRAID TO LOVE. THIS GOES BEYOND JUST EROS LOVE, THIS IS AGAPE LOVE.

Now back to the proverbs wife, she's a diligent business woman. She makes things with her hands; she does real estate and trading with her own money.

I'm not suggesting you have to own your own business or it's wrong to be a stay at home wife/mom. I just want to dispel the myth that men have to be the only financial providers. God has given us this example with the Proverbs 31 wife. It's nothing wrong with a woman pulling herself up by her bootstraps and going to work to contribute to the household to make it better. That's what a suitable helper was ordained to do.

Again, this is the word, not my opinion. Not only that, since you're created to be a helper, God may give you more than your husband; more education, money, resources and connections. However, God doesn't give you more to Lord over him, or to reject the man that doesn't make a lot of money. Remember God is your source. He gives you more so that you can help *him*. Perhaps your husband has already visited you but because you had more resources, you rejected him. I know a novel idea huh?

The Proverb 31 woman is diligent in the affairs of her home taking care of her family and servants getting an early start on her day. Let's be clear, just because you're efficient and can provide doesn't make you the head. That order *never* changes. You will always be the body and help meet!

> **Proverbs 31:27**
>
> She watches over the affairs of her household and does not eat the bread of idleness.

Single women may not have this mentality because their only concern is themselves. God wants us to have healthy successful marriages and families. So God begins the paradigm shift in our psyche, by preparing you while you're single through his caring for the affairs of the Lord system. That's the practice. The word is giving us a preview of the new schedule we'll have as a wife. Even I had a problem adjusting to this one because I'm not a morning person. I like the message version for Proverbs 31:15-17:

> **Proverbs 31:15**
>
> *She's up before dawn*, preparing breakfast for her family and organizing her day. ¹⁷First thing in the morning, she dresses for work, rolls up her sleeves, eager to get started. She senses the worth of her work, is in no hurry to call it quits for the day.

You see, God does have a system. I believe a lot of newlyweds end up in divorce court because they didn't expect the pace of marriage to be so fast and furious! Work, school, soccer practice, piano lessons, cheerleading practice, church, cook, clean, make love and maybe sleep! They weren't prepared for the rigorous schedule and lifestyle of married life with a family of their own day after day.

In the scriptures, the virtuous woman made sure that everyone was taken care of. As a result, she was taken care of:

> **Proverbs 31:28**
>
> [28]Her children respect and bless her; her husband joins in with words of praise: *"Many women have done wonderful things, but you outclass them all!"*
> [30]Charm can mislead and beauty soon fades, The woman to be admired and praised is the woman *who lives in the Fear of God.*
> [31]*Give her everything she deserves*! Festoon her life with praise.

Sound great right? I thought I'd start out with where we want to be before I show you where some are and why a good wife is so hard to find. This will be deep and if you're guilty of this lifestyle/behavior it's not to condemn you. The purpose is for deliverance so that you'll be single on purpose instead of alone and lonely. You may not be a wife already due to the consequences of sin. If you're not saved the lifestyle that I'm referencing may sound familiar, maybe even normal. But if you're a Christian and still allowing sin in your life, this applies to you according to the open doorway created by that sin.

Hosea 2:2 (Message version)

²"Haul your mother into court. Accuse her! *She's no longer my wife. I'm no longer her husband. Tell her to quit dressing like a whore, displaying her breast for sale.*
³If she refuses, I'll rip off her clothes and expose her, naked as a newborn. I'll turn her skin into dried-out leather, her body into a badlands landscape, a rack of bones in the desert. ⁴*I'll have nothing to do with her children born one and all in a whorehouse.*
⁵Face it: *Your mother's been a whore, bringing bastard children into the world.* She said, 'I'm off to see my lovers! They'll wine and dine me, dress and caress me, perfume and adorn me!'. ⁶But I'll fix her: I'll dump her field of thistles, then lose her in a dead-end alley. ⁷*she will go on the hunt for lovers but not bring down a single one*. Then she'll say, 'I'm going back to my husband, the one I started out with. That was a better life by far than this one.'
⁸*She didn't know this it was I all along who wined and dined and adored her, That I was the one who dressed her up in the big-city fashions and jewelry that she wasted on wild Baal-orgies.* ⁹I'm about to bring her up short: No more wining and dining! Silk lingerie and gowns are a thing of the past. ¹⁰I'll expose her genitals to the public. All her fly by night lovers will be helpless to help her.
¹¹Party time is over. I'm calling a halt to the whole business, her wild weekends and unholy holidays. ¹²I'll wreck her sumptuous gardens and ornamental fountains, of which she bragged, "whoring paid for all this!" They will soon be dumping grounds for garbage, feeding grounds for stray dogs and cats. ¹³I'll make her pay for her indulgences in promiscuous religion-all that sensual Baal worship. And all the promiscuous sex that went with it, stalking her lovers but me she forgot.

The lifestyle in this scripture reference is the death cycle of worldly women. Some of you may be in this cycle right now. It's empty, degrading and in direct violation to God. The Lord lets us know in this passage that he's the one who made you. He's the element that makes you special. When he chose you and married you that was a gift and honor we didn't deserve.

This godly walk requires faith and faithfulness. Living righteously transforms us into virtuous women. Sin breaks our covenant with the Lord sending us plummeting to the world system which pulls us farther and farther away from God. Consequently, pulling us farther and farther away from the love we really desire.

Keeping Your Word

> **Ephesians 5:6**
>
> "Let no man deceive you with vain words: for because of these things cometh the wrath of God upon the children of disobedience".

Everybody, God, men and women alike, desires to have someone who is faithful. Women are quick to say they're faithful because they're intimate with one man at a time. But if you profess to be a Christian and your walk doesn't match your word, men lose respect because it is a form of unfaithfulness. If you don't keep your word, you got nothing!

Believe it or not, men are secretly rooting for you. Even though they may pressure you, they really want you to win the battle within yourself because it makes them feel safe with you. When you give in and don't keep your word, physically they're relieved but inwardly, they're disappointed. Matter of fact, unsaved people are secretly rooting for you as well. As long as you walk in righteousness you bring salt and light to their lives.

Unsaved people are living in darkness and when you come around with truth and righteousness it's refreshing. But when they come to you and you're a light that is darkness, that attraction turns to distain.

Keeping your word regarding your body can be a challenge. I'm not exempt. As a Christian single myself, I found being celibate rather easy. That is of course, when there was no man in my life. There were times when I was alone I would feel waves of intense urges but as quick as they came, they left. The key, I noticed was rather simple, don't *entertain* those feelings. It was nothing but a spirit that had come to tempt me. When I made the decision in my heart that I will not violate God's will by indulging, the feelings left.

But what do you do when you meet a man that you really like? You believe that God has sent him; everything seems to be lining up but things are not moving as fast as you want it to?

Right here is where things gets really dicey because you know you can't have sex until you're married and at the same time he doesn't want to rush into a marriage.

First, let me tell you what the enemy will do. He will make you feel like you are responsible for maintaining this relationship. He'll take you back to a worldly state of mind where women often believe that if men don't get sex from you they'll get it somewhere else, causing you to panic and give in. You tell yourself, "I'm only human", "you tried", "I can only do so much" or since you believe he's the man you're going to marry anyway it's ok.

All of that is a trick of the devil for you to sabotage your blessing before it's fully matured. God is a merciful God, so if this already happened to you, repent immediately and start walking in obedience again. He knew that you would fall before you fell and he'll forgive you.

✒ PURPOSE PRINCIPLE #61 ✑

WHATEVER GOD PUTS TOGETHER, LET NO MAN PUT ASUNDER. HE WILL HELP YOU MAINTAIN WHAT *HE HAS GIVEN YOU*. HE'S NOT RESPONSIBLE FOR WHAT *YOU* PUT TOGETHER.

> **John 1:9**
>
> If we confess our sins, he is faithful and just to forgive us *our* sins, and to cleanse us from all unrighteousness.

So how do you stand and be faithful? How do you resist the temptation of having what you want right in front of you without touching it until the appropriate time? It's done by keeping your word. As a Christian, Christ lives in you, The Holy Spirit, which is the word. It is your assignment to be faithful to what God has entrusted you with. Your decision to know the word, what God told you to do and choose to be faithful is the ultimate act of love and is the sum total of your purpose. You don't stand on *your word*, you stand on *his*!

✒ PURPOSE PRINCIPLE #62 ✑

GOD DOESN'T HONOR *YOUR* WORD, HE HONORS *HIS*.

> **John 1:1-3**
>
> ¹In the beginning was the Word, and the Word was with God, and the Word WAS God. ²He was with God in the beginning. ³All things *came to be through him*, and without him nothing made had being.

Therefore, your character, who you are, what's in you should line up with the word. You have to keep the word of God in you. God created us in his image and his likeness. One thing that we all know about God and should emulate is this; *God keeps his word.*

> **Isaiah 55:11**
>
> So shall my word be that goes forth out of my mouth: it shall not return unto me void, but it shall accomplish that which I please, and it shall prosper in the thing for which I sent it.

> **Matthew 24:35**
>
> Heaven and earth will pass away, but my words will never pass away.

Who put the tree of the knowledge of good and evil in the middle of the garden? The devil or God? The answer: God put it there. But why? Why would God create an Eden for you and place temptation right in the middle of it?

Well, God revealed this to me. The tree was not placed there to be a temptation. Adam and Eve were not thinking about the tree until the serpent planted seductive *words* in Eve's head. She took her focus off of God (the word) and started *listening to the serpent*. Eve was led astray by her own lust, which caused her to disobey the words of the Lord.

The tree was placed there because God desires for us to choose him! It's never about the tree, it's not about temptation, and it's not about restriction. It's a no brainer! To know God is to love him and he expects us to always love him over everything because what else can compare?!

Truth is your future husband will feel this way as well. Because you're married to him, you gave your word that you will be his wife. Therefore, no matter how handsome, rich, nice or whatever another man may be, your vow should prevent you from entertaining the idea of cheating. Even if you're not necessarily happy in your marriage because of some trials you're going through it still doesn't give you a pass to commit adultery. You chose to be in covenant, so you must honor your word.

A handsome snake will always show up in the garden of your mind whispering something in your ear that's contrary to the word of God. This snake will offer you something that seems better than what you already have. The bottom line comes back to…words. Whose words are you going to believe, God or another? Every garden has snakes and tree of the knowledge of good and evil in the middle of it.

✌ PURPOSE PRINCIPLE #63 ✌

GOD WILL NEVER TEMPT YOU WITH A MAN. HE EXPECTS US TO ALWAYS CHOOSE HIM ABOVE ALL ELSE NO MATTER WHAT!

When you decide to honor your word, you're basically saying; I'll keep the covenant, our agreement, your presence (because the word is God), your laws, your ordinances and your precepts. The reason many fall is they don't have enough word in them! Scary thing is far too many Christian women have relatively no fear of the Lord and the consequences of disobedience. It's true! If you could see the physical manifestation of Jesus standing in front of you before you sin, you wouldn't do it. Although, you don't see him with your natural eyes, he's there. It is imperative that we reverence God, know, understand and obey his word.

> **Proverbs 3:3**
>
> Let not mercy and truth forsake thee: bind them about thy neck; write them upon the table *of thine heart:*

> **2 Corinthians 3:3**
>
> You show that you are a letter from Christ, the result of our ministry, *written* not with ink but with the Spirit of the living God, not on tablets of stone but *on tablets of human hearts.*

> **Deuteronomy 11:18**
>
> Fix these words of mine in your *hearts and minds*; tie them as symbols on your hands and bind them on your foreheads.

I've learned you cannot resist temptation in your own strength. It's only through the strength of God to stand and endure. What does that mean? Through prayer, obedience and surrender to the word and will of God you'll find his strength. Your love for him *is your strength*.

When you're in covenant with the Lord, you're under contract. In a legal contract both parties are bound to the words of the document or agreement. Therefore, since you're in covenant with God, his word lives in you. When you cry out the terms of the contract (his word), *he will do what he says!*

> **Jeremiah 1:12 (AMP)**
>
> Then said the Lord to me, You have seen well, for *I am alert and active, watching over My word to perform it.*

> **Isaiah 55:11 (AMP)**
>
> *So shall My WORD be that goes forth out of My mouth:* it shall not return to Me void [without producing any effect, useless], but *it shall accomplish that which I please and purpose,* and *it shall prosper* in the thing for which I sent it.

You *stand* on *his* promises that he has in his word for you. If he told you to "seek ye first the kingdom of God and his righteousness and all these things shall be added unto you", believe it!

If he says, "care for the things of the Lord and devote yourself body and spirit" do it. If he told you that he has someone for you believe it and wait on it. But when it comes…when your Eden comes, there *will be* a tree of the knowledge of good and evil.

Stand on the word that God gave you. Obey and stay faithful to the covenant you have with God. It's designed to protect and prepare you for the level of commitment required in life and marriage.

❧ Purpose Principle #64 ☙

You cannot resist temptation in your own strength. Your strength comes from the Lord, through the word, the Holy Spirit.

> Beware; the tempter comes when you're weak in the flesh. The key is to be strong in the spirit. We were created in his image and his likeness. We are most like him when we're in the word! Satan came to tempt Jesus in the wilderness after he fasted 40 days & nights. The enemy knew this flesh would be weak. But Jesus knew that his strength to resist did not come from his flesh, it came from his spirit. He is the word and it was his will to do the will of the Father. That's what made him successful in his walk and his assignment. When we're in the word, we are like God. We have the strength, power and authority of God. If a person leaves because you're being faithful to the word, let them leave.

Eden was full of trees and fruit God provided for them that they were able to enjoy. Missing one tree will not kill you. Likewise, God has plenty of men available. If you didn't get the man that you liked, know that God has a whole Eden full of others! That's how you do it! Trust God's word more than anything and be willing to lose what you *think* you want. Everything will be all good because your relationship with God is more important than anything else. Please, don't feel deprived.

> **Psalm 84:11**
>
> For the LORD God is a sun and shield: the LORD will give grace and glory: *no good thing will he withhold from them that walk uprightly.*

Your word, your character is everything! You can't bypass this fact. It's what you are judged by, from God, man, society, your children, everyone! We're looking for God to grant certain petitions in our life based on his word/character and yet, we have not honored ours.

Look at it this way. You are building. You're building a future for yourself and your family on this earth and for the world to come. The words you speak today is what you will see manifested in your life tomorrow. But it's not your words alone; it is you speaking in agreement with the power and authority of the word of God that you willingly agree with.

Therefore, the bible tells us before we start building, count the cost. The house you're building, if it's going to stand it has to be built on the rock, which is Jesus, the word of God. The cost to build this house is your word and discipline. Look at what the following scriptures tell us about character and your house:

> **Proverbs 14:1**
>
> The wise woman builds her house, but with her own hands the foolish one tears hers down.

> **Proverbs 9:1**
>
> Wisdom has built her house; she has hewn out its seven pillars.

> **Proverbs 24:4**
>
> Through wisdom is a house built; and by understanding it is established: And by knowledge shall the chambers be filled with all precious and pleasant riches.

The bible is talking about a wise woman who "builds" her house. She is wise because she is taking the time to gather the necessary materials in her life to bring shelter to herself and all she's responsible for. It's built through wisdom.

Well, where does this wisdom come from? I have to be specific because there are unsaved women who are considered smart or wise. But the word tells us where true wisdom is derived from. Wisdom begins with the fear of the Lord. There is a standard, a foundation that is instantly laid when you fear the Lord. You have boundaries and there are some things that you just won't do. The mere acknowledgement of God's presence, authority, in its fullness according to knowledge should bring reverential fear. When a woman builds her house, the house she lives in and the body which houses our spirit with the fear of the Lord, she's building a sure foundation. Whether you understand at first or not why you're obeying his word, if you do it, you'll be blessed and build a sure house.

> **Psalm 111:10**
>
> The fear of the LORD is the beginning of wisdom: a good understanding have all they that do his commandments: his praise endures forever.

The world doesn't have to nor do they (for the most part) keep their word. That's why their houses fall apart. I'm not just talking about a building; I'm also talking about the body. People fall apart because they don't keep their word. They tell you that they love you, sleep with you, take your money, time and then change their mind. The bible tells us that the foolish woman, tears her house down with her own hands. Yes, even the bible tells us if you're building your house without the fear of the Lord, without wisdom, the demise of your house will be your own fault!!

✌ PURPOSE PRINCIPLE #65 ✌

IF YOU BUILD A HOUSE OUTSIDE THE WILL OF GOD ON YOUR OWN, YOU'LL EVENTUALLY TEAR IT DOWN WITH YOUR OWN HANDS.

Your words reflect your character. It's either built on truth or a lie. The more word you have within you, the stronger your house will be. There's no need to be in any relationship built on a lie. A lie will never hold because a lie is nothing (pause. think about that). If you're shacking up with someone, that relationship, situation is a lie. You're living like your married and you're not. That's a lie, it won't hold. The truth just is. It will hold forever. Know and keep the word of truth in you.

I can imagine how you feel. You may be in love with someone that you don't want to leave. You know they're not right for you but the feelings are strong and it's complicated. There may even be children involved.

No matter how complicated it may appear the word is clear. Although it may be hard to let go now, it really boils down to, who you are going to believe? Do you believe that God is God? Is Jesus Lord over your life? Did he tell you to live the way your living? If what you're holding on to does not match what the word says, let it go and keep your word, the word of God! He will give you the wisdom you need to get through this and how to move forward. Truly, that's all you need. One word from the Lord!

The Idol of Relationship

When you've made the decision in your heart, mind, body and soul to do things God's way, I feel like God says to you, "now we can do business"! Then the purification process begins. Part of this development is the recognition and removal of idols and idolatry in your life.

Mistakenly, people assume the only idols that exist are the ones like a statue or some tangible item. Those idols are obvious (or at least it should be). If you have those types of things in your life they must be removed and destroyed immediately and forever! There are however, other idols unconsciously present in our lives that we're not aware of. Nevertheless they exist. Although intangible idols may not be obvious to the naked eye it can be revealed by the Holy Spirit.

Idolatry in any form in your life will indefinitely be a hindrance to you meeting your purpose, destiny and possibly your future spouse. Worship is reserved for our heavenly Father, Jesus Christ. Anything else is idolatry. The enemy is so crafty that he would try to confuse you by making the line between worship and honor/love for someone very hazy. In other words, worship defined says, "to honor and love as a deity". You see, God wants us to love one another and give honor where honor is due but not the same kind of love you give a deity. Once you cross over into that, its idolatry.

IDOL/IDOLATRY DEFINED:

Idol:

1. a representation or a symbol of an object of worship
2. a: a likeness of something b.obsolete: pretender, impostor
3. a form or appearance visible but without substance (an enchanted phantom, a lifeless idol-P.B. Shelley)
4. an object of extreme devotion
5. a false conception: fallacy

Idolatry:

1. worship of idols
2. Blind or excessive devotion to something.
3. excessive devotion or reverence

> **WORSHIP DEFINED:**
>
> **Worship**:
>
> 1. a. The reverent love and devotion accorded a deity, an idol, or a sacred object. B. The ceremonies, prayers, or other religious forms by which this love is expressed.
> 2. Ardent devotion; adoration.
> 3. To honor and love as a deity.
> 4. To regard with ardent or adoring esteem or devotion.
> 5. To participate in religious rites of worship.
> 6. To perform an act of worship.
> 7. To show profound religious devotion to (ones god) for example by praying
> 8. To have intense love and admiration for (a person)

We've seen this idolatrous behavior in people who've become obsessed with lovers. What some call "love" isn't love, its manipulation and control. People in this situation try to control their lover feelings/will/choices by making sacrifices expecting love in return. Sacrifice of self esteem, time, money, resources, even children for a man! Idolatrous women will do anything to provoke their god to make them feel good again. The devoted worshipper has no idea that they are blinded and led by their lust. They think their sacrifice is valid and will be accepted by their beloved because they do it in the *name* of love.

If you're in this situation you've crossed the line into idolatry. No man is worthy of that type of worship. Man cannot handle it because of the flesh. The person who has become obsessed got that way because the Holy Spirit told them "no", but their flesh told them "yes" and they obeyed. Instead of having faith in God, obeying his word and will by letting him control the situation, you put faith in your idol which never reciprocates. Never!

Now there is a difference between having an idol and idolatry. The idol is the *symbol or object* of worship. Idolatry is what *you do* with the idol. Worship, devotion or reverence of an idol may be visibly obvious or you could be spiritually blinded by your level of admiration. The Holy Spirit helps with this because the word says that the Holy Spirit is the Spirit of Truth and will bring all things to your remembrance.

> **1 Corinthians 6:9-10**
>
> Know ye not that the unrighteous shall not inherit the kingdom of God? Be not deceived: neither fornicators, nor idolaters, nor adulterers, nor effeminate, nor abusers of themselves with mankind, Nor thieves, nor covetous, nor drunkards, nor revilers, nor extortionist, shall inherit the kingdom of God.

Worship defined says, " to regard with ardent (passionate) or adoring esteem or devotion". How many relationships have you been in where you were completely absorbed by your partner with this type of esteem or devotion? That was a form of worship. Idolatry defined says its "blind excessive devotion or reverence". You've heard the phrase, "love is blind"?! What about after you've broken up with someone and persist in getting back with them, acting as if God is not able to replace him or ever give you someone better? This is a form of idolatry!

Why do I say this? When you're in that worship mode you're more connected to the gift than the giver. You're basically saying that God is not God enough to meet your need. When you're totally consumed mind body and soul with someone, you're committing idolatry. Anything can be made an idol in your life. People, money, things, a time in your life, a place, etc... In order to walk in your purpose, every idol must be torn down. God is very, very serious about this.

What does God say about idolatry?

> ### Exodus 20-1-8
>
> And *God spake* all these words, saying, *I am the LORD thy God*, which have brought thee out of the land of Egypt, out of the house of bondage. *Thou shalt have no other gods before me.* Thou shalt not make unto thee any graven image, or any likeness of anything that is in heaven above, or that is in the earth beneath, or that is in the water under the earth: *Thou shalt not bow down thyself to them, nor serve them: for I the LORD thy God am a jealous God, visiting the iniquity of the fathers upon the children unto the third and fourth generation of them that hate me;* And shewing mercy unto thousands of them that love me, and keep my commandments. *Thou shalt not take the name of the LORD thy God in vain; for the LORD will not hold him guiltless that taketh his name in vain.*

I cannot make this stuff up! This scripture starts out by saying "God spoke"! He said that "Thou (you) shalt have no other gods before me." The mere fact that he mentioned "thou shalt not have any other gods before me" clearly is an indication that people have other gods in their life. "Thou shalt not bow down thyself to them, nor serve them: for me the Lord thy God is a jealous God".

ॐ Purpose Principle #66 ॐ

When the Holy Spirit reveals to you the idols in your life, tear them down. Walk away and shut the door forever!

What do you bow yourself down to? The dictionary defines the word "bow" as "to comply and consent". Do you comply and consent to men with money and all the bling that comes to you with indecent proposals? Is it that handsome man that you have insane chemistry with that you will give compliance, consent (bow) to sleep with even though you know you shouldn't? Is it money, power, sex, food, material wealth? What or whom do you bow (give compliance and consent) to? Your (vanity), excessive shopping, keeping up appearances? Think about it, do you worship relationships so much so that you spend the majority of your time thinking about getting a partner, talking about why you're not married and what you could do to "get a man". Do you worship this idea and concept so much that you max out your credit cards get in debt, spending all your money to look good and find someone? Does your *want* trump that of what God desires for you? Whom do you serve? Are you serving your credit cards? Are you serving men? Are you serving yourself?

> **Matthew 6:24**
>
> "No one can serve two masters. Either he will hate the one and love the other, or he will be devoted to the one and despise the other. You cannot serve both God and money".

This is far from the first time God made a commandment about idols. See, you want to get married, you want to be successful but are you *really* ready? Your house must be swept clean and put in order to receive your blessing and maintain it. This may not be fun to hear but I promise you, keep reading and listen to what the Lord is saying to you. It will set you free. See where you have been hindered and why.

Listen:

> **Romans 1:18-25**
>
> *For the wrath of God is revealed from heaven against all ungodliness and unrighteousness of men, who hold the truth in unrighteousness*; Because that which may be known of God is manifest in them; for God hath *shewed* it unto them. For the invisible things of him from the creation of the world are clearly seen, being understood by the things that are made, even his eternal power and Godhead; so that they are without excuse: *Because that, when they knew God, they glorified him not as God, neither were thankful; but became vain in their imaginations, and their foolish heart was darkened. Professing themselves to be wise, they became fools*, And changed the glory of the incorruptible God into an image made like to corruptible man, and to birds, and four footed beasts, and creeping things. *Wherefore God also gave them up to uncleanness through the lusts of their own hearts, to dishonor their own bodies between themselves: Who changed the truth of God into a lie, and worshipped and served the creature more than the Creator*, who is blessed forever. Amen.

Idols and idolatry in your life can be so vast yet so undetectable that you could be guilty of it and feel normal about it. That is the trick of the enemy. The bible says:

> **Hosea 4:6**
>
> My people are destroyed for a lack of knowledge.

Let's not continue to be in ignorance! God told us to study and show thy*self* approved.

Listed below are some of the hidden places of idolatry to watch out for and recognize in your own life. Pray to the Holy Spirit that he show you ALL idols/high places around you.

Once revealed, destroy them completely, repent and turn your back on it.

Self Exaltation

How art thou fallen from heaven, O Lucifer, son of the morning! How art thou cut down to the ground, which didst weaken the nations! For thou hast said in thine heart, I will ascend into heaven, I will exalt my throne above the stars of God: I will sit also upon the mount of the congregation, in the sides of the north: I will ascend above the heights of the clouds; I will be like the most High. Yet thou shalt be brought down to hell, to the sides of the pit.

> **Isaiah 14:12-15**
>
> Your own godhood. And the serpent said unto the woman, Ye shall not surely die: For God doth know that in the day ye eat thereof, then your eyes shall be opened, and ye shall be as gods, knowing good and evil. And when the woman saw that the tree was good for food, and that it was pleasant to the eyes, and a tree to be desired to make one wise, she took of the fruit thereof, and did eat, and gave also unto her husband with her; and he did eat. And the eyes of them both were opened, and they knew that they were naked; and they sewed fig leaves together, and made themselves aprons.

Lovers of Themselves

This know also, that in the last days perilous times shall come. For men shall be lovers of their own selves, covetous, boasters, proud, blasphemers, disobedient to parents, unthankful, unholy, Without natural affection, trucebreakers, false accusers, incontinent, fierce, despisers of those that are good, Traitors, heady, high minded, lovers of pleasures more than lovers of God; Having a form of godliness, but denying the power thereof: from such turn away.

> **2 Timothy 3:1-5**
>
> Lust of the Flesh, Lust of the Eyes, & the Pride of Life.

Love not the world, neither the things that are in the world. If any man love the world, the love of the Father is not in him. For all that is in the world, the lust of the flesh, and the lust of the eyes, and the pride of life, is not of the Father, but is of the world. And the world passeth away, and the lust thereof: but he that doeth the will of God abideth for ever.

> **1 John 2:15-17**
>
> The Work of Their Own Hands.

Their land also is full of idols; they worship the work of their own hands, that which their own fingers have made: And the mean man boweth down, and the great man humbleth himself: therefore forgive them not. Enter into the rock, and hide thee in the dust, for fear of the LORD, and for the glory of his majesty. The lofty looks of man shall be humbled, and the haughtiness of men shall be bowed down, and the LORD alone shall be exalted in that day. For the day of the LORD of hosts shall be upon every one that is proud and lofty, and upon every one that is lifted up; and he shall be brought low:

Vanity

> **Proverbs 31:30**
>
> Charm is deceitful, and beauty is vain: but a woman that fears the LORD, she shall be praised.

> **2 Peter 2:18**
>
> For when they speak great swelling words of *vanity*, they allure through the lusts of the flesh, through much wantonness, those that were clean escaped from them who live in error.

Manipulation/control/witchcraft

When thou art come into the land which the LORD thy God giveth thee, thou shalt not learn to do after the abominations of those nations. There shall not be found among you any one that maketh his son or his daughter to pass through the fire, or that useth divination, or an observer of times, or an enchanter, or a witch, or a charmer, or a consulter with familiar spirits, or a wizard, or a necromancer. For all that do these things are an abomination unto the LORD: and because of these abominations the LORD thy God doth drive them out from before thee.

Covetousness

> **Colossians 3:5**
>
> Mortify therefore your members which are upon the earth; fornication, uncleanness, inordinate affection, evil concupiscence, and covetousness, which is idolatry:

Stubbornness

> **1 Samuel 15:23**
>
> For rebellion is as the sin of witchcraft, and stubbornness is as iniquity and idolatry. Because thou hast rejected the word of the LORD, he hath also rejected thee from being king.

The Thief

Many of you have been waiting for a man to come into your life who will be your husband. In the process of waiting for your "husband", you've come across men who you like and are interested in you. Obviously, all of your suitors are not going to be the one. As you probably already know, most of them will be impostors.

> **John 10:10 RSV**
>
> "The thief comes only to steal and kill and destroy; I came that they may have life, and have it abundantly."

The worst part about imposters is they're thieves. If unrecognized, they'll devour your time, money, body, youth, looks, self esteem and lord forbid, your life. They're there to take up the spot of the real blessing God has for you. Not only does he want to prevent the arrival of your future husband, he wants to intercept your purpose and cancel every good thing you already have in your life. The word of God is black or white, no gray areas. Either you're the real thing or

> **Galatians 5:7-10**
>
> You were running a good race. Who cut in on you and kept you from obeying the truth? *⁸That kind of persuasion does not come from the one who calls you.* ⁹"A little yeast works through the whole batch of dough." ¹⁰I am confident in the Lord that you will take no other view. The one who is throwing you into confusion will pay the penalty, whoever he may be.

you're not. When the right man of God comes into your life, he will do right by you. He will love you like Christ loves the church. But when an imposter comes into your life he comes to rob, steal, kill and destroy.

~ PURPOSE PRINCIPLE #67 ~

LOVE GIVES, LUST TAKES. –BISHOP T.D. JAKES

So why does he keep coming to you? What does he want from you? He wants to abort your purpose. It's what you're impregnated with that the enemy wants to destroy. You're full of destiny. I don't mean that in a catchy phrase sort of way. It's not always about your destination it's about what happens along the way. While *single on purpose*, you're ministering to people with your life, depositing seeds into the kingdom of God. Multiplying and manifesting the sons and daughters of God, tearing satan's kingdom down. Do you think the enemy is going to just sit back and let that happen without contesting you? Absolutely not!

Satan specifically assigns familiar spirits to you from birth. The assignment of a familiar spirit is to study you, know your strengths and weakness, likes and dislikes, then inflict pain where they know it will hurt. Or they send the appropriate demon to torture you. Their ultimate goal is to cancel your purpose and kill your spirit. When you're in your rightful position, doing the right thing, the enemy cannot touch you. Now that doesn't mean the he won't come for you, he will. Since the enemy understands that he cannot directly attack you, he attempts to get *you* to *move out of position*.

> How does satan get you out of position?
> 1. Disobedience
>   a. For we ourselves also were once foolish, **disobedient**, deceived, serving various lusts and pleasures, living in malice and envy, hateful, and hating one another.
> 2. Fear
> 3. Sin
> 4. Following:
>   a. lust of the eyes
>   b. lust of the flesh
>   c. the pride of life

❧ PURPOSE PRINCIPLE #68 ☙

WATCH OUT FOR "THE CHURCH GOER", THE MAN THAT GOES TO CHURCH BUT INSIDE IS A DEVIL. HOW HE LIVES OUTSIDE THE CHURCH AND HOW HE TREATS YOU WILL REVEAL WHO HE REALLY IS.

All of these short comings are done by our own hands. Yes, the enemy will come. He will seduce you, expect it. Many of you are like me where I was living righteously and met men claiming to be Christian. They go to church, tithe, pray etc… Yet, when you tell them you cannot have sex until marriage, they pressure you. Or, they live worldly lives outside of the church and when you try to live according to the word they call you "religious". I personally was dumbfounded by this type of guy because I thought we *both* were Christians. Now, I understand as believers, we all have different measures of faith and we're all growing, walking out this journey. But all Christians should be in uncontested agreement with the word. Therefore, we must beware of the deceivers and thieves.

So how does one identify a real man of God from the imposter? The word of God provides insight on the character, heart and actions of a counterfeit. God instructs us to *watch*. Not just to watch out for the enemy around us but for the enemy within… our flesh. Below is a comprehensive list of scriptures and pointers showing how to identify thieves and things women of God should be conscious of:

God is not the author of confusion

If you had peace in your life, home and spirit before you got involved with a certain person that's a good indication God did not send them. If God is not the author of confusion, then guess who just entered? Satan.

> 1 Corinthians 14:33 For God is not *the author* of confusion, but of peace, as in all churches of the saints

If the man refuses to do what's right

> *This is how* we *know* who the children of God are and who the children of the devil are: Anyone who does not do what is right is not a child of God; nor is anyone who does not love his brother.1 John 3:10

You will know a tree by its fruit

If someone you're seeing professed to be Christian and are interested in a future with you, their life should match what they're saying. If what you see and hear manifested from their mouth does not line up with actions, don't make excuses for it. The Holy Spirit's helping you to see this person is not the one, at least not while in that condition.

 📖 Yes, just as you can identify a tree by its fruit, so you can identify people by their actions.-Matt 7:20

 📖 By their fruit you will recognize them. Do people pick grapes from thornbushes, or figs from thistles? Matthew 7:16

 📖 My brothers, can a fig tree bear olives, or a grapevine bear figs? Neither can a salt spring produce fresh water. James 3:12

 📖 The fruit of righteousness will be peace; the effect of righteousness will be quietness and confidence forever.

 📖 Hear, O earth: behold, I will bring evil upon this people, *even the fruit of their thoughts*, because they have not hearkened unto my words, nor to my law, but rejected it - Jeremiah 6:19

 📖 But the Holy Spirit produces this kind of fruit in our lives: love, joy, peace, patience, kindness, goodness, faithfulness

He's a thief and imposter if he lies to you

 📖 You belong to your father, the devil, and you want to carry out *your father's desire.* He was a murderer from the beginning, *not holding to the truth,* for *there is no truth in him. When he lies, he speaks his native language,* for he is a liar and the father of lies. John 8:44

Try or Test the Spirit

📖 Dear friends, do not believe every spirit, but *test the spirits* to see whether they are from God, because many false prophets have gone out into the world. 1John 4:1

📖 *Hereby know ye the Spirit of God*: Every spirit that confesseth that Jesus Christ is come in the flesh is of God- 1John 2:19

If they're a thief, they will not want to do things the right way

📖 I tell you the truth, *the man who does not enter the sheep pen by the gate, but climbs in by some other way, is a thief and a robber.* ²The man who enters by the gate is the shepherd of his sheep. ³The watchman opens the gate for him, and the sheep listen to his voice. *He calls* his own sheep *by name* and leads them out. ⁴When he has brought out all his own, he goes on ahead of them, and his sheep follow him because they know his voice. ⁵But *they will never follow a stranger; in fact, they will run away from him because they do not recognize a stranger's voice.*" ⁶Jesus used this figure of speech, but they did not understand what he was telling them. ⁷Therefore Jesus said again, "I tell you the truth, I am the gate for the sheep. ⁸All who ever came before me were thieves and robbers, but the sheep did not listen to them. ⁹I am the gate; *whoever enters through me will be saved.* He will come in and go out, and find pasture. ¹⁰The thief comes *only* to *steal and kill and destroy*; I have come that they may have life, and have it to the full. ¹¹"I am the good shepherd. The good shepherd lays down his life for the sheep.

They're thieves and imposters if they are lovers of themselves/selfish people

> People will be lovers of themselves, lovers of money, boastful, proud, abusive, disobedient to their parents, ungrateful, unholy, ³without love, unforgiving, slanderous, without self-control, brutal, not lovers of the good, ⁴treacherous, rash, conceited, lovers of pleasure rather than lovers of God— ⁵having a form of godliness but denying its power. *Have nothing to do with them.*

Imposters will be faithless and disloyal

This man will not commit to you. If he's not willing to do the honorable thing for you, than he's an imposter. If he is disrespecting you he's showing disloyalty. This behavior is not that of a true man of God.

> ⁵⁷*Like their fathers* they were *disloyal and faithless*, as unreliable as a faulty bow – Psalm 78:56, 57

Is he a true believer?

The bible tells us to not be unequally yoked with unbelievers. Many people misinterpret what this means. That scripture is not talking about just being unequally yoked together with non Christians. It means what is says, "unbelievers".

There are many people who profess to be Christians but do not believe in the power of the word of God. They are *church goers*. God tells us not to be unequally yoked with them.

This applies when you are seeing someone and you want to wait until marriage (as you should) and they tell you "that was in the bible days, today it's different". Or, "we love each other so it's ok". This is not true. We know what the word says. And if you believe what the word says, you have to do what the word says do. Watch, I say, watch out for unbelievers! Those are the ones that can really trip you up!

> [14] Do not be yoked together with *unbelievers*. For what do righteousness and wickedness have in common? Or what fellowship can light have with darkness? [15] What harmony is there between Christ and Belial? *What does a believer have in common with an unbeliever?* [16] What agreement is there between the temple of God and idols? For we are the temple of the living God. As God has said: "I will live with them and walk among them, and I will be their God, and they will be my people." [17] "Therefore come out from them and be separate, says the Lord. Touch no unclean thing, and I will receive you." [18] "I will be a Father to you, and you will be my sons and daughters, says the Lord Almighty."

Are you both in agreement?

> Can two walk together, except they are agreed? Amos 3:3

These signs shall follow them that believe

> And these signs shall follow them that believe; In my name shall they cast out devils; they shall speak with new tongues; They shall take up serpents; and if they drink any deadly thing, it shall not hurt them; they shall lay hands on the sick, and they shall recover.

Are they clean?

> 📖 ⁴³"When an impure spirit comes out of a person, it goes through arid places seeking rest and does not find it. ⁴⁴Then it says, 'I will return to the house I left.' When it arrives, it finds the house unoccupied, *swept clean and put in order*. ⁴⁵Then it goes and takes with it seven other spirits more wicked than itself, and they go in and live there. And *the final condition of that person is worse than the first*. That is how it will be with this wicked generation." Matthew 12:43-45

> 📖 "Woe to you, scribes and Pharisees, hypocrites! For you *clean the outside of the cup and of the platter, but within they are full of extortion and unrighteousness*. Matthew 23:25

Do they tithe?

If not, then they're cursed with a curse. Marrying someone who doesn't tithe will bring a curse over your whole family because he is the head. It's best to wait on the Lord for the man of God he prepared for you instead of connecting with a non believer that won't tithe.

> 📖 ⁶"I the LORD do not change. So you, the descendants of Jacob, are not destroyed. ⁷Ever since the time of your ancestors you have turned away from my decrees and have not kept them. Return to me, and I will return to you," says the LORD Almighty."But you ask, 'How are we to return?'⁸"Will a mere mortal rob God? Yet you rob me."But you ask, 'How are we robbing you?'"In tithes and offerings. ⁹*You are under a curse—your whole nation—because you are robbing me.*

¹⁰Bring the whole tithe into the storehouse, that there may be food in my house.

If they leave you

📖 They went out from us, but they were not of us; for if they had been of us, they would no doubt have continued with us: but they went out, that they might be made manifest that they were not all of us –John 2:19

Here's what the scriptures tell us to watch out for:

📖 Proverbs 1:10 My son, if sinners entice you, do not give in to them.

📖 For such men are false apostles, deceitful workmen, masquerading as apostles of Christ. 14And no wonder, for Satan himself masquerades as an angel of light. 15 It is not surprising, then, if his servants masquerade as servants of righteousness. *Their end will be what their actions deserve.*-2 Corinthians 11:13-15

📖 *Be self-controlled and alert*. Your enemy the devil prowls around like a roaring lion looking for someone to devour.- 1 Peter 5:8

📖 James 4:7 *Submit yourselves*, then, *to God. Resist the devil*, and he will flee from you.

📖 1 Peter 1:13 Therefore, *prepare your minds for action*; be *self-controlled*; set your hope fully on the grace to be given you when Jesus Christ is revealed

- 📖 . Matthew 7:15 Be on the *watch* for false prophets, who come to you in sheep's clothing, but inside they are cruel wolves.

- 📖 Matthew 26:41 *Watch* and *pray*, that you don't enter into temptation. The spirit indeed is willing, but the flesh is weak

- 📖 Luke 11:21 When the strong man armed keeps *watch* over his house, then his goods are safe

- 📖 Galatians 6:1 Brethren, if anybody be detected in any misconduct, you who are spiritual should restore such a one in a spirit of meekness. And let each of you keep *watch* over *himself*, lest he also fall into temptation.

- 📖 *2Watch out for those dogs, those men who do evil, those mutilators of the flesh. 3For it is we who are the circumcision, we who worship by the Spirit of God, who glory in Christ Jesus, and who put no confidence in the flesh*—Phil 3:2,3

- 📖 Corinthians 2:11 in order that Satan might not outwit us. For we are not unaware of his schemes.

- 📖 I will not allow deceivers to serve in my house (your body), and liars will not stay in my presence. (this is why your relationships with certain men do not work. They are deceivers)

- 📖 In fact, everyone who wants to live a godly life in Christ Jesus will be persecuted, 13while *evil men* and *impostors* will go from bad to worse, deceiving and being deceived 3:12,13

Do Not Be Yoked With Unbelievers

- 📖 2 Corinthians 4:2 Rather, we have renounced secret and shameful ways; *we do not use deception*, nor do we distort the word of God. On the contrary, by setting forth the truth plainly we commend ourselves to every man's conscience in the sight of God.

- 📖 2 John 1:7 Many deceivers, who do not acknowledge Jesus Christ as coming in the flesh, have gone out into the world. Any such person is the deceiver and the antichrist

- 📖 Dear friend, do not imitate what is evil but what is good. Anyone who does what is good is from God. Anyone who does what is evil *has not seen God.*

- 📖 Judges 2:22 *I will use them to test* Israel and **see** *whether they will keep the way* of the LORD and walk in it as their forefathers did."

- 📖 But evil men are all to be cast aside like thorns, which are not gathered with the hand.

Watch out for dogs:

- 📖 Outside are the dogs and sorcerers and the sexually immoral and murderers and idolaters, and everyone who loves and practices falsehood. Revelation 22:15

- 📖 Like a dog that returns to his vomit is a fool who repeats his folly. Proverbs 26:11

- 📖 Look out for the dogs, look out for the evildoers, look out for those who mutilate the flesh. Philippians 3:2

> The dogs have a mighty appetite; they never have enough. But they are shepherds who have no understanding; they have all turned to their own way, each to his own gain, one and all. Isaiah 56:11

23

High Places, Strongholds & Soul Ties

Ever wonder why people get into relationships they don't belong in and stay for long lengths of time? One main reason people stay too long when it's unhealthy and not right is idolatry. They've created an image in their mind, an ideal fantasy of what they want; who they think their soul mate should be. When someone comes along that fits the description they hold onto them and place them on a pedestal. In *reality* that person doesn't match the perception, yet they continue cleave to the *image* until it becomes a high thought.

In other words, imagination has become reality...to them. Non acceptance of the truth of who a person really is becomes denial and if it lingers on too long, becomes a stronghold.

For instance, I knew a woman who aspired to marry a tall, dark and handsome, wealthy athlete. She confided that she wanted to be a well-kept woman who stays at home with the kids and take care of her man. So she would only date men that fit this description.

Eventually she met an NBA player who, in the beginning appeared to be genuinely interested in her (which was the bait) and had all the things she was looking for. Fairly shortly after they got together, he constantly cheated on her, disrespected her and simply wasn't good for her. Yet she remained in this relationship because she was holding on to and replaying the picture in her mind of the "short lived" good times they had. I mean, he did fly her to a couple of places and invited her to a few games but that's about it.

Mind you, all of this was in the beginning. Years later, the relationship drastically worsened, and she still hasn't evolved with reality because she's stuck in imagination. She was committed to the disrespectful lifestyle and treatment because she wanted that dream so badly. In reality, the man never lived up to the *image* she had of him. She was more concerned with the image, than who *he really was*.

～ PURPOSE PRINCIPLE #69 ～

STAY CURRENT. DON'T WORSHIP THE IDOL OF RELATIONSHIP BY REPLAYING OLD IMAGES IN YOUR MIND. FOCUS ON THE LORD AND DEAL WITH PEOPLE ACCORDINGLY.

They continued to see each other off and on for years. Each year drained more and more from who she was, depleting her self esteem to almost nothing.

Finally, he lost so much respect for her that he broke up with her, replaced her with a younger woman whom he married within 6 months. During the relationship and long after, she was bound to the image of this guy and the relationship. Every time she would reminisce, she would talk about their good times like they were yesterday.

Because I was there, I knew these times weren't as good as she perceived them to be. They were brief, worthless moments, but because she wanted it so badly she was blinded. These fantasies she had for this man and what the relationship really was became a stronghold. It took her years to get over him and the disappointment of all the wasted time.

Honestly, most of us have been there. You might not have wanted the same things as my friend but we all have had at one point or another, a image in our mind of how our lives should go, how the person we marry should look and how they'll mesh into our world.

Here's my point. Although, we're comfortable with these images, we cannot worship them. We cannot govern our lives behind an image of what we want because it becomes idolatry. The *image* becomes *imagination*. It's not real! The Lord doesn't want us to be bound to or by anything. He knows these fantasy thoughts can bind you into a stronghold. This is one of the reasons why it's so hard to get over people.

High places in life are often your *thoughts*. For instance, you can break up with a man you knew wasn't right for you but he still consumes your thoughts. If he calls you jump to answer, you entertain him as a friend with the hopes that things will change. You're still holding on to what God told you to release.

Aside from promulgated images occupying your mind, something much bigger is happening here. When someone has you in a stronghold, he binds up your house. I'm not talking about your physical home (although manifestation of the enemies presence ultimately ends up there as well) I'm talking about your body. When you're intimate with someone sexually, your souls intertwine.

That's why it's so much harder for women when they break up with a man. Their soul has been tied to the person they've been with. That's where you hear the term "soul tie". The terrible thing about this is that you don't know the demon or how many demons men are carrying and depositing. Some demons are stronger than others.

I found it interesting that the bible says in order to take over a house, first the strongman has to be bound. Then the house has to be swept clean. Where did this strongman come from? The strongman came from impartation of the man or men you were sleeping with! I know it's gross to think of such a thing but unfortunately this is very real.

Have you ever seen a house that used to be nice get taken over by drug addicts? It is amazing that an entire building can be torn down from wear and tear from people. Not because they're deliberately trying to do so. It happens from years of neglect, abuse, no maintenance, high traffic and no love. This is exactly what happens to women that have sex out of the confines of marriage. The strongman has taken over and the wear and tear begins.

You, yes you, the one reading this book. If you or someone you know is in a soul tie, bound in a stronghold, don't dismay. You have the power through Jesus Christ to end this right now! If you're bound to a man living with you, either put him out or you leave. God will give you the strength and wisdom to do so (trust me!).

If his presence continues to linger in your spirit, you must cast down that imagination, bind up the strongman (that spirit holding you) and cast it out in the name of Jesus. He no longer has right to be there. Originally the enemy obtained authority from you through disobedience. However you can *evict the strongman* with *obedience* to the word and through the power of the name of Jesus!

---

2 Corinthians 10:5

Casting down imaginations, and every *high thing* that exalteth itself against the knowledge of God, and bringing into captivity *every thought* to the *obedience* of Christ;

> **Ephesians 6:12**
>
> For we wrestle not against flesh and blood, but against principalities, against powers, against the rulers of the darkness of this world, against spiritual wickedness in *high places*.

That "I/self" has exalted itself again. The man that you're worshipping is the imagination but your high place is your "I/self". Kill your eye and replace it with the eyes of the Lord. In the mind you are listening to the voice of your "I". "I" love him, "I" want him, "I" need someone to love me, "I" need companionship, "I" don't care what anybody thinks, I, I, I! When you put God's will ahead of your own will, the "I" will come down. You'll resist the enemy and he will flee from you!

There are some women who've been in these strongholds for years. Whether it's been years or a couple of months it doesn't matter. A soul tie is very hard to break if you're not willing to break it. A soul tie is a spiritual bondage. It's not a natural mind over matter thing. Some people think that if you just stop thinking about someone they will go away. It's not that simple, it's a spiritual thing that has to be addressed on the spiritual level. Sometimes, to sever the tie it will require prayer, fasting and intercession. Ask God to release you from the bondage of that person and he'll do it.

> **Mark 9:29**
>
> And he said unto them, This kind can come forth by nothing, but by prayer and fasting

> **Mark 3:27**
>
> No man can enter into a strong man's house, and spoil his goods, except he will first *bind the strong man*; and then he will spoil his house.

> **2 Kings 12:2**
>
> ²Joash *did what was right in the eyes of the Lord* all the years Jehoida the priest instructed him. ³*The high places, however were not removed.*

> **2 Kings 14:3**
>
> ³He did what was right in the eyes of the Lord but not as his father David had done. In everything he followed the example of his father Joash. ⁴The high places, however, were not removed; the people continued to offer sacrifices and burnt offerings there.

> **2 Kings 15: 3**
>
> ³He *did what was right in the eyes of the Lord*, just as his father Amaziah had done. ⁴*The high places, however, were not removed.*

> **2 Kings 18:3**
>
> ³He did what was right in the eyes o f the Lord, just as his father David had done. ⁴*He removed the high places, smashed the sacred stones and cut down the Asherah poles.*

So what do you do with the high place? The bible addresses that in second Corinthians chapter of 10:5 the King James version is says: casting down imaginations and every high thing that exalted itself against the knowledge of God's and bringing into captivity every *thought to the obedience of Christ.* That Scripture talks about the knowledge of God. If you have the knowledge of God then you should not entertain those imaginations because the knowledge of God tells you to care for the things of the Lord and devote yourself body and spirit (see how that works?!). When these carnal idolatrous thoughts and imaginations hold you in a stronghold the Bible tells *us* to bring it down. You cast down imaginations with the power of the word of truth. Speak scriptures to yourself and declare it to the spirit that had you in bondage. Remind yourself of who you are in Christ.

SCRIPTURAL SELF ESTEEM BOOSTERS

1. I will praise thee; for I am fearfully *and* wonderfully made: marvellous *are* thy works; and *that* my soul knoweth right well. Psalm 139:14
2. For the LORD God *is* a sun and shield: the LORD will give grace and glory: no good *thing* will he withhold from them that walk uprightly. Psalm 84:11
3. No weapon that is formed against thee shall prosper; and every tongue *that* shall rise against thee in judgment thou shalt condemn. This *is* the heritage of the servants of the LORD, and their righteousness *is* of me, saith the LORD. Isaiah 54:7
4. For my thoughts are not your thoughts, neither are your ways my ways," declares the LORD Isaiah 55:8
5. your kingdom come, your will be done, on earth as it is in heaven Matthew 6:10
6. I, *even* I, *am* the LORD; and beside me *there is* no saviour. Isaiah 43:11
7. Wait for the LORD; be strong and take heart and wait for the LORD. Psalm 27:14
8. For God hath not given us the spirit of fear; but of power, and of love, and of a sound mind 2 Timothy 1:7
9. How shall I curse, whom God hath not cursed? or how shall I defy, *whom* the LORD hath not defied? Numbers 23:8
10. Depart, depart, go out from there! Touch no unclean thing! Come out from it and be pure, you who carry the articles of the LORD's house. Isaiah 52:11
11. Can two walk together, except they are agreed?
12. Do not set foot on the path of the wicked or walk in the way of evildoers. Proverbs 4:14
13. When Jesus saw him lie, and knew that he had been now a long time *in that case*, he saith unto him, Wilt thou be made whole? John 5:6
14. Jesus saith unto him, Rise, take up thy bed, and walk. John 5:8
15. Do not put your trust in princes, in human beings, who cannot save. Psalm 146:3

Disobedience is also a high place. Oftentimes, instead of casting down negative, false thoughts and images making them captive to the obedience of Christ through the word, we hold on to what God commands us to release. Understand "wants" and "imaginations" do not have authority to just come into your mind, set up shop, take root and do what it wants to do. God has given you power in the name and blood of Jesus to bring these thoughts and imaginations into subjection. But if *you disobey the word*, you give the enemy authority and make the word of no effect in your life.

~ PURPOSE PRINCIPLE #70 ~

THE WORD OF GOD IS NOT JUST RANDOM WORDS YOU SPEAK. YOU MUST BELIEVE IN THE WORD AND OBEY AT THE SAME TIME. FAITH AND OBEDIENCE IS THE KEY THAT UNLOCKS THE DOOR TO THE POWER OF GOD IN YOUR LIFE.

God's will concerning our purpose in this world is to manifest the sons and daughters of God. That mandate is not only for single people but for all Christians. As singles, we ought to care for the things of the Lord and we ought to be the light of the world. Obedience to the calling in the single office makes us good sons and daughters. We're manifesting sons and daughters by walking in that power so when lustful cravings come upon your flesh to sin, you have the strength to abstain.

Once you've manifested the power through Jesus to break that stronghold, you'll be free and clear, making better choices. Now you're a light showing other people that yes, you can be happy, satisfied, whole and healthy as a single Christian woman. Love will eventually find you in his perfect timing.

If you don't cast down imaginations and high thoughts, you'll continue be bound to a lifeless image. If this image is in an exalted place in your mind it's an idol! And every day and minute you waste, thinking and dwelling on a person and relationship it's idolatry.

You need to know this. This is so important because we all want to know why sometimes our desire feels so far from us. We need to break free of strongholds.

Adultery

The Adulterous Woman

When one thinks of adultery, we normally picture someone married who has an affair with someone outside of the marriage. Like many of you, I only considered adultery in the physical sense. There are however, other forms of adultery that causes hindrances to our purpose and blessings.

I had a couple of friends who were really nice women that got caught up in adulterous affairs. Although they were my friends, I made it clear to them that I didn't approve. Of course, that was just my opinion, you can't make people do what they don't want to do and who am I to judge? In my heart of hearts though, I felt what they were doing to those families were devastating.

Now, it's easy to look down on someone's sin when it not your struggle. Adultery in the physical sense was not my struggle. So I just couldn't understand why they had to mess with someone else's husband with all the single men out there in the world. I thought they were selfish, weak and faithless. But God has a way of showing us that he's the only one that's perfect. And that we're only made perfect through him and his righteousness. He showed me that *I* had become an adulterous woman!

> **ADULTERY DEFINED:**
> - extramarital sex that willfully and maliciously interferes with marriage relations; "adultery is often cited for grounds for divorce".
> - Adultery is the voluntary sexual intercourse between a married person and another person who is not his or her spouse.
> - Adultery is referred to extramarital sex, philandery, or infidelity, but does not include fornication. The term "adultery" for many places carries a moral or religious association, while the term "extramarital sex" is morally judgementaly neutral.
> - Adulterer-someone who commits adultery or fornication.

I was like, what?! How can this be? I wasn't sleeping with a married man. No, that wasn't my sin. I broke my covenant in a different way. I had *an adulterous heart* in the respect that I put my wants above God which is idolatrous behavior.

I had been celibate for a long time; dedicated my life to the Lord, seeking him diligently with my whole heart. That's when he began to put this book in my spirit. I was so full of the word and Gods spirit that I thought that I was invincible. That is until I ran into my ex boyfriend.

When we ran into each other I was honestly looking at him as just a friend. We hadn't seen each other in about 6yrs, so we both have matured physically and spiritually (so I thought). I would visit him at his house where we would have long talks about God and the things he revealed to us. I loved those conversations.

Then one day he was sitting across from me and he told me that he was looking at me like I could be his wife. At that moment, I started looking at him as more than a friend. So I told him that was fine but I'm not having sex until marriage. At first he was cool with it. Later on it became a problem. He began to put the pressure on and I eventually gave in.

✒ Purpose Principle #70 ✒

Fight the good fight of faith. Resist the enemy. If you open the door to the enemy, it gets harder and harder to shut.

After the first time we were intimate, I went into the bathroom and cried because I broke my covenant. I asked God to forgive me and told the guy that we couldn't do this anymore. But one time led to another, then another and another. You see, once the door is open it is harder to shut. He made me believe that God loves us and knows we are only human. He persuaded me that I can't expect a grown man I'm seeing seriously, to not have sex.

I truly believed that he was a man of God and that he was just weak in this area. I even tried to use a scripture that I found to support what I was doing.

All along, God was showing me signs that I was going the wrong way. I ignored the signs and inevitably the relationship ended in disaster. It was like watching my own movie. I knew how it was going to end.

❧ Purpose Principle #71 ❧

THE HOLY SPIRIT ALWAYS GIVES YOU WARNING ABOUT A PERSON. IT'S THAT STILL SMALL VOICE YOU HEAR IN THE BEGINNING. LISTEN TO HIM. IF HE TELLS YOU TO RUN (I DON'T CARE HOW FINE, WEALTHY, RICH, SMART, ETC)...RUN!!!

You see a few things happened here. Before this man came into my life, I asked God to make me a wife. God showed me through scripture that when I gave my life to God, I entered into covenant with him and that agreement made me a wife.

When my ex mentioned making me his wife that was a tactic of the enemy because he knew that's what I *wanted*. I should have continued with my faith in God on what he said.

God told me I was already a wife! When I decided to listen to man instead of listening to God I became adulterous. Remember one of the definitions of adulterer?

> **Adultery is the voluntary sexual intercourse between *a married person* and another person who is not his or her spouse.**

Once I decided to listen to my man instead of God my character began to change. I stopped going to church as much, I didn't pray as much. The guilt of what I had done made me not want to go. I began to get reacquainted and more comfortable with the world again. My focus changed, God had given me specific instructions that required faith and I stopped doing it.

My ex didn't believe what I told him about what God instructed me to do. He often would argue that women today didn't know how to be submissive. Basically, he wanted me to do things the way *he believed* things should go.

He didn't have the level of faith that I had. Yet, I allowed the enemy to lie to me, submitting to a boyfriend instead of my husband (God).

Lured by the pride of life (wanting to be married) and the lust of the flesh (sex), I spent the majority of my time trying to cater to him and his wishes. The irony of it all was that he didn't appreciate or respect any of it!

> **1 Corinthians 6:13**
>
> [13]*The body is not meant for sexual immorality* but for the Lord and the Lord for the body. [15]Do you not know that your bodies are members of Christ himself? Shall I then take the members of Christ and unite them with a prostitute? Never! [16]Do you not know that he who unites himself with a prostitute is one with her body? For it is said, "the two will become one flesh.". [17]*But he who unites himself with the Lord is one with him in spirit.* [18]Flee from sexual immorality. All other sins a man commits are outside his body, but *he who sins sexually sins against his own body.* [19]Do you not know that your body is a temple of the Holy Spirit, who is in you, whom you have received from God? You are not your own; [20]you were brought with a price. Therefore honor God with your body.

When I broke up with my ex, I prayed and asked God to forgive me. I repented for what I did and asked God to cleanse me from all unrighteousness and get me back on track. I believe that God forgave me but he used my situation for this chapter.

He let me know that I committed fornication, adultery and idolatry! He showed me that when you disobey God's (your husband) laws and his word (the truth) and believe another (man), you have committed high treason (idolatry & adultery).

> **1 Corinthians 6:17**
>
> But he that is joined unto the Lord is one spirit.

Do you not know that we are members of the body of Christ himself? Do you not know that your body is a temple of the Holy Spirit, who is in you, whom you have received from God? *You are not your own.* You desecrate God and his name when you commit this adulterous act.

God will not allow himself to share space with sin. He is too Holy! Your name changes from Jesus to a prostitute because you have changed characteristics according to your actions.

Your character, (which is the manifestation of the description of a name) has changed from a Holy, consecrated character to that of a whore and prostitute. You're literally worshiping and having sex with a demon with your actions.

In the Old Testament Israel sinned against God by committing whoredom and adulterous acts, by their actions.

How can a nation be considered adulterous? Israel was in covenant (marriage/agreement) with God. Instead of staying *faithful* to the covenant by obeying his laws and statues they chose to *worship* other Gods by following their *idolatrous ways*.

I found it rather interesting that one of the main deity figures Israel prostituted with was Asherah. This pagan god was considered the goddess of *war*, *sex* and *fertility*. They erected sex and worship shrines, housed male prostitutes, and engaged in lewd sexual activity. To signify the presence of this demon was the Asherah pole.

What's really interesting to me is that I felt like even though I committed fornication, I was still a Christian (Christ-like). I said to myself, God knew that I was just struggling in this area.

To a degree, I still believe that to be true. I believe that God will have mercy on us while it's a struggle. But once we say yes and commit with our whole mind, body and soul to the temptation, that's when sin has totally conceived.

As I pondered this theory, I came across the following scriptures:

> **2 Kings 12:2**
>
> ²Joash *did what was right in the eyes of the Lord* all the years Jehoida the priest instructed him. ³*The high places, however were not removed.*

> **2 Kings 14:3**
>
> ³He did what was right in the eyes of the Lord but not as his father David had done. In everything he followed the example of his father Joash. ⁴The high places, however, were not removed; the people continued to offer sacrifices and burnt offerings there.

> **2 Kings 15: 3**
>
> ³He *did what was right in the eyes of the Lord*, just as his father Amaziah had done. ⁴*The high places, however, were not removed; the people continued to offer sacrifices and burnt offerings there.*

> **2 Kings 18:3**
>
> ³He did what was right in the eyes o f the Lord, just as his father David had done. ⁴*He removed the high places, smashed the sacred stones and cut down the Asherah poles.*

We're only perfect through Jesus. There is a state of being where overall you can be doing what is right in the eyes of the Lord but there are still *high places* in your life. In these particular scriptures, the Kings of Judah attempted to live righteously but did not remove the high places. But when they finally got it right, they removed the high places and cut down the *Asherah poles*!

The Asherah pole is a symbol for the pagan goddess of Asherah, the fertility deity. It's also indicative of the male genitalia. Women, when you have a man in your life that you're fornicating with, you're symbolically placing this demonic pole in the temple of the Holy Spirit.

That relationship is a high place in your life. And even though you may have a relationship with the father, this is a high place that needs to come down.

To go even deeper, there was also another demon by the name of Ashtaroth that they worshiped back then. Before I go into that, I'm going to briefly share my experience.

While I was still dating my ex, each time I was intimate with him it became easier and easier to do it without guilt. I justified it within myself saying, "he's the one I'm going to marry anyway" or "he's my man and its only him so God understands".

> **Proverbs 30:20**
>
> "This is the way of an adulteress; she eats and wipes her mouth and say, 'I've done nothing wrong".

Meanwhile, one night I had a strange dream. I was eating a mango and at the same time I was curiously observing a mango tree. The tree itself looked normal but the fruit looked distorted. The fruit actually looked like a giant mango with a dingy looking fetus inside.

When I woke up, I looked online at a dream book and it said that the fruit represented sex and lust. It could also mean let the "man-go". The fetus meant that I may be expressing difficulty in my relationship.

I thought the dream was weird, so I ignored all of that and forgot about it. Then a couple of days later I had another dream. In this dream there was a huge black rat on the kitchen floor that looked like it was dying. It was kind of crawling and moving very slow.

While I was pondering this sight, I saw a green snake crawling up the wall. There was a door to the kitchen next to the rat and the singer Madonna opened the door and was looking at the rat. Now my attention turned to her, I didn't want her to touch the rat. But when I looked back at the rat, a baby fetus was on the floor about a foot away from the rat and now the rat was trying to get to it.

I told Madonna, "You better get your baby before the rat gets it," and she just stood there. I looked back at the rat and it was lying partially on top of the fetus and then I woke up.

This particular dream really disturbed me. So I prayed that God would reveal to me what this was all about. I also looked into the dream book and was quite disturbed at what I found.

Rats

To see rats in your dream, signifies feelings of doubts, guilt and envy. You are feeling unworthy. Something that you are keeping to yourself is eating you up inside. Alternatively, it denotes repulsion, decay, dirtiness and even death. The dream may also be a pun on someone who is a rat. Are you feeling betrayed?

To see a black rat, represents deceit and covert activities.

Snakes

To see a snake or be bitten by one in your dream signifies hidden fears and worries that are threatening you. Your dream may be alerting you to something in your waking life that you are not aware of that have not yet surfaced. Alternatively, the snake may be seen as phallic and thus symbolize temptation, dangerous and forbidden sexuality.

Of course, these things concerned me deeply. I thought it was just my guilt about having sex out of wedlock. But God used my situation to show me what was really happening.

As I was writing this book, I did research on Ashtaroth, Asherah and Astarte (considered the daughter of RA, sex war and fertility goddess). When I saw the picture of Ashtaroth I literally gagged. The depiction of this demon is a naked man sitting on top of a giant black rat. Very much like the one in my dream! Even more chilling, this demon is known as the prince of hell, named after the goddess Ashtoreth! According to Wikipedia Ashtaroth is depicted as:

"A nude man with dragon-like wings, hands and feet a second pair of feathered wings after the main, wearing a crown, holding *a serpent* in one hand."

According to Sebastien Michaelis he is a demon of the first hierarchy, who seduces by means of laziness, vanity and rationalized philosophies.

To others, he teaches mathematical sciences and handicrafts, can make them invisible and lead them to hidden treasures, and answers every question formulated to him. He was also said to give mortal beings the power over serpents.

God revealed to me that this was the demon that I was sleeping with. He was ordered to come after me to try to kill my seed.

This stuff is real people! Look in your bible, you'll see these demons in there. Not once, not twice but several times. These are demons that seduce you and set up high places within your spirit and in your lives.

A couple of months later, I got pregnant by my ex. He broke up with me the day that I told him and the months thereafter he refused to do anything until we got a blood test.

As infuriated as I was, I knew that *I* brought this on my*self*. This is what God was trying to warn me about. By now of course I realized he definitely was not the one for me. I didn't want a child with him but I refused to get an abortion. I cried out to God and all I can say to him was that I was sorry and to please fix this (whatever that meant), just fix it. And He did. About 3 days later I miscarried.

The dream about the fetus, the black rat etc. was prophetic. The Holy Spirit was trying to warn me in every way. I knew that God didn't want me with him but I was simply tired of waiting. I was so determined to have a man that I was willing to settle for less. That is until I got less and realized I didn't want it. Well, that's just me.

You see, in the bible, Jerusalem was set aside as the Holy Place, where the temple of God resided at that time. Jerusalem is symbolic of our physical bodies. We are to present our bodies as a living sacrifice because it is the temple of the Holy Spirit. Fornication, adultery, is forms of idolatry.

The loving act of sexual intercourse in the confines of marriage is a beautiful form of worship. Satan's job is to attempt to pervert the good will of God. He got kicked out of heaven because of his pride. He wanted to exalt his *self* over God so that *he* can be worshipped.

This is part of the reason why we're attacked with the temptation of sexual sins. Satan understands it's a form of worship. When you have sex out of wedlock, you're sinning with your body, your temple.

The enemy loves this because he has an opportunity to be worshiped by you right in God's face in his temple. Armed with this renewed consciousness, you must decide whom you're going to follow. God or man?

What does this have to do with you being single? Everything. You must guard your heart from spiritual adultery.

> **Ezekiel 43:6-10**
>
> While the man was standing beside me, I heard someone speaking to me from inside the temple ⁷He said: "Son of man, this is the *place of my throne and the place for the soles of my feet.* This is where I will live among the Israelites forever. The house of Israel will never again *defile my holy name*-neither they nor their kings-by their prostitution and the *lifeless idols* of their kings at their *high places.* When they placed *their threshold* next to *my threshold* and their *doorpost* beside *my doorpost,* with only a wall between me and them, they defiled *my Holy name* by their detestable practices. So *I destroyed them in my anger.* ⁹*Now let them put away from me their prostitution and the lifeless idols of their kings* and I will live among them.

These demons are very real and they're after you. God sanctified me and while I was intimate with the Lord, I heard him very clearly and I lived completely by faith. God told me not to work a job at that time. I didn't have a job for almost a year and all of my bills every month were taken care of. I didn't worry because I knew God had me. I was full of the anointing.

But when I allowed that demon into my realm, I found myself drifting and I didn't even realize it. I was seduced farther and farther away from the truth. Even after my ex and I broke up, I felt so distant from God. It was harder to hear him. I had to consecrate myself again and rededicate my life to him. I didn't realize the impact of my actions until the spell was broken. I had to ask God to help me break down the high places in my life.

You cannot be a wife and an adulterous woman at the same time. Whatever you follow that causes you to sin is an adulterous, idolatrous affair. THIS IS A HINDERANCE TO YOU FULFILLING YOUR PURPOSE!

A faithful man of God will respect and comply with your standard of waiting until marriage. Although, most men will not go for this, that's ok. You're not in the dating game and don't need a lot of men. All you need is the *one* that God has for you. And he does have one for you! That one is ordained to wait with you and when he can't wait no longer he will marry you.

We have to hold fast to this. The devil has lied to you and he has lied to me. The rules to the game haven't changed. God's laws and principles are like the theory of gravity. It works every time. So if it takes a while before that man shows up, don't sweat it. Continue to love the Lord. Enjoy being his faithful wife.

The Process

Transition

Often times as Christians we're so quick to say the devil has done something to us when things go wrong. Yes, demonic attack is very real, however this is not always the reason for your trials. Sometimes we misinterpret the situation all together.

There are times when the Lord has a plan and will shut things up. When God closes something no man can open it and vice versa. All in all, this is a good thing because we know that all things work together for the good of those who believe and are called according to his purpose. He's not shutting you in to imprison you.

For his divine purpose, there are times when he gives you an assignment that you must be processed for. God himself transitions you from one stage of your life to another.

I say this because many of you have been single for a long time. So long that it seems peculiar. It just doesn't make sense. Nevertheless, you continue to be faithful to the Lord. For some, God has shut you in. I'm here to tell you that he's preparing you. The good news is the transition is seasonal for a set time.

A great example is Noah. His process provides a great illustration of how the Lord himself shut him in.

Noah and his family entered the Ark (symbolic of our covenant with him through Jesus Christ). The rain fell 40 days and 40 night's (theologians say 40 is the number for transition). Notice, once Noah and his family entered the ark "The Lord shut him in". Once you are in covenant with God you are locked in. He sets you aside to process you.

Genesis 7:17 says "for 40 days the flood kept coming" While you're in the ark the flood will keep coming but you'll be safe, you and your family. The rain continuously beat upon the ark, but it didn't sink…it floated. The rain stopped after 40 days but the earth was still flooded for 5 months. Can you imagine how miserable Noah and his family must have felt stuck in the ark with all those animals for that long? Think about it, after the rain stopped I'm sure they thought, well it won't be long now. But it was long. Five months longer!

Nevertheless, all along God had a plan that was greater than the discomfort of the moment. The additional time spent inside the boat was designed to kill everything that was not of God outside the boat.

Although I'm referring to Noah, I'm really talking about you. Here's the process:

- Noah and his family entered the ark (you entering covenant)
- God shut him in (separation and protection from the world/cocoon state/hidden)
- Rain (problems) came while Noah and his family were in the ark (process) 40 days 40 nights. (problems are coming in at the same time)
- That also represents God processing your spiritual house, changing your heart and mindset simultaneously setting you apart from everyone else during this process. Problems *will come* to distract you at the same time.

- As the rain came, Noah and his family were dry and the ark floated. The bible says that "as the waters increased they lifted the ark high above the earth.
- After the rain stopped the flood remained for 150 days. *This is not designed to keep you trapped.* This is to kill off everything that's not of God around you.
- *God remembered* Noah (God will remember you).
- The ark stopped on a mountain (Jesus, the rock).
- Then after 40 days Noah opened the window (he looked for his opportunity to come out). God is about perfect timing.
- God told him when to come out and what to do.
- Noah built an altar to God.

Whenever God shuts you in, he has a planned time for you to come out. There's a perpetual instruction given to man from the beginning, "be fruitful, multiply, replenish and subdue".

Noah is a perfect example of process. First he got a word from the Lord, obeyed it and got to work. He worked on the ark for 120yrs *before* the flood! Although he had a word of promise from the Lord, he was still shut in. Still, in the end, God brought them out. He didn't bring them out to do what they wanted to do. He brought them out to do his will." *bring them out so they can* multiply on the earth and be fruitful and increase in number". The entire process of shutting in and bringing out, from beginning to end is for his purpose.

Sometimes God will shut your womb (spiritual production). That could be in the literal or spiritual sense of the meaning. The womb is defined as the place in which anything is formed and produced. In the single position, at times you'll find yourself with a shut womb. God is forming things in you that upon maturity will be multiplied. As much as we would like to accelerate the process, we have no idea exactly what God is developing within us until we run the entire course.

There's an example in the bible which illustrates this concept. A woman named Hannah was barren because *God shut up her womb*. Of course at the time she didn't know that God had a divine purpose in doing this. Like most of us, she had just about everything a woman could ask for except for the one thing she desired the most. For Hannah, she wanted a child.

Hannah was married to a man that loved her, Elkanah. Sounds good right? Well, he also had another wife by the name of Peninah. Now, the problem here is that Peninah was fertile myrtle! Every time Hannah turned around this woman was pregnant! And she was not gracious about it either. Peninah flaunted the fact that she was producing in Hannah's face. This was torture for Hannah. Since Elkanah loved Hannah and knew she was barren he tried to over compensate with *other things*. The bible says that he gave her a worthy portion. But it wasn't money or things that she wanted. What she wanted a baby.

> Peninah was able to bare children but her husband didn't love her like Hanna. Beware of losing focus by paying attention to the "Peninah" archetype. Most of those women are insecure themselves, which is why they try to show off the things they have. More than likely they envy who you are.
>
> Other "Peninahs" are women who sleep their way to the top, manipulate and seduce to get what they want. You see them with things you would like to have; sometimes material things, children, a great career, good looks or a good man. These women enjoy flaunting their stuff in your face. Their only doing that because they're not satisfied. Ignore her... it's not about her or anything she has because it's *just things*. You have the one thing that she wants and doesn't have... real love!

We can all relate to her situation in one way or the other. Hannah was in a situation where she waited a long time in a hostile environment to get what she desired most. While waiting on the Lord, there was an adversary, a tormentor, Peninah. Hannah was so distraught about her situation that when she went to the temple, she cried out to the Lord. She cried so hard that the priest thought she was drunk. Isn't that how heavy we feel sometimes while waiting for a husband?

It seems like every trifling, mean, dirty woman out there has a good man, while you're being faithful, single, watching from afar. It's hard. You don't want what's theirs, you want what's yours. In your heart you just what to know, when?

And like Hannah's cry, some people don't understand that kind of pain because they're not going through it. But she was so determined to get an answer from the Lord that she made a vow. Hannah's vow put her right where God wanted her to be. She repositioned her request from a self-centered position to a God given purpose position. Purpose inspires God to unlock shut doors.

> **Samuel 1:11**
>
> And *she made a vow*, saying, "O LORD Almighty, if you will only look upon your servant's misery and remember me, and not forget your servant but give her a son, then I will give him to the LORD for all the days of his life, and no razor will ever be used on his head."

The interesting thing to me about this story is the end. Hannah finally receives the promise (a son) and returns him to God to let him serve in the temple. Her son Samuel turned out to be one of the most influential, powerful prophets in the bible! So we see that it was never about Hannah and what she wanted! It was the vehicle of pain that drove Hannah to seek God with all of her heart and soul.

At first God allowed her enemy to flaunt their children in her face. Not to hurt Hannah. Peninnah was the person God used to induce labor in the spirit. So don't discount your enemies, you need them at the table that God is preparing for you!

> **Psalm 23:5**
>
> 5You prepare a table before me in the presence of my enemies.

Also, after Hannah honored her vow by giving Samuel back to God, he blessed her with 5 more children! After she did the will of God, he opened her womb and gave her the promise!

Process

You must understand that in order to be single on purpose God has to be Lord over your life. Once you do that, you'll embark on an exciting new journey. Your operating systems change from worldly/self serving to Godly/giving service. Everything about you is about to change for the better.

When I made the decision to let God be Lord over my life, he did just that. He began to process me. This process was not easy; in fact it was very painful at first. I'm telling you this not to discourage you but to be honest.

When you live in darkness, you cannot see the garbage, the ugliness and the filth that's all around you. When God begins to process you, he turns the light on and you begin to see the stinking filth that you used to think was good.

It's hard when you have to point the finger at your own self. But I assure you, after your spiritual house is swept clean and the light shining bright in your spirit, you come alive! So it's worth the work.

Below are 10 steps that I went through in my process. When I was going through these stages I didn't know that it would work out to be a 10 steps. The idea of listing the steps of my process came to me when a friend asked me what I was reading and doing to stay strong and faithful. I told her that I was just reading and studying the word but I knew she wanted more than that. So I prayed and asked God what to tell her. He told me to write down the stages he walked me through. I did just that and here are the 10 steps of process he walked me through:

STEP 1. I acknowledged God. I acknowledged him as my Lord and savior. I acknowledged, accepted and *received* the message that he is faithful.

STEP 2. I *genuinely repented* from my sins. To repent means to stop what you're doing wrong (sins) immediately and turn around in the right direction.

STEP 3. I actually decided to really have faith in God. He spoke to me and said I will receive what I desire according to my faith. I know that my desire is to have a happy, healthy family and marriage so I believe that God has ordained my husband for me from the beginning of time. I believed that the moment I prayed it.

What that did for me was take away the loneliness of singlehood, I no longer felt like I needed to *find myself a partner* or that I had to be out on the scene (visible) to be found. I realized that God is God and he doesn't need my help to find my husband. He knows how to get me into position as well as the man he has for me. It doesn't matter what I'm wearing, my weight, how much money I have, whether I have emotional baggage or not. God knows exactly where I am in my life and he knows the best match for me for where I am.

Have you ever gone to the supermarket looking a hot mess (to you) and someone flirts with you? This has happened to almost everyone at one time or another. You never know what people find attractive. Remember God is faithful! He hasn't forgotten you and he will not forget you. He will not withhold any good thing from you. Rest in this and wait on the Lord.

STEP 4. I began to be grateful for where I am. When I lived in LA, I had friends out of state who were in relationships and they would call me and ask, "what are you doing tonight"? I noticed I would always be doing something exciting and they were either getting rushed off the phone by their partner, had to make dinner or had to tend to their children while trying to have a conversation. Or, if I wanted to travel somewhere either they couldn't go or had to consult with their partner.

Then it dawned on me, I don't have to deal with any of that. When I came home, I could relax, watch whatever I wanted on TV, listen to the radio, leave dishes in the sink if I wanted to, if I didn't feel like cooking I didn't have to and I could leave and go where ever I wanted to without notice or question. I finally began to enjoy the single side of life. Because once you're married there will be another person to consider. Many married people envy single people for the very things I was dying to give up. So I decided to be grateful for where I am in my life.

STEP 5. I committed myself to God's ways. I stopped fornicating, manipulating, rebelling, coveting and being fearful. God will reveal to you what sins need to be removed from your life. When he does, remove them instantly. Forget about it being easy, no one said it would be easy. It may be the hardest thing you've ever done. But you have to remember your way doesn't and haven't worked. This time, try God, I promise it will work.

STEP 6. I changed my environment. I no longer frequent nightclubs and bars searching for something or someone to fill my lonely void. I quit surrounding myself with unbelievers. I found a church home that speaks the word of truth to help strengthen my walk.

STEP 7. I asked God to make me a wife. He then led me to Habakkuk 2, and showed me that he is my husband. Through him, I'm already a wife. That's why he said that a man that finds a wife finds a good thing. If you're not saved livings by his word, you're not a wife. You're a woman. There's a difference. This is why our lives must line up with his word and do it his way.

STEP 8. I begin to pray and ask God to release me from demonic spirits and soul ties that have controlled and influenced me. When you are sexually intimate with people, part of their spirit is imparted into you. This is why when you try to leave people or get left it is often times hard to heal and get over. I began to delete every phone number and contact to all of my exes. I decided to completely eliminate contact because I wanted God to give me my husband. God is not the author of confusion and I knew that the people that I had already been with weren't my husband even though there were people that I wanted it to be.

I had to show God through my actions that I seriously wanted his choice and not my own. I also wanted to be released from those soul ties. In doing this act of faith, I was showing God that I trust he will deliver. I know that I don't have to cling to the past to make me feel desired, appreciated, accepted or loved. I refused to lie to myself any longer by keeping "friendships" where I was the only one being friendly.

Clean your house! Be honest with yourself and when God tells you to remove someone, remove them immediately and completely. I don't care if you were with them a hundred years. It doesn't matter. You want what God has for you because when he gives a gift he adds no sorrow to it. Whatever door God opens, no man can shut! This is the type of fireproof relationship you really want.

STEP 9. Forgive. Forgive the people that have hurt you and forgive yourself. Then forget it. Yes, it really is that simple. I made the decision to do so. And it is so liberating! It really doesn't matter what other people think.

Forgiveness is more for you. You're spiritually clearing the path to receive all that God has for you. He forgave you. Think about all of the lies you told, the people you slept with, the hearts you broke. God forgave you. Free yourself, don't let the enemy have that leverage over you. Whatever and I mean whatever happened in the past, you cannot do anything about, nor can the ones that hurt you. Period! So forgive and forget you'll feel much better. You will even start to look better too.

STEP 10. Wait on the Lord. Don't give God a time frame. He knows your age and stage in life. Have faith in him only. Put all of your trust in him. You won't be disappointed and if you're really focused on him you won't really notice the time. God will satisfy you.

I asked him to satisfy my soul and he did. I no longer hunger and thirst for a relationship with a man. I hunger and thirst after righteousness and God's love. This is better because man will disappoint you, even when they don't mean to. God's love is perfect.

He wants your time

Your ministry and purpose is carried, birthed through process. Before you were saved, your behavior was sinful like that of the world. Your walk, your talk, everything about you was of the world. People you associated with, places you frequent, things you were interested in, all reflected the nature and the character within.

But when you gave your life to the Lord, a change began inside of you and in your life. A light came on in your eyes and you've begun to see things clearer. Now the things that you used to do, places you used to go and people you used to associate yourself with became less appealing. Why? Not because they've changed … you changed.

There's a mystery in this transformation. Its undeniably public. You living a Holy, righteous life, is a witness. People are watching your process whether you're aware of it or not.

How you live speaks volumes! This is why you have to devote yourself to the Lord body and spirit.

26

TIRED OF WAITING

The most critical part of waiting is...you guessed it...*waiting*. It's not the concept of faith that baffles us it's the ugly in-between stage from belief to manifestation where we struggle the most. It's easy to believe what you were taught to have faith in. Basic things like sitting in a chair. You believe the chair will hold you so you sit in it with confidence (if it looks sturdy of course). You don't question each time before you sit, "will it hold me"? Yet even though God has come through for us time and time again, we question that seat almost every time.

This is paramount when you talk about divine purpose in your life. Right now, you're single so we're going to focus on that. You're in the waiting phase. But what IS waiting? Did you know there are different types of waiting? One form of waiting is where you sit tapping your feet waiting from one minute to the next. Waiting in this manner is what I call *"weighting"*. It's an oppressive, heavy, dragging, passing of time. That form of waiting is riddled with unbelief. "Weighting" my friend, is the most dangerous. The other type of waiting is like that of a server. Service unto God...*waiting*.

Let's talk about the weighting/waiting. *Weighting* creates massive problems in a believer's life. The enemy uses your lack of faith in the process to weaken you, making it so heavy and overwhelming that you abort your assignment. He wants to distract you from the source of your power which is your faith in God. Some of you refuse to help other people, volunteer or even help at the church because it will remove you from the "find a man campaign". So instead of waiting on God, you wait on a man.

Look at the children of Israel. When they were in the wilderness, Moses would go up to Mount Sinai to talk to the Lord on behalf of the people. One time in particular Moses went up to talk to the Lord in the mountain and took longer than usual. They assumed Moses was dead, so they became *afraid.* That's how some of us are when we are waiting for a husband. When God takes too long for our liking, we become afraid that he will never return.

Let's look at this closely because this is what we do today and don't even realize the magnitude of what we are doing:

> [1] When the people saw that Moses *was so long in coming down* from the mountain, they gathered around Aaron and said, "*Come, make us gods* who will go before us. As for this fellow Moses who brought us up out of Egypt, we don't know what has happened to him."
> [2] Aaron answered them, "Take off the gold earrings that your wives, your sons and your daughters are wearing, and bring them to me." [3] So all the people took off their earrings and brought them to Aaron. [4] He took what they handed him and made it into an idol cast in the shape of a calf, fashioning it with a tool. Then they said, "These are your gods, O Israel, who brought you up out of Egypt." [5] When Aaron saw this, he built an altar in front of the calf and announced, "Tomorrow there will be a festival to the LORD." [6] So the next day the people rose early and sacrificed burnt offerings and presented fellowship offerings. Afterward they sat down to eat and drink and got up to indulge in revelry.

First of all, the children of Israel just experienced a major move of God. They witnessed PHAROAH/Egyptians, their oppressor of 400 years defeated by miracle after miracle. Even if that thought didn't register, at least they were finally in a safe place. They had a time to rest. Whatever they needed God provided them. In all actuality, there really wasn't any reason to doubt him. If you look at your own life and think of all that God has done for you, it is easy to sound just like them.

Nevertheless, they freaked out when Moses took too long. So you're thirty something no kids, never been married and he taking too long. What happens when you get tired of waiting? You say, I'm gonna find me a man, I need someone to love me and take care of me ("Come, make us gods who will go before us) You create your own golden calf. You take all of your valuables and give it to an idol that you create. Lust of the eyes, lust of the flesh, the pride of life.

Now you have a man. He's not a Christian but he pays the bills. He's not a Christian but the sex is great. He's married but he says he's separated so it's all good. He's not a Christian but he's a really nice guy. He's not what I've been praying for but at least I have a man. I'm not getting any younger and just because he's not a Christian doesn't mean that he doesn't love God. So you make excuses and give in; you take off your gold valuables and create the golden calf. You act as if prior to them God hasn't taken care of you. Now you're so consumed with your man that you don't go to church anymore, don't pray any more, don't talk to God anymore. Everything becomes about keeping and pleasing your man. You turn more and more worldly every day. The idol demands this.

Remember, satan is not an originator. He's an impostor and he uses the same tricks over and over. It's amazing that it still works so well. He uses the same tools: lust of the eyes, lust of the flesh and the pride of life. When you are "weighting", you're the most vulnerable and the enemy will always show up to tempt you. No different from when Jesus was fasting for 40 days and 40 nights in the wilderness. Satan approached Jesus the same way. Why did satan choose this moment to confront Jesus? He knew Jesus was physically weak at this time. Jesus CHOSE to fast DEPRIVING the FLESH by his own will. Jesus was able to do this because he had a purpose. He was doing the will of the father. That is something that you constantly hear Jesus say, "not my will, but my father", "I'm doing the will of the father". Satan HAD TO COME to tempt Jesus. His goal wasn't to fail in his mission to get Jesus to sin. Of course he was trying to distract and destroy Jesus anyway he could. We're no different! Our purpose as children of God is to fulfill the will of the father! Satan waits for your time in the wilderness (your season for waiting) to tempt you. He knows that you're close to your blessing and desires to catch you in a weakened state.

Now let's go back to the children of Israel. Why was it so easy for them to fall so fast and so hard? There are a few reasons for this. One, they were carnal (fleshly, worldly) minded. They were so used to the world system that their hearts haven't been fully converted. They experienced the blessings of the lord without the personal experience of the *presence* of the Lord like Moses. Like many of us today, they didn't understand their purpose. The bible says:

> ### Hosea 4:6
>
> *"My people are destroyed for lack of knowledge: because thou hast rejected knowledge, I will also reject thee, that thou shalt be no priest to me: seeing thou hast forgotten the law of thy God, I will also forget thy children."*

God chose them to be his people. Just like God chose you. What a blessing! When God delivers you out of bondage, he leads you to your promised land. However, your deliverance is conditional. There is a price for looking back. When I say looking back, I mean looking back to the world system, your old way of doing things.

It may seem natural for you to you to divert to your old ways when the new way doesn't *seem* to be working. Please understand that going back is not an option. This is real serious and real talk. There's a war going on for your soul. If you're smart you'll voluntarily choose the Lord. With or without you, the war is going on and if you don't choose you'll lose by default.

This is what happen to the children of Israel who decided to rebel and build the golden calf. They lost everything! You don't think this is real? You, reading this book right now, can you tell me that after giving your life to God that when you went back to your old ways it went well with you? I'm sure you cannot tell me that. Oh sure on the surface it may seem like it, just like that golden calf was pretty too…until Moses came back.

What do you do, when your Moses/Boaz finally comes for you and you are out there dancing, reveling and rebelling in the streets? Do you think he is going to want you then? Out in the clubs dressed half naked, looking like a whore, acting like a whore to please this calf because you think this is all you have to offer. Do you think the man of your dream (Moses, Boaz etc) is going to want you like that?

No! It's a trick of the enemy it's a distraction and a set up designed for you to sabotage your own blessing.

This is why you have to wait (serve) on the Lord. If you haven't fully converted yet, renewed your heart and mind, this will be hard for you at first. But that is the first thing that you have to do. Fully convert yourself to the Lord's way of doing things. No more straddling the fence.

Ladies, this is for your very survival! Once you do this, it will be much easier to serve the Lord and do things his way. It will be easier to wait. Serve the Lord with all of your heart, mind body and soul.

You don't have to look for a man, seduce or convince a man to be with you. The heart of the King is in *his hands*. God is a rewarder of them that diligently seek him. God arranges marriages.

Remember, God said:

> **Proverbs 21:1**
>
> The *king's heart is in the hand of the LORD,* as the rivers of water: *he turns it wherever he will.*

The other reason why the children of Israel fell so easily is they lost their focus. They weren't focused on the Lord they were focused on Moses (a man, something physical, tangible, visible). They did not establish faith in God himself. When they lost their FOCUS, they lost their FAITH.

Now think back to the chapter on names, I explain how the Lord operates with names and words and satan operates with numbers and formulas?

OK, check this out. When you subtract FOCUS from God you lose FAITH. When you lose faith you add and idol. You add an idol over God = Death.

> ²²"Do not be angry, my lord," Aaron answered. "You know how prone these people are to evil. ²³They said to me, 'Make us gods who will go before us. As for this fellow Moses who brought us up out of Egypt, we don't know what has happened to him.' ²⁴So I told them, 'Whoever has any gold jewelry, take it off.' Then they gave me the gold, and I threw it into the fire, and out came this calf!"
> ²⁵Moses saw that the people were running wild and that Aaron had let them get out of control and *so become a laughingstock to their enemies*. ²⁶So he stood at the entrance to the camp and said, *"Whoever is for the LORD, come to me."* And all the Levites rallied to him.
> ²⁷Then he said to them, "This is what the LORD, the God of Israel, says: 'Each man strap a sword to his side. Go back and forth through the camp from one end to the other, each killing his brother and friend and neighbor.' " ²⁸The Levites did as Moses commanded, and that day about three thousand of the people died. ²⁹Then Moses said, *"You have been set apart to the LORD today,* for you were against your own sons and brothers, and he has blessed you this day."

Aaron was the Priest but he was overwhelmed by the influence of the people. We see this today in some churches, Pastors that compromise the truth to keep large memberships and money. But God is not mocked. That is why he wants you to focus on him.

> **Matthew 6:33**
>
> But seek first his kingdom and his righteousness, and all these things will be given to you as well.

He wants to make it easy for you. Although waiting may be hard sometimes there are many benefits. You don't lose. There is nothing to look back to. Leave the ex's behind. Looking back into your past can turn you into to a pillar of salt (bitter) like Lot's wife. As you continue to serve the Lord, you'll love him more and more and the weight/wait will lift. When your husband comes (Moses/Boaz etc) you'll be ready to receive him.

> [29]Then Moses said, "You have been set apart to the LORD today, for you were against your own sons and brothers, and he has blessed you this day."

> **Psalm 37:9**
>
> For evil men will be cut off, *but those who hope in the LORD will inherit the land.*

> **Isaiah 40:31**
>
> but those who hope in the LORD *will renew their strength.* They will soar on wings like eagles; they will run and not grow weary, they will walk and not be faint.

There is inevitable disaster when you think God's way is taking too long and decide to take matters into your own hand. This never works! Please, please, please, my brothers and my sisters, remain faithful. The price for disobedience, rebellion and unfaithfulness is too high. In the meantime, look around you, find ways to serve. Start loving on people, your family, friends, colleagues and even strangers. They need you and they're waiting for you. God set you aside, right now…today… to be the one to intercede and serve. He made you *single on purpose.*

> **Revelation 2:7**
>
> He that hath an ear, let him hear what the Spirit saith unto the churches; To him that overcometh will I give to eat of the tree of life, which is in the midst of the paradise of God.

The End

A WORD TO MY DAUGHTERS:

~~

Daughters of Zion, the Kings daughters are in fact, devoted things. We are set aside for use in the Kingdom. Below, I've taken the liberty to write down what God says his daughters should look like, how they should carry themselves, what to do and what not to do. Think for a second of how many hours we spend with our girlfriends and relationship gurus trying to figure out how what would make us more attractive. Now, give God this moment to tell you who you are and what to expect.

What are the duties of a daughter of the King?

Single women

    📖 1 Corinthians 7:34 An unmarried woman or virgin is concerned about the Lord's affairs: Her aim is to be devoted to the Lord in both body and spirit.

Older women

    📖 Titus 2:4 that they may *train the young women* to love their *husbands*, to love their children.

What does a daughter of the King wear?

Salvation & Righteousness

- Isaiah 61:10 I will greatly rejoice in the LORD, my soul shall be joyful in my God; for *he hath clothed me* with the garments of *salvation*, he hath covered me with the robe of *righteousness*, as a bridegroom decketh *himself* with ornaments, and *as a bride adorneth herself with her jewels.*
  - This is how a daughter prepares for her husband. God clothes her with salvation which reveals that she was adopted as a daughter but she *dresses herself* with righteousness, not expensive clothes, makeup or hair but righteousness!

Truth, peace, faith, salvation, armed with the word of God

- Ephesians 6:14 Stand therefore, having *your loins girt about with truth*, and having on the *breastplate of righteousness*; 15And your feet shod with the preparation of *the gospel of peace*; 16Above all, taking *the shield of faith*, wherewith ye shall be able to quench all the fiery darts of the wicked. 17And *take the helmet of salvation, and the sword of the Spirit, which is the word of God:*

Righteous Acts

- Revelation 19:8 And to her was granted that *she should be arrayed in* fine linen, clean and white: for the fine linen is the *righteous acts* of saints.

Power

- Luke 24:49 Behold, I send forth the promise of my Father on you. But wait in the city of Jerusalem until you are *clothed with power* from on high."

The anointing/Christ/the word

- Galatians 3:27 for all of you who have been baptized into Christ, have *clothed yourselves with Christ.*
- Ephesians 6:14 Take your place, then, having your body *clothed* with the true word, and having put on the breastplate of righteousness

Your new self

📖 Colossians 3:10 and have *clothed yourselves* with the *new self* which is being remolded into *full knowledge* so as *to become like Him* who created it.

Gladness

📖 Psalms 30:11 You have turned my mourning into dancing for me. You have removed my sackcloth, and *clothed* me with *gladness*.

Good works

📖 Timothy 2:10 But *clothed* with good works, *as is right for women* who are living in the fear of God.

Humility

📖 1 Peter 5:5 Likewise, ye younger, submit yourselves unto the elder. Yea, all of you be subject one to another, and be *clothed with humility*: for God resisteth the proud, and giveth grace to the humble.

Soft clothing

📖 But what went ye out for to see? A man clothed in soft raiment? behold, they that wear soft *clothing* are in kings' houses.
- Ecclesiastes 9:8 Let your clothing be white at *all times*, and let not your head be without oil.

The blood of Jesus

📖 Proverbs 31:21 She is not afraid of the snow for her household; for all her household are *clothed* with *scarlet*.

How should she look?

📖 Your beauty should not come from outward *adornment*, such as braided hair and the wearing of gold jewelry and fine clothes. 4Instead, it should be that of great worth in God's sight. 5For this is the way the *holy women* of the past *who put their hope in God used to make themselves beautiful*. They were submissive to their own husbands, 6like Sarah, who obeyed Abraham and called him her master. *You are her daughters* if you do what is right and *do not give way to fear*.

What is her character like?

Honorable

📖 Psalms 45:9 Kings' *daughters* are among your *honorable* women. At your right hand the queen stands in gold of Ophir.

Meek

📖 Matthew 5:5 Blessed are the meek, for they will inherit *the earth*.

What a daughter should NOT be found doing:

📖 Deuteronomy 23:17 There shall be no prostitute of the *daughters* of Israel, neither shall there be a sodomite of the sons of Israel

📖 Isaiah 3:16 16 The Lord says, "The women of Zion are *haughty*, walking along with outstretched necks, flirting with their eyes, tripping along with mincing steps, with ornaments jingling on their ankles. 17Therefore the Lord will bring sores on the heads of the women of Zion; the Lord will make their scalps bald." 18In that day the Lord will snatch away their finery: the bangles and headbands and crescent necklaces, 19the earrings and bracelets and veils, 20the headdresses and ankle chains and sashes, the perfume bottles and charms, 21the signet rings and nose rings, 22the fine robes and the capes and cloaks, the purses 23and mirrors, and the linen garments and tiaras and shawls.

Isaiah 32:9 Rise up, you women who are at ease! Hear my voice! You careless *daughters*, give ear to my speech!

Why a Kings daughter cannot marry a non believer:

- 📖 Ezra 9:12 now therefore don't give your *daughters* to their sons, neither take their daughters to your sons, nor seek their peace or their prosperity forever; *that you may be strong, and eat the good of the land, and leave it for an inheritance to your children forever*
- 📖 Nehemiah 5:5 Yet now our flesh is as the flesh of our brothers, our children as their children: and behold, we bring into bondage our sons and our *daughters* to be servants, and some of our daughters are brought into bondage already : neither is it in our power to help it; for other men have our fields and our vineyards.
- 📖 Matthew 9:16 16 No man puts a piece of *new cloth* onto an *old garment*, for that which is put on to fill it up takes from the garment, and the tear is made worse.17Neither do men put new wine into old wineskins: else the wineskins break, and the wine runs out, and the wineskins perish: but they put new wine into new wineskins, and both are preserved.

Your inheritance as a Kings Daughter:

- 📖 Matthew 5:5 Blessed are the meek, for they will inherit *the earth*.
- 📖 Ephesians 1:11-14 In whom also we have obtained an inheritance, being predestinated according to the purpose of *him who works* all things after the counsel of *his own will*
- 📖 Titus 3:7 That being justified by his grace, *we should be made heirs* according to the hope of eternal life.
- 📖 Romans 8:17 And if children, then heirs; heirs of God, and joint-heirs with Christ; if so be that we suffer with him, that we may be also glorified together.

- Acts 20:32 And now, brothers, I commend you to God, and to the word of his grace, which is able to build you up, and to give you an inheritance among all them which are sanctified.
- Matthew 5:5 Blessed are the gentle, for they shall *inherit* the earth
- Matthew 19:29 Everyone who has left houses, or brothers, or sisters, or father, or mother, or wife, or children, or lands, for my name's sake, will receive one hundred times, and will *inherit* eternal life.
- Romans 4:13 Again, the promise that he should *inherit* the world did not come to Abraham or his posterity conditioned by Law, but by *faith-righteousness*
- 1 Peter 3:9 not rendering evil for evil, or reviling for reviling; but instead blessing; knowing that to this were you called, that you may *inherit* a blessing
- Revelation 21:7 He that overcometh shall *inherit all things*; and I will be his God, and he shall be my son.
- Leviticus 20:24 But I have said to you, "You shall *inherit their land*, and I will give it to you to possess it, a land flowing with milk and honey." I am Yahweh your God, who has *separated you from the peoples.*
- Numbers 33:54 You shall *inherit* the land by lot according to your families; to the more you shall give the more inheritance, and to the fewer you shall give the less inheritance: wherever the lot falls to any man, that shall be his. You shall inherit according to the tribes of your fathers
- Psalms 25:13 His soul shall dwell at ease. *His seed* shall *inherit the land.*
- Psalms 37:9 For evildoers shall be cut off, but *those who wait* for Yahweh shall *inherit the land*
- Psalms 37:29 The righteous shall *inherit the land*, and live in it forever
- Psalms 37:34 Wait for Yahweh, and keep his way, and he will exalt you to *inherit the land.* When the wicked are cut off, you shall see it.

- 📖 Proverbs 3:35 *The wise* will *inherit glory*, but shame will be the promotion of fools. (WEB KJV JPS ASV DBY WBS YLT NAS RSV NIV)
- 📖 Proverbs 8:21 That I may cause *those that love me* to *inherit substance*; and I will fill their treasures.
- 📖 Isaiah 57:13 When you cry, let those who you have gathered deliver you; but the wind shall take them, a breath shall carry them all away: but he who takes refuge in me shall possess the land, and shall *inherit my holy mountain*."

How do you know that you are entitled to the inheritance?

- 📖 You must be related, family, part of the body of Christ to be eligible for your inheritance. You became family, a daughter when you received Jesus as Lord and savior.

Through covenant

- 📖 Genesis 15:8-9 But Abram said, "O Sovereign Lord, how can I know that I will gain possession of it?" ⁹So the Lord said to him, "Bring me a heifer, a goat and a ram, each three years old, along with a dove and a young pigeon."
- 📖 Deuteronomy 16:20 You shall follow that which is altogether just, that you may live, and inherit the land which Yahweh your God gives you.
- 📖 When you start to increase in the land.
- 📖 Exodus 23:30 Little by little I will drive them out from before you, until you have increased and inherit the land.

You will not have an inheritance if:

- 📖 Corinthians 6:9 Or don't you know that the unrighteous will not inherit the Kingdom of God? Don't be deceived. Neither the sexually immoral, nor idolaters, nor adulterers, nor male prostitutes, nor homosexuals
- 📖 1 Corinthians 6:10 nor thieves, nor covetous, nor drunkards, nor slanderers, nor extortioners, will inherit the Kingdom of God
- 📖 1 Corinthians 15:50 Now I say this, brothers, that flesh and blood can't inherit the Kingdom of God; neither does corruption inherit incorruption.
- 📖 Galatians 5:21 envyings, murders, drunkenness, orgies, and things like these; of which I forewarn you, even as I also forewarned you, that those who practice such things will not inherit the Kingdom of God.

> I took the time to write out all of those scriptures so that you may know what the word of God has to say about his daughters. Please take it to heart, read and re-read these scriptures over and over again and start to live your life like the princess you are! For your father is God of God, King of Kings and Lord of Lords!

*Eye of Ra/Horus Illustration

The *Eye of Ra* or *Eye of Re* is a being in ancient Egyptian mythology that functions as a *feminine counterpart* to the sun god Ra and a violent force that subdues his enemies. The Eye is an extension of Ra's power, equated with the disk of the sun, but it also behaves as an independent entity, which can be personified by a wide variety of

Egyptian goddesses, including *Hathor, Sekhmet, Bastet, Wadjet,* and *Mut. The Eye goddess acts as mother, sibling, consort, and daughter of the sun god. She is his partner in the creative cycle in which he begets the renewed form of himself that is born at dawn.* The Eye's violent aspect defends Ra against the agents of disorder *that threaten his rule.* This dangerous aspect of the Eye goddess is often represented by a lioness or by the uraeus, or cobra, a symbol of protection and royal authority. As an apotropaic power, *the Eye is often equated with the Eye of Horus*, which in other cases is a separate concept.

The Eye of Ra was involved in many areas of ancient Egyptian religion, including in the *cults* of the many goddesses who are equated with it. Its life-giving power was celebrated in *temple* rituals, and its dangerous aspect was invoked in the protection of the *pharaoh*, of sacred places, and of ordinary people and their homes.

The Eye of Ra could be equated with the disk of the sun, with the cobras coiled around the disk, and with the red and white crowns of Lower and Upper Egypt.

The Egyptians often referred to the sun and the moon as the "eye"s of particular gods. The right eye of the god *Horus*, for instance, was equated with the sun, and his left eye equated with the moon. At times the Egyptians called the lunar eye the "*Eye of Horus*", a concept with its own complex mythology and symbolism, and called the solar eye the "Eye of Ra"—Ra being the preeminent sun god in *ancient Egyptian religion*. However, in Egyptian belief, many terms and concepts are extremely fluid, so the sun could also be called the "Eye of Horus".

The yellow or red disk-like sun emblem in Egyptian art represents the Eye of Ra. Because of the great importance of the sun in Egyptian religion, this emblem is among the most common religious symbols in all of Egyptian art. Although Egyptologists usually call this emblem the "sun disk", its convex shape in Egyptian relief sculpture suggests that the Egyptians may have envisioned it as a sphere. The emblem often appears atop the heads of solar-associated deities, including Ra himself, to indicate their links with the sun. *The disk could even be regarded as Ra's physical form.* At other times, the sun god, in various forms, ****is depicted inside the disk shape as if enclosed within it.* The Egyptians often described the sun's movement across the sky as the movement of a barque carrying Ra and his entourage of other gods, and the sun disk can either be equated with this solar barque or depicted containing the barque inside it. The disk is often called Ra's "daughter" in Egyptian texts.

As the sun, the Eye of Ra is a source of heat and light, and it is associated with fire and flames. It is also equated with the red light that appears before sunrise, and with the morning star that precedes and signals the sun's arrival.

The eyes of Egyptian deities, *although they are aspects of the power of the gods who own them,* sometimes take active roles in mythology, possibly because *the word for "eye"* in Egyptian, *resembles another word meaning "do" or "act".* The presence of the feminine suffix *t* in jrt may explain why these independent eyes were thought of as female.

The Eye of Ra, in particular, is deeply involved in the sun god's creative actions.

In Egyptian mythology, the sun's emergence from the horizon each morning is likened to Ra's birth, an event that revitalizes him and the order of the cosmos. *Ra emerges from the body of a goddess* who represents the sky—usually Nut. Depictions of the rising sun often show Ra as *a child contained within the solar disk.* In this context, *the disk may represent the womb from which he is born or the placenta that emerges with him.* The Eye of Ra, therefore, can also take the form of a goddess: the mother who brings Ra forth from her womb or a sister who is born alongside him like a placenta. *Ra was sometimes said to enter the body of the sky goddess at sunset, impregnating her and setting the stage for his rebirth at sunrise. Consequently, the Eye, as womb and mother of the child form of Ra, is also the consort of the adult Ra. The adult Ra, likewise, is the father of the Eye* who is born at sunrise. *The Eye is thus a feminine counterpart to Ra's masculine creative power, part of a broader Egyptian tendency to express creation and renewal in terms of sexual reproduction. Ra gives rise to his daughter, the Eye, who in turn gives rise to him, her son, in a cycle of constant regeneration.*

Ra is not unique in this relationship with *the Eye. Other solar gods may interact in a similar way with the numerous goddesses associated with* the Eye. Hathor, a goddess of the sky, the sun, and fertility, is often called the Eye of Ra, and she also has a relationship with Horus, who also has solar connections, that is similar to the relationship between Ra and his Eye.–Hathor can even be called "the Eye of Horus"—one of several ways in which the distinctions between the ***two eyes are blurred. The Eye can also act as an extension of and companion to Atum, a creator god closely associated with Ra. Sometimes this eye is called the Eye of Atum, although at other times the Eye of Ra and the Eye of Atum are distinct, with Ra's Eye the sun and Atum's

***Eye the moon.

The uraeus on the royal headdress of <u>Amenemope</u>

A myth about the Eye, known from allusions in the *Coffin Texts* from the Middle Kingdom (c. 2055–1650 BC) and a more complete account in the Bremner-Rhind Papyrus from the Late Period (664–332 BC), demonstrates the Eye's close connection with Ra and Atum and her ability ***to act independently. The myth takes place before the creation of the world, when the solar creator—either Ra or Atum—***is alone. Shu and Tefnut, the children of this creator god, have drifted away from him in the waters of Nu, the chaos that exists before creation in Egyptian belief, so he sends out his Eye to find them. ****The Eye returns with Shu and Tefnut but is infuriated to see that ***the creator has developed a new eye***, which has taken her place.* The creator god appeases her by giving her an exalted position on his forehead in the form of the uraeus, the emblematic cobra that appears frequently in Egyptian art, particularly on royal crowns.

The equation of the Eye with the uraeus and the crown underlines the Eye's role as a companion to Ra and to the pharaoh, with whom Ra is linked. Upon the return of Shu and Tefnut, the creator god is said to have shed tears, although whether they are prompted by happiness at his children's return or distress at the Eye's anger is unclear. These tears give rise to ***the first humans. In a variant of the story, ***it is the Eye that weeps instead, so the Eye is the progenitor of humankind.*

The tears of the Eye of Ra are part of a more general connection between the Eye and moisture. In addition to representing the morning star, the Eye can also be equated with the star Sothis (Sirius).

Every summer, at the start of the Egyptian year, Sothis' heliacal rising, in which the star *rose above the horizon just before the sun itself*, heralded the start of the Nile inundation, which watered and fertilized Egypt's farmland. Therefore, the Eye of Ra precedes and represents the floodwaters that restore fertility to all of Egypt.

Aggressive and Protective

The Eye of Ra also represents the destructive aspect of Ra's power: the heat of the sun, which in Egypt can be so harsh that the Egyptians sometimes likened it to arrows shot by a god to destroy evildoers. The uraeus is a logical symbol for this dangerous power. In art, the sun disk image often incorporates one or two uraei coiled around it.

The solar uraeus represents the Eye as a dangerous force that encircles the sun god and guards against his enemies, spitting flames like venom.–Four uraei are sometimes said to surround Ra's barque. Collectively called "Hathor of the Four Faces", they represent the Eye's vigilance in all directions.

***Ra's enemies are the forces of chaos, which threaten *maat*, the cosmic order that he creates. They include both humans who spread disorder and cosmic powers like Apep, the embodiment of chaos, whom Ra is said to combat every night.-In some Egyptian texts, the Eye's fiery breath assists in Apep's destruction.

This apotropaic function of the Eye of Ra is another point of overlap with the Eye of Horus, which was similarly believed to ward off evil.

***The Eye's aggression may even extend to deities who, unlike Apep, are not regarded as evil. Evidence in early funerary texts suggests that at dawn, Ra was believed to swallow the multitude of other gods, who in this instance are equated with the stars, which vanish at sunrise and reappear at sunset. In doing so, he absorbs the gods' power, thereby renewing his own vitality, ***before spitting them out again at nightfall. ***The solar Eye is said to assist in this effort, slaughtering the gods for Ra to eat. The red light of dawn therefore signifies the blood produced by this slaughter.[16]

In another myth, related in the <u>Book of the Heavenly Cow</u> from the <u>New Kingdom</u> (c. 1550–1070 BC), ****Ra uses*the Eye as a weapon against humans who have rebelled against his authority.* ***He sends the Eye—Hathor, in her aggressive manifestation as the lioness goddess Sekhmet—to massacre them. She does so, but after the first day of her rampage, Ra decides to prevent her from killing all humanity. He orders that beer be dyed red and poured out over the land. ****The Eye goddess drinks the beer, mistaking it for blood, and ***in her inebriated state returns to Ra without noticing her intended victims.* Through her drunkenness she has been returned to a harmless form.

***The solar Eye's volatile nature can make her difficult even for her master to control. In a third myth, known in several variants, the Eye goddess becomes upset with Ra and runs away from him. In some versions the provocation for her anger seems to be her replacement with a new eye after the search for Shu and Tefnut, but in others her rebellion seems to take place after the world is fully formed. With the

solar Eye gone, Ra is vulnerable to his enemies and bereft of a large part of his power. The Eye's absence and Ra's weakened state may be a mythological reference to solar eclipses.[18]

Meanwhile, the Eye wanders in a distant land—Nubia or Libya—as a wild feline, as dangerous and uncontrolled as the forces of chaos that she is meant to subdue. *To restore order, one of the gods goes out to retrieve her.* In one fragmentary version, the war god Anhur searches for the Eye, which takes the form of the goddess Menhit, using his skills as a hunter. In other accounts, it is Shu who searches for Tefnut, who in this case represents the Eye rather than an independent deity. In a third version, known from a Late Period papyrus dubbed "The Myth of the Eye of the Sun", Thoth, the messenger and conciliator of the Egyptian pantheon, persuades the goddess to return through a combination of lectures, enticement, and entertaining stories.

His efforts are not uniformly successful; at one point, the goddess is so enraged by Thoth's words that she transforms from a relatively benign cat into a fire-breathing lioness, making Thoth jump.[19]

When the goddess is at last placated, the retrieving god escorts her *back to Egypt*. Her return marks the beginning of the inundation and the new year. ***The pacified Eye deity is once more a procreative consort for the sun god, or, in some versions of the story, for the god who brings her back.* Menhit becomes the consort of Anhur, Tefnut is paired with Shu, and Thoth's spouse is sometimes Nehemtawy, a minor goddess associated with this pacified form of the Eye.

In many cases, the Eye goddess and her consort then produce a divine child who becomes the new sun god. The goddess' transformation from hostile to peaceful is a key step in the renewal of the sun god and the kingship that he represents.

Manifestations

The characteristics of the Eye of Ra were an important part of the Egyptian conception of female divinity in general, and the Eye was equated with many goddesses, ranging from very prominent deities like Hathor to obscure ones like Mestjet, a lion goddess who appears in only one known inscription.

Sekhmet as a woman with the head of a lioness, wearing the sun disk and uraeus

The Egyptians associated many gods who took felid form with the sun, and many lioness deities, like Sekhmet, Menhit, and Tefnut, were equated with the Eye. Bastet was depicted as both a domestic cat and a lioness, and with these two forms she could represent both the peaceful and violent aspects of the Eye. Yet another goddess of the solar Eye was Mut, the consort of the god Amun, who was associated with Ra. She, too, could appear in both leonine and cat form.

Likewise, cobra goddesses often represented the Eye. Among them was Wadjet, a tutelary deity of Lower Egypt who was closely associated with royal crowns and the protection of the king. Other Eye-associated cobra goddesses include the fertility deity Renenutet, the magician goddess Weret-hekau, and Meretseger, the divine protector of the burial grounds near the city of Thebes.

The deities associated with the Eye were not restricted to feline and serpent forms. Hathor's usual animal form is a cow, as is that of the closely linked Eye goddess Mehet-Weret. Nekhbet, a vulture goddess, was closely connected with Wadjet, with the Eye, and with the crowns of Egypt. Many Eye goddesses appear mainly in human form, including Neith, an arrow-shooting deity sometimes said to be the mother of the sun god, and Satet and Anuket, who were linked with the Nile cataracts and the inundation.[29] Other such goddesses include Sothis, the deified form of the star of the same name, and Maat, the personification of cosmic order, who was connected with the Eye because she was said to be the daughter of Ra.[30] Even Isis, who is usually the companion of Osiris rather than Ra, or Astarte, a deity of fertility and warfare who was imported from Canaan rather than native to Egypt, could be equated with the solar Eye.[32]

Frequently, two Eye-related goddesses appear together, representing different aspects of the Eye. The juxtaposed deities often stand for the procreative and aggressive sides of the Eye's character, as Hathor and Sekhmet sometimes do. Wadjet and Nekhbet can stand for Lower and Upper Egypt, respectively, along with the Red Crown and White Crown that represent the two lands. Similarly, Mut, whose main cult center was in Thebes, sometimes served as an Upper Egyptian counterpart of Sekhmet, who was worshipped in Memphis in Lower Egypt.

These goddesses and their iconographies frequently mingled. Many combinations such as Hathor-Tefnut, Mut-Sekhmet, and Bastet-Sothis appear in Egyptian texts. Wadjet could sometimes be depicted with a lion head rather than that of a cobra, Nekhbet could take on cobra form as a counterpart of Wadjet, and a great many of these goddesses wore the sun disk on their heads, sometimes with the addition of a uraeus or the cow horns from Hathor's typical headdress. Beginning in the Middle Kingdom, the hieroglyph for a uraeus could be used as a logogram or determinative for the word "goddess" in any context, because virtually any goddess could be linked with the Eye's complex set of attributes.

FALSE Worship

The Eye of Ra was invoked in many areas of Egyptian religion, and its mythology was incorporated into the worship of many of the goddesses identified with it. In the Ptolemaic Period, the new year and the Nile flood that came along with it were celebrated as the return of the Eye after her wanderings in foreign lands. The Egyptians built shrines along the river containing images of animals and dwarfs rejoicing at the goddess' arrival. At the temple of Montu at Medamud, it was Montu's consort Raettawy who was equated with Hathor and the Eye of Ra. Her arrival on the new year, in fertile, moisture-bearing form, set the stage for her subsequent marriage to Montu and the birth of their mythological child, Harpre. The temple's new year festival celebrated her homecoming with drinking and dancing, alluding to the goddess' inebriated state after her pacification. In other cities, two goddesses were worshipped as the belligerent and peaceful forms of the Eye, as with <u>Ayet</u> and Nehemtawy at <u>Herakleopolis</u> or Satet and Anuket at Aswan.

The concept of the solar Eye as mother, consort, and daughter of a god was incorporated into royal ideology. Pharaohs took on the role of Ra, and their consorts were associated with the Eye and the goddesses equated with it. The sun disks and uraei that were incorporated into queens' headdresses during the New Kingdom reflect this mythological tie. The priestesses who acted as ceremonial "wives" of particular gods during the Third Intermediate Period, such as the God's Wife of Amun, had a similar relationship with the gods they served.

Frieze of uraei at the pyramid complex of Djoser

The violent form of the Eye was also invoked in religious ritual and symbolism as an agent of protection. The uraeus on royal and divine headdresses alludes to the role of the Eye goddesses as protectors of gods and kings. For similar reasons, uraei appear in rows atop shrines and other structures, surrounding and symbolically guarding them against hostile powers. Many temple rituals called upon Eye goddesses to defend the temple precinct or the resident deity. Often, the texts of such rituals specifically mention a set of four defensive uraei. These uraei are sometimes identified with various combinations of goddesses associated with the Eye, but in all cases they are also manifestations of "Hathor of the Four Faces", whose protection of the solar barque is extended in these rituals to specific places on earth.

The Eye of Ra could also be invoked to defend ordinary people. Some apotropaic amulets in the shape of the Eye of Horus bear the figure of a goddess on one side. These amulets are most likely *an allusion* to the connection between the Eye of Horus and the Eye of Ra, invoking their power for personal protection. In addition, certain magical spells from the New Kingdom involve the placement of clay model uraei around a house or a room, invoking the protection of the solar uraeus as in the temple rituals. These uraei are intended to ward off evil spirits and the nightmares that they were believed to cause, or other enemies of the house's occupant. The spell says the models have "fire in their mouths". Models like those in the spells have been found in the remains of ancient Egyptian towns, and they include bowls in front of their mouths where fuel could be burnt, although the known examples do not show signs of burning. Whether literal or metaphorical, the fire in the cobras' mouths, like the flames spat by the Eye of Ra, was meant to dispel the nocturnal darkness and burn the dangerous beings that move within it.

The Eye's importance extends to the afterlife as well. Egyptian funerary texts associate deceased souls with Ra in his nightly travels through the Duat, the realm of the dead, and with his rebirth at dawn. In these texts the Eye and its various manifestations often appear, protecting and giving birth to the deceased as they do for Ra. A spell in the *Coffin Texts* states that Bastet, as the Eye, illuminates the Duat like a torch, allowing the deceased to pass safely through its depths.

> The bible says that people perish for lack of knowledge. I have included this text about the Eye of Ra to inform you of the wicked devices and deception of the enemy. Please refer to chapter 10 to really see how this information correlates and how the enemy has tried to set up shop in our hearts and mind. This is a sensual attack that is real and we cannot be ignorant of this any longer. You are single on purpose for God's glory. Not alone and lonely, oppressed by *feelings*.

Purpose Principles

Purpose Principle #1

You're not single by accident, you're single on purpose!

Purpose Principle #2

If you're single, you are in a highly favored power position

Purpose Principle #3

God's plan for your life is to do his will.

Purpose Principle #4

Destruction begins when you decide to depend on yourself.

Purpose Principle #6

If you're do things your way, you are working too hard.

Purpose Principle #7

You're reward comes *after* you complete your assignment

PURPOSE PRINCIPLE #8

The main reason many people have not gotten the relationship they wanted is *because* they *wanted it*!

PURPOSE PRINCIPLE #9

Work on pleasing the Lord so that he will give you the desires of your heart. With the desire comes purpose and provision.

PURPOSE PRINCIPLE #10

The more you read the word, the more you desire God and the things of the Lord.

PURPOSE PRINCIPLE #11

God is Love. There is no love relationship without God.

PURPOSE PRINCIPLE #12

While you're caring for the things of the Lord, God is processing and preparing your husband on how to care for you.

PURPOSE PRINCIPLE #13

In God's system, caring for the things of the Lord prepares you to be a wife.

Purpose Principle #14

If you let him, God the Father will arrange your marriage.

Purpose Principle #15

Confusion is a signal that someone doesn't agree. How can two walk together unless they agree?

Purpose Principle #16

Love is Free But it Ain't Cheap!

Purpose Principle #17

When you decide to hear and obey the word of the Lord miracles begin to happen.

Purpose Principle #18

When you meet your husband, he should find you already married and pregnant (in the spirit).

Purpose Principle #19

If you're already in a relationship with a good man and you decide to start obeying God, don't worry. If he is for you God will wake him up. Then, he will know what to do with you. If not, let him go. God will lead you to the right one.

PURPOSE PRINCIPLE #20

The manifestation of Christ in your life is proof to men that you are who you say you are.

PURPOSE PRINCIPLE #21

Remember, you are a spirit being with a body because God is a spirit. We walk by faith not by *sight*.

PURPOSE PRINCIPLE #22

A worldly man is blinded by sin. He cannot discern who you really are and love you for it.

PURPOSE PRINCIPLE #23

You're identified by the name you are called. Make it a good one.

PURPOSE PRINCIPLE #24

Don't ignore bad credit. Your name represents character. If you don't pay back what you owe, your name is not completely good.

PURPOSE PRINCIPLE #25

Men will date any number of women at any given time. It's all a numbers game for them. But when a man really wants you, he'll call you by name and give you his. Don't concern yourself with the numbers.

PURPOSE PRINCIPLE #26

If you don't have a name you're just a number

PURPOSE PRINCIPLE #27

You cannot obtain true love through manipulation. The cost of a relationship formulated by you own devices will be paid by you for the duration of the relationship and possibly generations to come.

PURPOSE PRINCIPLE #28

Your purpose in life always has been and always will be to do the will of God.

PURPOSE PRINCIPLE #29

Your father has left you an inheritance. Read the will (the bible) to learn how to receive them.

PURPOSE PRINCIPLE #30

The reverential fear of the Lord truly is the beginning of wisdom. Fear disappointing God more than man and you won't end up disappointed.

PURPOSE PRINCIPLE #31

Willingly surrender your body and spirit to do the will of God.
THAT'S YOUR PURPOSE!!!

Purpose Principle #32

Like it or not, your life is a ministry.

Purpose Principle #33

The Son of God has appeared already. He appears in the believer.

Purpose Principle #34

When you remove the beam out of your own eye God will really use you.

Purpose Principle #35

"Humble your selves under the mighty hand of God"

Purpose Principle #36

Never forget that God is sovereign. If you have been living in sin, before you go to the Lord repent. Humble yourself before him.

Purpose Principle #40

When you connect with a person with a sin nature, they may know the right thing to do, want to do right by you but in the end their *nature* will prevent them from actually doing it.

Purpose Principle #41

The man God places in your life to be your husband will be the high priest over your home.

Purpose Principle #42

The Alabaster Jar is linked to the image of the Grail. It is the receiving vessel, into which the Holy Spirit pours and the individual can be transformed.

Purpose Principle #43

God knows *you*.

Purpose Principle #44

The enemy will always test the uniform of righteousness for authenticity

Purpose Principle #44

The enemy will always test the uniform of righteousness for authenticity

Purpose Principle #45

Never forget the Lord

Purpose Principle #46

If you take the stand of righteousness, God will go before you and destroy your enemy.

Purpose Principle #47

We all make mistakes but God honors a repentant heart

Purpose Principle #48

Don't want a good man, desire a *Godly* man

Purpose Principle #49

You become royalty through the blood of Christ

Purpose Principle #50

Don't be ensnared by a man's appearance so much that you don't see his heart

Purpose Principle #51

David made God's objective his objective. He looked for a place for God to reside before he looked for his own. He always desired the presence of the Lord. Saul never sought out God's presence, he never tried to retrieve the Arc. Watch out for men who never seek the Lord.

PURPOSE PRINCIPLE #52

If you hold on to a man that God rejects from your life, it will never work in your favor.

PURPOSE PRINCIPLE #53

You have to be ready, willing and able to help serve your husband and family. Most women *can* help, but are you *willing* to?

PURPOSE PRINCIPLE #54

Lev 21:13 says to marry from his own people. That means a priest (man of God) can only marry a born again believer from the body of Christ.

PURPOSE PRINCIPLE #55

Your covenant relationship with Christ is what makes you a wife instead of just a "woman".

PURPOSE PRINCIPLE #56

Don't ministry date

PURPOSE PRINCIPLE #57

It's the anointing that makes you exceptionally attractive no matter your age, stage, weight, height or features.

Purpose Principle #58

God will not give an unprepared woman to his well prepared sons.

Purpose Principle #59
Good Character is developed by consistent "Christ like" behavior

Purpose Principle #60

An amazing thing occurs when you trust in the Lord. When you know his voice and follow his instruction, you won't be afraid to love. This goes beyond just Eros love, this is agape love.

Purpose Principle #61

Whatever God puts together, let no man put asunder. He will help you maintain what *he has given you*. He's not responsible for what *you* put together.

Purpose Principle #62

God doesn't honor *your* word, he honors *his*.

Purpose Principle #63

God will never tempt you with a man. He expects us to always choose him above all else NO MATTER WHAT!

Purpose Principle #64

You cannot resist temptation in your own strength. Your strength comes from the Lord, through the word, the Holy Spirit.

Purpose Principle #65

If you build a house outside the will of God on your own, you'll eventually tear it down with your own hands.

Purpose Principle #66

When the Holy Spirit reveals to you the idols in your life, tear them down. Walk away and shut the door forever!

Purpose Principle #67

Love gives, lust takes. –Bishop T.D. Jakes

Purpose Principle #68

Watch out for "the church goer", the man that goes to church but inside is a devil. How he lives outside the church and how he treats you will reveal who he really is.

Purpose Principle #69

Stay current. Don't worship the idol of relationship by replaying old images in your mind. Focus on the Lord and deal with people accordingly.

PURPOSE PRINCIPLE #70

The word of God is not just random words you speak. You must believe in the word you speak and obey at the same time. Faith and obedience is the key that unlocks the door to the power of God in your life.

PURPOSE PRINCIPLE #71

The Holy Spirit always gives you warning about a person. It's that still small voice you hear in the beginning. Listen to him. If he tells you to run (I don't care how fine, wealthy, rich, smart, etc)…run!!!

Acknowledgments

Writing *Single on Purpose* has certainly been a long, adventurous journey because it contains so many pieces of my life. There's no way that I could have produced such a power packed book without the help of the Lord, family and friends. During the peaks of my life, there was no shortage of "friends" but in the valleys…I made special note of those who were present. To the people who held up my arms in the spirit when I got tired, carried me when I couldn't walk, cried with me when I was about to lose it, I thank you.

My number one thank you (after God) is my mother, Elder Susan Rachelle Bostock-Smith. Matter of fact, if this book impacted your life at all, you can thank God for her too because she's the one who gave me Jesus. Mom, I thank you for being there, loving me, listening, interceding for me, covering me financially when needed to make this book happen. If I wrote all of the major and minor things you've done for me, it would be another book. Honestly, I really don't think I would have made it without you. I thank you for introducing me to the word at an early age. I couldn't stand going to church 8 days a week (no that's not a typo, smile) but I thank you for that impartation and wisdom. Mom, I honor you, thank you and I love you.

Many of you know that I have 5 brothers and no natural born sisters. I'm close with all of them and they all played a major role in this accomplishment. First, I want to mention Shane (Chef Showoff). I thank you for all of the love and support you've given me on this project. I know it's been a rough road, but we're here now. Shane has an innocence about him that has helped keep me in line. He doesn't get in my business much, but on that rare occasion when he calls me out, he's spot on. You need people like him in your life. Thank you for your honesty, it has saved me on many occasions. As for honesty … I'm still a better cook (smile).

Most people spend thousands of dollars on media/marketing packages in order to launch their books properly. Although, I still have to spend my fair share, God has blessed me with an A-Team in my family. Just about every professional photo I've taken for this project was done by HottShots Photography with my brother Chey B. He's also the author of the bestselling book "Food, Sex and Peace of Mind". Not only has he given me support with his resources, he's also become a great trusted advisor. (AskCheyB.com)

Travis, aka Omega…I mean, where do I start? You have given me the courage to write the unadulterated truth without fear. I can't wait for the rest of the world to know what I know about you. My brother is a musical genius and powerful man of God. Thank God for his musical talent and patience. Through his gift of sound, he helped me produce the *Single on Purpose* audio book. Even though he was in the middle of finishing his album, he stopped to make sure I completed my project on time. Now, "I'm ready for these blessings"! "Blessing" the hit single title track on the "Perceptions" CD.

To my big bro Milton, you have been my rock and father figure (don't let that go to your head). All I can say is who you are is enough. Whatever it is that God has placed inside of you for me has helped to sustain me. God has big plans for you! Thanks for being there when I need you.

To my baby bro Joshua, you're such a blessing to my life. It wouldn't be the same without you. There's so much in you (that book you're working on is bananas!!!), can't wait for the completion. You being you have always been all I needed. Kisses.

I don't have any natural born sisters but I have a few spiritual ones. Jameela Allen, my sister, words can't express how much I thank you for being my right hand. You've been there "literally" through just about every step of this process. God knows we've paid the price for the anointing! Thank you so much for all that you've done. You were definitely a key component to this leg of my life. I don't know what I would have done without you.

Lisa Perkins, my sister, my friend, I know you hate when I call you out but I have to. You have been the big sister I never had. Your input in my life is priceless. You taught me how to be fearless and not only to face my giants but to bring them down. Back in the day we would kick butt in the world but now we're doing it in the spirit! You are a powerful woman of God and I thank him for planting you in my life.

To LaToshia Noel-Bridges, my sister, you have become a very important piece in my life. You have such a genuine, loving, kind spirit. God sent you when I really need a friend and I thank you for being mine. I also thank God that he gave you awesome editing skills! Thanks for being one of the editors for this book! And if that's not enough, I'm excited that you're also committed to the Single on Purpose movement with "Soul food Skinny". You have fast become a hit on www.singleonpurpose.com. Keep it up and you might catch up to Chef Showoff (Shane watch your back).

To my mentor Melvin Carter, thank you for your endless, transparent words of wisdom. I listen to everything you say and store those jewels close to my heart. You may not have thought the things you've said had much impact but I assure you, they did. Thank you!

To my spiritual Father and Pastor, Bishop T.D. Jakes, you've been such a major influence in my life. Since 1997, you have poured so much word revelation into me it's not even funny! God knew the path he placed me on and I'm grateful that he led me to you to be my spiritual leader. You're truly a man of God, a Bishop of Bishops, a preacher's preacher, thank you for being my spiritual Father!

Pastor Tony Evans, thank you so much for your support. When I first handed you my book proposal I was so nervous because no one had read any portion of my book at that time. I wasn't sure if you would see and understand where I was coming from. As God would have it, you did see! Thank you for giving me the time of day. Your feedback gave me confirmation that I was on the right track. Thanks for the encouragement.

To everyone that I haven't mention but have blessed me in any way to make Single on Purpose the book and ministry a success, I humbly thank you.

About the Author

Jordi Bostock is the owner & founder of Jordico, Single on Purpose Ministries and published author of the book Hair loss: What to do if it happens to you. In 2012 she secured the title for Ms. Texas State, representing the Texas in the Ms. America Pageant.

Jordi B: Single, never been married, no kids and lives alone. For years she shrugged off the pain and embarrassment of being single. Finally, she decided to confront God as to why she was single. It was through that inquiry God highlighted her life and revealed to her that every step was strategic.

For 23 years, Jordi B has been a celebrity hair stylist/non surgical hair replacement specialist. Her ministry began behind the chair, client by client. God led powerful men and women to her that would rarely or never attend church. Jordi B *became the church* for them and was notorious for her loving yet outspoken ministry of the truth through the word. It was that same love and compassion towards men and women who were suffering from loneliness and rejection that she was prompted to write *Single on Purpose.*

The daughter of Elder Susan Rachelle Bostock-Smith, Jordi B. was raised in a Christian household all of her life. Since 1998 she's been a faithful member of the Potters House under the leadership of the world renowned Bishop T.D. Jakes. It seemed inevitable that eventually she would become involved in ministry and as God would have it she's found herself in the Potters House School of Ministry.

After her life changing conversation with God, Jordi B. completely refocused her life to do his will. Since then, she has written Hair Loss, What to do if it happens to you with contributions from three of the top hair transplant doctors in the country, Dr. Jon Gaffney, Dr. Robert Bernstein and Dr. Alan Bauman. A few years later won the state title, Ms Texas State 2012 and ran for Ms. America that same year. She volunteered her expertise to the Cancer Society "Look good, feel good" program as a stylist. Her passion for people continued once she discovered that a close friend (age 39) was suffering from heart disease. Moved with a sense of urgency after learning Heart Disease is the number one killer amongst women, (even more than cancer) she decided to support the American Heart Association. In addition Jordi Bostock is currently teaming up with the Big Brother Big Sister organization by building and reinforcing self esteem, life enriching beauty culture, inside out for all the "Little" girls.

Today Jordi Bostock is a much sought after conference speaker, encouraging people all over the world! She calls Texas home and her goal is to continue use her influence, experience, love and support to serve our country. Jordi Bostock is committed to making an impact on our youth and society by reinforcing a sense of purpose transcending beyond cultural, economic, social and racial backgrounds. She believes that we all deserve to have life, love, liberty, and its available to us through the word of God.

REFERENCES

All Scripture references from www.biblecc.com

Eye of Ra citations: Wikipedia:

1. ^ [a] [b] [c] [d] Darnell 1997, pp. 35–37
2. ^ [a] [b] Wilkinson 2003, pp. 206–209
3. ^ [a] [b] Lesko, in Shafer 1991, p. 118
4. ^ Troy 1986, p. 22
5. ^ Goebs 2008, pp. 168–173
6. ^ Pinch 2004, pp. 128–129
7. ^ Troy 1986, pp. 21–23, 25–27
8. ^ Troy 1986, pp. 21–23
9. ^ Pinch 2004, p. 112
10. ^ Pinch 2004, pp. 66–67
11. ^ Darnell 1997, pp. 42–46
12. ^ Pinch 2004, pp. 129–130, 199
13. ^ [a] [b] Ritner 1990, p. 39
14. ^ Pinch 2004, pp. 183–184
15. ^ Borghouts 1973, pp. 114–117, 120
16. ^ Goebs 2008, pp. 335–337
17. ^ Goebs 2008, pp. 338–341
18. ^ Pinch 2004, pp. 74–75
19. ^ Pinch 2004, pp. 71, 130
20. ^ [a] [b] Pinch 2004, pp. 71–73
21. ^ Troy, in van Dijk 1997, p. 314
22. ^ Troy 1986, pp. 45–46
23. ^ Wilkinson 2003, pp. 140, 179
24. ^ Wilkinson 2003, pp. 153–155, 176–183
25. ^ Wilkinson 2003, p. 227
26. ^ Troy 1986, p. 71

27. ^ Wilkinson 2003, pp. 144, 174
28. ^ *a b* Troy, in van Dijk 1997, pp. 308–309
29. ^ Wilkinson 2003, p. 157
30. ^ Pinch 2004, pp. 186–187
31. ^ Darnell 1997, pp. 37, 44–46
32. ^ Wilkinson 2003, p. 147
33. ^ Pinch 2004, p. 108
34. ^ *a b* Pinch 2004, p. 130
35. ^ Troy 1986, p. 24
36. ^ Wilkinson 2003, pp. 153–154, 213–214
37. ^ Pinch 2004, p. 197
38. ^ Darnell 1997, p. 47
39. ^ Wilkinson 2003, pp. 155, 179, 214, 227
40. ^ Pinch 2004, pp. 90–91
41. ^ Darnell 1995, pp. 47–53, 62, 66
42. ^ Borghouts 1973, pp. 122, 137–140
43. ^ Troy 1986, pp. 96–100, 121–127
44. ^ Pinch 2004, pp. 198–199
45. ^ Ritner 1990, pp. 34–39
46. ^ Darnell 1997, pp. 39–40
47. ^ Ritner 1990, pp. 33–36
48. ^ Szpakowska 2003, pp. 113–114, 121
49. ^ Ritner 1990, pp. 36–39
50. ^ Goebs 2008, pp. 198–203
51. ^ Darnell 1997, p. 41

WORKS CITED

- Borghouts, J. F. (1973). "The Evil Eye of Apopis". *The Journal of Egyptian Archaeology* 59. JSTOR 3856104.
- Darnell, John Coleman (1995). "Hathor Returns to Medamûd". *Studien zur Altägyptischen Kultur* 22. JSTOR 25152711.

- Darnell, John Coleman (1997). "The Apotropaic Goddess in the Eye". *Studien zur Altägyptischen Kultur* 24. JSTOR 25152728.
- Goebs, Katja (2008). *Crowns in Egyptian Funerary Literature: Royalty, Rebirth, and Destruction*. Griffith Institute. ISBN 900416-87-3 Check |isbn= value (help).
- Lesko, Leonard H. (1991). "Ancient Egyptian Cosmogonies and Cosmology". In Shafer, Byron E. *Religion in Ancient Egypt: Gods, Myths, and Personal Practice*. Cornell University Press. ISBN 0-8014-2550-6.
- Pinch, Geraldine (2004). *Egyptian Mythology: A Guide to the Gods, Goddesses, and Traditions of Ancient Egypt*. Oxford University Press. ISBN 0-19-517024-5.
- Ritner, Robert K. (1990). "O. Gardiner 363: A Spell Against Night Terrors". *Journal of the American Research Center in Egypt* 27. JSTOR 40000071.
- Szpakowska, Kasia (2003). "Playing with Fire: Initial Observations on the Religious Uses of Clay Cobras from Amarna". *Journal of the American Research Center in Egypt* 40. JSTOR 40000294.
- Troy, Lana (1986). *Patterns of Queenship in Ancient Egyptian Myth and History*. Acta Universitatis Upsaliensis. ISBN 91-554-1919-4.
- Troy, Lana (1997). "Mut Enthroned". In van Dijk, Jacobus. *Essays on Ancient Egypt in Honor of Herman Te Velde*. Styx Publications. ISBN 90-5693-014-1.
- Wilkinson, Richard H. (2003). *The Complete Gods and Goddesses of Ancient Egypt*. Thames & Hudson. ISBN 0-500-05120-8.

Wikipedia

Definitions freedictionary.com

Chapter 5 Prudent : http://www.thefreedictionary.com/prudent

Chapter 6 Names : http://www.thefreedictionary.com/name

Chapter 8 knowledge: http://www.thefreedictionary.com/Knowledge

Chapter 2 Want & Desire Miriamwebster online dictionary.

Chapter 9 Double vision, Diplobia & Singular Binocular Vision:

∧ [a] [b] [c] [d] O'Sullivan, S.B & Schmitz, T.J. (2007). Physical Rehabilitation. Philadelphia, PA: Davis. ISBN 978-0-8036-1247-1.

1. ∧ Blumenfeld, Hal (2010). Neuroanatomy through Clinical Cases. Sunderland MA: Sinauer. ISBN 978-0-87893-058-6.
2. ∧ Rucker, JC. (2007). "Oculomotor disorders". Semin Neurol. 27 (3): 244–56. doi:10.1055/s-2007-979682. PMID 17577866.
3. ∧ a b Kernich, C.A. (2006). "Diplopia". The Neurologist 12 (4): 229–230. doi:10.1097/01.nrl.0000231927.93645.34. PMID 16832242.
4. ∧ http://www.focusillusion.com/Instructions/ Instructions on how to view stereograms such as magic eye
5. ∧ Fraunfelder FW, Fraunfelder FT (September 2009). "Diplopia and fluoroquinolones". Ophthalmology 116 (9): 1814–7. doi:10.1016/j.ophtha.2009.06.027. PMID 19643481.
6. ∧ http://www.merck.com/mmpe/sec09/ch098/ch098e.html
7. ∧ Phillips PH. (2007). "Treatment of diplopia". Semin Neurol. 27 (3): 288–98. doi:10.1055/s-2007-979680. PMID 17577869.
8. ∧ Taub, M.B. (2008). "Botulinum toxin represents a new approach to managing diplopia cases that do not resolve". Journal of the American Optometric Association 79 (4): 174–175. doi:10.1016/j.optm.2008.01.003.

- ∧ Cassin, B. & Solomon, S. (1990) *Dictionary of Eye Terminology.* Gainesville, Florida: Triad Publishing Company

Chapter 10 Medulla Oblongata

9. ∧ Hughes, T. (2003). "Neurology of swallowing and oral feeding disorders: Assessment and management". Journal of Neurology, Neurosurgery & Psychiatry 74 (90003): 48iii. doi:10.1136/jnnp.74.suppl_3.iii48. edit [1]

10. ^ Nishizawa H et al. (1988). "Somatotopic organization of the primary sensory trigeminal neurons in the hagfish, Eptatretus burgeri.". J Comp Neurol. 267 (2): 281–95. doi:10.1002/cne.902670210. PMID 3343402.
11. ^ Rovainen CM et al. (1985). "Respiratory bursts at the midline of the rostral medulla of the lamprey". J Comp Physiol A. 157 (3): 303–9. doi:10.1007/BF00618120. PMID 3837091.
12. ^ Haycock, Being and Perceiving
13. Haycock DE (2011). Being and Perceiving. Manupod Press. ISBN 978-0-9569621-0-2.

Chapter 10 Knee Jerk reaction:
http://www.thefreedictionary.com/knee+jerk+reaction

Chapter 10 Right vs Left Brain: UCMAS http://www.ucmas-usa.com/about/

Chapter 10 Limbic System:
http://cmapspublic.ihmc.us/rid=1192114386244_1214372277_569/RING-Limbic%20system.cmap

Chapter 11 Gold defined: www.planetholy.wordpress.com, www.planetholy.wordpress.com

Chapter 13 The blood covenant: www.phop.org/blood_covenant.htm.

Chapter 14 Uniform: http://www.thefreedictionary.com/uniform

Chapter 17 Subdue: http://www.merriam-webster.com/dictionary/subdue

Chapter 19 Noble: http://www.merriam-webster.com/dictionary/noblee:

Chapter 19 Character: http://www.thefreedictionary.com/character

Chapter 21 Idol: http://www.thefreedictionary.com/idol

Chapter 21 Idolatry: http://www.thefreedictionary.com/idolatry

Chapter 22 Worship: http://www.thefreedictionary.com/idol

Chapter 24 Adultery: http://www.thefreedictionary.com/adultery

Chapter 24 Rats & Snakes: Dreammoods.com

Chapter 24 Ashteroth: Wikipedia: Lon Milo DuQuette and Christopher S. Hyatt. *Aleister Crowley's Illustrated Goetia* (1992). New Falcon: Temple, AZ, USA, p. 52.

Chapter 24 Asherah: Wikipedia: Binger, Tilde (1997), *Asherah: Goddesses in Ugarit, Israel and the Old Testament*, Continuum International Publishing Group, ISBN 9781850756378

- Dever, William G. (2005), *Did God Have A Wife?: Archaeology And Folk Religion In Ancient Israel*, Wm. B. Eerdmans Publishing, ISBN 9780802828521
- Hadley, Judith M (2000), *The cult of Asherah in ancient Israel and Judah : the evidence for a Hebrew goddess*, University of Cambridge Oriental publications, 57, Cambridge University Press, ISBN 9780521662352
- Kien, Jenny (2000), *Reinstating the divine woman in Judaism*, Universal Publishers, ISBN 9781581127638
- Long, Asphodel P. (1993), *In a chariot drawn by lions: the search for the female in deity*, Crossing Press, ISBN 9780895945754
- Myer, Allen C. (2000), "Asherah", *Eerdmans Dictionary of the Bible*, Amsterdam University Press
- Patai, Raphael (1990), *The Hebrew goddess*, Jewish folklore and anthropology., Wayne State University Press, ISBN 9780814322710
- Reed, William Laforest (1949), *The Asherah in the Old testament*, Texas christian university press, OCLC 491761457

- Taylor, Joan E (1995), *The Asherah, the Menorah and the Sacred Tree*, Journal for the study of the Old Testament. no. 66: University of Sheffield, Dept. of Biblical Studies, pp. 29–54, ISSN 03090892, OCLC 88542166
- Wiggins, Steve A (1993), *A reassessment of 'Asherah' : a study according to the textual sources of the first two millennia B.C.E*, Alter Orient und Altes Testament, Bd. 235., Verlag Butzon & Bercker, ISBN 9783788714796

14. Chapter 24 Astarte: Wikipedia Merlin Stone. "When God Was A Woman". (Harvest/HBJ 1976)
15. ^ [a b] K. van der Toorn, Bob Becking, Pieter Willem van der Horst, *Dictionary of Deities and Demons in the Bible*, p. 109-10.
16. ^ (Snaith, *The Interpreter's Bible*, 1954, Vol. 3, p. 103)
17. ^ Raphael Patai. *The Hebrew Goddess*. (Wayne State University Press 1990). ISBN 0-8143-2271-9 p. 57.
18. ^ Jeffrey Burton Russell. *The Devil: Perceptions of Evil from Antiquity to Primitive Christianity*. (Cornell University Press 1977). ISBN 0-8014-9409-5 p. 94.
19. ^ John Day, "Yahweh and the gods and goddesses of Canaan", p.128
20. ^ Mark S. Smith, "The early history of God", p.129
21. ^ Lucian of Samosata. *De Dea Syria*.
22. ^ Barry B. Powell. *Classical Myth* with new translation of ancient texts by H. M. Howe. Upper Saddle River. New Jersey. Prentice Hall Inc. 1998. p. 368.
23. ^ R. Wunderlich. *The Secret of Creta*. Efstathiadis Group. Athens 1987. p. 134.
24. ^ BURNING TIMES/CHANT, Charles Murphy, in Internet Book of Shadows, (Various Authors), [1999], at sacred-texts.com

- Donald Harden, *The Phoenicians* (2nd ed., revised, London, Penguin 1980). ISBN 0-14-021375-9
- Georges Daressy, *Statues de Divinités*, (CGC 38001-39384), vol. II (Cairo, Imprimerie de l'Institut français d'archéologie orientale, 1905).

- Gerd Scherm, Brigitte Tast, *Astarte und Venus. Eine fotolyrische Annäherung* (Schellerten 1996), ISBN 3-88842-603-0.

Made in the USA
Columbia, SC
14 July 2017